POLICE : THE HUMAN FACE

POLICE : THE HUMAN FACE

R.C. Dikshit

GYAN PUBLISHING HOUSE

NEW DELHI-110002

Police : The Human Face

(Crime, Law, Police)

ISBN : 81-212-0662-6

Published in 2000 in India by
Gyan Publishing House
5, Ansari Road, Darya Ganj
New Delhi-110002

Laser Typesetting: at Manas Typesetter
Printed at: Mehra Offset Press

Contents

Preface

The instinct of preservation and procreation must have been the basic considerations of family units. When such family units came together, then the clan, tribe, race and nation came into existence that founded village, towns and established kingdoms and empires. The rules of governance for enforcing normative behaviour must have been considered essential and this was the beginning of the rule of law.

In society some people do not conform to the normative behaviour. To avoid the clashes and consequential disintegration the judicial system is evolved. The rules of the governance and the means evolved for ensuring adherence to rules and objectivity of the people reflect the level of social life and decide the quantum of influence exercised on the work of the community and contemporary thought process.

Quite early in human history it was realized that observance of rules cannot be ensured without proper sanction. This sanction could be in the form of social disapproval, corporal punishment, apprehension of evil consequences in this life or beyond it. In the course of human history, various means were adopted to ensure the observance of rules in the interest of well-being of the community, nation, state or the empire. The means employed, for the above and in view, depended on the ingenuity of the tribal leader or the arbiter or the leader of the community who secured observance by tribal patriotism or loyalty of his people, by popular disapproval of breakers of tribal laws and deference shown to the custom and tradition by the contact with supernatural influence which he professes by fear of his own or the magical power of tribal religious leaders by giving material or spiritual reward for law observance, by instilling, for neglect of it fear of punishment in this life or the next but always he depended on and was obliged to use, as ultimate sanction, the physical or military force of the young men of the tribe. Ultimate dependence on the physical force for long period of time must have brought to the force the disadvantages of the system, necessitating the discovery of viable alternative in the form of some sort of policing.

The policing could be done either by the force exercised by the people indirectly through some persons selected for the purpose or it could be done by the force appointed by the ruler or the chief in authority. One flows from below upwards known as 'kin police' and the other one from above downwards and may be termed as 'gendarmerie' or totalitarian police system. In the course of history the two systems can be seen at times to blend partially with one another, especially in early times and particularly in the early history of city, states and in some respects to have borrowed from each other in methods.

The ruler appointed police was the general rule for the empires while in smaller democracies the community elected police was the norm. The empires of Sumer, Babylonia, Egypt, Persia, Rome, Byzantine and Islamic empires had ruler appointed police while in India both ancient and medieval we had a mixture of two systems. The capital cities and other cities of importance had ruler appointed police with elaborate system to check espionage and sabotage while the rural areas continued to be governed by an elaborate but informal system of Panchayats at time organized on the pattern of castes or clans but always being the representative bodies.

'Without liberty law loses its nature and its name and becomes oppression. Without law liberty also loses its nature and name becomes licentiousness' (James Wilson-1742-98). When the community felt the need of parting with a portion of its freedom in exchange for peace and harmony in society, it developed an elaborate system of policing. Policing was evolved along with the evolution of community life and as the community life became more complex and system of policing and administration of justice also became equally intricate. The checks and balances were invented and various controls were introduced restraining hitherto free and unrestrained community life which made an eminent scholar say "Man is born free but he is everywhere in chains". The legal system so evolved was initially the reflection of social life but later on it became a flexible instrument of social order (J. Homes). It created new social values and gave new vision to the society and thus paved the way for a new social order.

The contradictions between individual interest and social interest are not the only troubles in the path of smooth social order. There are incompatibilities between the interests of individual and group. It is one of the most important functions of law to adjust and conciliate these conflicting interests and incompatibilities. This conciliation can be achieved by promulgation of general rules and evolving general standard principles for adjustment. Without the principles of adjustment or standard normative behaviour the society will flung around in uncertaintity. For effecting social cohesion and element of chance or happenstance, due process of law was evolved.

In India the system given by Manu and others was still prevalent, when invaders from west established their foot-holds on the western coast. The invaders in the territories under their occupation tolerated indigenous system but for they had their own community law. Similarly when Mughals established their empire they could introduce their system only in bigger cities while rural areas were still governed by old traditional judicial system of Panchayat. With the arrival of French, Spanish, Portuguese and British colonizers again plurality of systems was introduced by new arrivals. Gradually the influence of other Europeans declined leaving a major part of the country for the British rule and a new colony was added to British empire. Growth of the judicial system during British period in India was very slow initially as they retained indigenous system in most parts of the country but introduced Anglo-Saxon judicial system in metropolitan cities. After first war of independence in 1857, this process of change in administrative system as well as judicial system, was hastened under pressure of socio-political changes.

The policing during the early period was under the direct control of kings in the capital cities while elaborate federal system existed in the rural areas under local or provincial chieftains. During Mughal period also same system continued for policing. But with the advent of Anglo-Saxon Law a new police system was evolved in India by rulers representing British Empire. This new system evolved in India was different from police system prevalent in England.

The police system as it evolved during British period, was to protect interests of British Empire. The political upheavals from 1857, onwards till India achieved freedom, change in the administration was brought about but aims and objectives of Police Department remained the same. At the dawn of independence, police being the strong arm of the administration, was most hated institution in the country as it was held responsible for brutalities inflicted on the people and inhuman treatment meted out to the political leaders during freedom movements both violent and non-violent. The political changes brought about by declaration of independence did not change the image, attitude and functioning of the police.

When the goals of society and the law enforcing wing including those who are entrusted with the job of framing laws are the same there is no social conflict and the problem of policing remains simple. Those who frame the laws think in terms of the wider interest of society and personal considerations take a back seat. The people who indulge in defiant behaviour are treated as criminals in the eyes of law as well as in the eyes of society and such persons or groups are treated harshly.

When few people act as think-tank and others blindly rely on their wisdom and far-sightedness then there is no conflict in the society so long as they are objective and impartial. But in every society a time may come when a few wise men take their followers for a ride or the gap between the thinkers and the followers widens. In such a situation the social tensions generate conflict in the different segments of the society. Policing becomes difficult in such circumstances in democratic countries. Such conflicts can be resolved in a democratic way while in a dictatorial set up violence remains the only alternative as was witnessed in countries of eastern Europe. Under the circumstances mentioned above not only police but whole of the administrative machinery finds itself in a dilemma whether to enforce rule of law or should it join hands with those who feel that those who control administrative machinery are the usurpers. At certain point of time a situation may arise when elected government may issue command to its own administrative arms to do certain things which are not lawful. In such circumstances it is the duty of administrative leadership to guide the organization in the correct direction otherwise the organization will lose credibility knocking off the very basis of its existence. In the present socio-political scenario, not only the police but even the political leadership has lost its credibility.

The policemen tend to think that total responsibility for maintaining law and order rests with them and as such they feel fully justified to transgress the limits set by law in controlling crime by adopting illegal preventive measures and questionable methods in eliciting information during the course of investigation. In this connection, it should be quite clear to everybody that the Constitution which created the police organization also created the body of law, therefore both enjoy equal amount of sanctity and respect. Police on their part cannot think of enforcing law by breaking it and community cannot maintain peace and order by demoralizing and dehumanizing the police force. In maintaining law and order one should always keep in mind that the methods adopted to maintain order and prevent crime in the society should not be more oppressive and intolerable then the effect of crime itself.

In brief one can say that police system does not only need to be efficient but also humane so that its operations do not alienate the people as has happened in certain regions affected by the extremism and separatism. It is true that 'government cannot be exercised without coercion but the coercion employed ought to be reduced to the lowest possible limit consistent with safety.

The ideal police force is one which affords a maximum of protection at the cost of a minimum of interference with the lawful liberty of the people. The real difficulty of police problem is, therefore, to fix the limits where non-interference should end and coercion should begin'.

Our society continues to develop at an unprecedented speed, and regrettably, so does the crime. It has become more sophisticated, organized and internationalized. Nonetheless, criminal justice has not necessarily developed sufficiently and quickly enough to meet the challenges of the present. As a result criminal justice administrators now have an even greater and more significant responsibility to realize justice fairly and efficiently.

Police is the part of judicial system which includes prosecution and judiciary as well. All the three agencies have to work in co-operation in the task of maintenance of order and administration of justice. Inefficiencies of one agency affect performance of other. The reforms in judicial system should therefore be taken together in all the three agencies so that prevention and detection of crime, prosecution of criminals in courts and dispensation of justice improves. The standard of investigation should improve, prosecution should be purposeful and court proceedings should be prompt and based on merits and not on personal likes and dislikes.

The economic scenario is changing fast and the lifestyle of people is also undergoing change. The people who decide to live on predatory pursuits are also adapting themselves to ever changing socio-economic pattern of their target groups resulting into emergence of well organized groups of criminals with very intelligent and well equipped members and efficient crime machine with inter-state and at times transnational linkage.

The economic crime is fast becoming one of the most important criminal activity of organized criminals. With the globalization of trade and commerce the crime has also become global. With the unprecedented growth of communication channels and growth of new banking system money laundering has become one of the most important activities of the financial wizards. All these developments need change in police working if society needs control over crime and criminals.

With the Universal Declaration of Human Rights of 1948, a new dimension has been added to police functioning. A new code of conduct has been prescribed for law enforcing agencies. With the new covenants and international treaties, new rights have been created in favour of people all over the world. The environmental protection has added entirely a new field of operation for the Police. Perhaps entirely new judicial system will have to be evolved for affective administration of environmental laws. Police as an organization, has to adjust itself and gear up to face new challenges that are likely to be thrown up in the next millennium.

The organized crime has also become universal as far as the operations connected with money laundering are concerned. The political and bureaucratic linkages have also given a new dimension to the problem of money laundering in particular. It has created practical operational problems for the police specially in the state where the dividing line between political leaders and leaders of the underworld has been obliterated. While discussing effectiveness and efficiency of police all those points have to be discussed and solutions are to be found out.

Finally, it may sound strange but it is true that more communities have perished by their inability to enforce laws than have been destroyed by nature or hostile aggression. In the history of communities, absence or weakness of effective law enforcement machinery can be seen to be very frequently the true cause of failure in battle. The prevention and deduction of crime has been the anchor sheet of Administration of Justice throughout the history. To keep pace with the development of the society to match the strength of the criminals, it is duty of leaders of the force to build and maintain its efficiency and morale, instil a sense of objectivity and impartiality and also to evolve a machinery so that the organization gathers sufficient strength and moral fibre to purge itself when required.

During my career as Police Officer I had occasions to meet and interact with persons of standing in different branches of administration as well as those engaged in different occupations and professions besides the victims of crime. This interaction almost compelled me to delve deep into the problems facing the people and their reaction to police responses. These reactions were from mild criticism to violent agitations, at times justified inview of Police inaction, over-reactions or lack of concern demonstrated for the people in general. While on other occasions I found that public reaction was based on total ignorance of facts and legal procedure on which police had no control. The book which is collection of independent articles written and published during last 8-9 years, is an attempt to analyse the prevailing situations and enlighten the people at large about the inherent factors responsible for typical Police behaviour in given situation. Being an insider to the system I got ample opportunity to introspect and suggest corrective measures which I have done in some of these articles included in this book.

The change in life-style has also brought about the radical changes in social responses in given situation necessitating upgradation in Police professional capabilities including attitudinal changes up to the cutting edge level.

The articles which have been included in this book were mostly published in professional journals having limited readership, are being published in book form to reach the wider section of society for proper understanding of Police problems so that in coming years they can shape the Police to cater to the needs of future generations. My endeavour will be more than rewarded if this book motivates the readers to resolve to create efficient and humane Police.

My thanks to the journals where my articles were published earlier and also to those who encouraged me by communicating their reactions. I am also thankful to my family members specially my wife Vimla for encouragement and assistance at every stage. I also thank Sri B.P. Garg for bringing about this publication in shortest time possible.

1

Police and Human Rights Issues

सर्वो दण्डजिते लोको दुर्लभो हि शुचिर्नरः।
दण्डस्य भयाद् भीतो भोगायैव प्रवर्तते।।

—शान्तिपर्व (15/34)-महाभारत

The Indian mind, thousands of years before the Christian era could perceive the existence of all living beings in *Paramatman* and visualized *Paramatman* in all creatures, thus leaving behind no room for hatred towards anyone. The Vedic rishis always prayed for the well-being of everyone in society. These rishis were first to conceive the whole world as one family *Vasudhaiv Kutumbakam*. In the above context it was considered the foremost duty of the State or King to protect the citizens (*Praja*). The protection of citizens in those days was considered necessary from high officials, criminals, enemies of the State and from the King himself and those who were close to him. One can very well realize how ancient is the concept of protecting rights of citizens against the avarice or greed of the king or the State.

Human rights are inalienable, sacrosanct and transcendental in nature and have been accepted as fundamental to our national life. From the time immemorial it has been maintained that without the protecting and directing hand of State through Army or police in the form of punishment (*dand*) man would degenerte into an animal and *Matsya Nyay* would prevail thus disintegrating the whole society. In the middle ages in Great Britain the debate on 'freedom or freedom from crime' ultimately gave birth to a permanent organization in the form of police. It was maintained that society would not prosper as a corporate body without curtailing liberty of some of the citizens to give protection to weaker sections in society.

Even the superficial study of the human civilization would reveal that these islands of civilization were nestled in protected places along the then prevalent routes of transport and communication but for the most part of their early existence they remained isolated from each other. This physical isolation helped the inhabitants in developing homogeneous lifestyle and evolving the value system most suited to their genius.

The careful study of early civilization will reveal that though these islands of early civilization had but limited contacts with each other but they developed strikingly similar value system to govern interaction with fellow beings. This universality of the Code of Conduct gave rise to certain basic concepts like basic rights, equality, justice including due process of law, etc. The writing of St. Thomas Acquinos and Grotious, the Magna Charta and Bill of Rights in Great Britain affirmed and recognised the basic and inalienable rights. The political movement in the wake of Industrial Revolution in Europe and general wave of freedom movements in the nineteenth and twentieth centuries culminating in vigorous growth in the number of membership of United Nations laid foundation for making the Universal Declaration of Human Rights to ameliorate the quality of life of teaming millions who were still languishing under the alien rule and suffering denial of basic rights considered so necessary for the dignity of man.

After the averages of two successive world wars the world organization was under tremendous pressure to proclaim the principles of future course of action of the world body to ameliorate the living conditions of the members of human family who suffered indignity, slavery and oppression which resulted in barbarous acts, killing millions of people, destroying thousands of human settlements and shaking human conscience. This was the momentous time which comes rarely in history, when we step out from the old to the new, when an age ends and when the soul of a nation, long suppressed finds utterance and when a country of sub-continental geographical assets like India becomes free after throwing away the yoke of foreign rule. On 10th December, 1948, Universal Declaration of Human Rights was proclaimed by the United Nations General Assembly when India was still framing its Constitution which explains the striking similarity with the provisions of Fundamental Rights and Directive Principles of the Constitution on one hand and human rights proclaimed by the United Nations in its General Assembly on the other. No wonder our Constitution included these in alienable, basic or fundamental rights of all members of the human family which serve as the foundation of freedom, justice and peace in the world and also affirmed faith in fundamental human rights, in the dignity and worth of human being and in the equal right of men and women.

The similarity between the fundamental rights and universal declaration of human rights made under the auspices of United Nations is quite striking. The Universal Declaration of Human Rights on 10th December, 1948 barely sixteen months after declaration of independence of India and almost one year before the Constituent Assembly gave final touches to our Constitution before its adoption on 26th January, 1950 explains this striking similarity in the provisions of our Constitution and instrument of Human Rights Declaration.

Some of the provisions which do not find place in our Constitution as Fundamental Rights have been included as Directive Principles of State Policy or given effect by including them in other Acts of Parliament. Even a separate Article (51-A) has been added in our Constitution regarding duties of a citizen.

The Universal Declaration of Human Rights was just beginning and the first step to enlist co-operation of member-State which enjoined upon them not to engage in any activity or to perform any act aimed at the destruction of any of the rights and freedoms set forth herein Article 30 of the Declaration on Human Rights'. The United Nations, in its anxiety to see implementations of their proclamation and also to monitor progress in this direction have been doing stock-taking of the compilation of legislations promulgated by the member-States. After the Declaration of Human Rights with a view to further ameliorating the living conditions and improving the quality of life of all members of human family the United Nations have adopted the following Resolutions/Covenants :

1. The Convention for the Protection of Human Rights and Fundamental Freedoms—4th November, 1950.
2. The Declaration of the granting of Independence to Colonial Countries and the Peoples—14th December, 1960.
3. The Declaration of the Elimination of All Forms of Racial Discrimination—20th November, 1963.
4. The Declaration of the Promotion among Youth of the Ideals of Peace, Mutual Respect and Understanding between peoples—7th December, 1965.
5. The Declaration of the Elimination of Discrimination against Women—7th November, 1967.
6. The Declaration of Social Progress and Development—11th December, 1969.
7. The Declaration of Principles of International Law concerning Friendly Relations and Co-operation among States in accordance with the Chapter of the United Nations—24th October, 1970.
8. The Charter of Economic Rights and Duties of the States—12th December, 1974.
9. The Declaration of the Use of Scientific and Technological Progress in the Interest of Peace and

for the Benefit of Mankind—10th November, 1975.

10. International Covenant on Civil and Political Rights—23rd March, 1976.
11. United Nations General Assembly Resolution (No. 34/169) adopting Code of Conduct for Law Enforcement Officials—17th December, 1979.
12. United Nations Resolution for Protection of all Persons under any Form of Detention or Imprisonment—9th December, 1988.
13. United Nations Convention on the Rights of the Child—20th November, 1989.

The Human Rights Declaration and inclusion in the Constitution notwithstanding the violations of different type of freedoms and rights to equality before law are very common. Instances have come to light when security forces as well as civilian arm of the government transgressed with impunity the limits set forth by the Constitution of India. Frequently complaints about torture, custodial deaths and assaults and illegal confinement have come to notice. Even on international fora the questions regarding violation of human rights have been raised again and again. Some of the Western countries in the General Assembly of the United Nations have also criticised the denial of basic rights to certain communities. The United States of America has gone even to the extent of imposing political and economic sanctions against some of the countries. South Africa suffered such isolation from all important members of United Nations for a long period of time resulting in abrogation of laws promoting apartheid. India was also subjected to severe grilling on many occasions.

The Amnesty International, People's Union for Civil Libertie, Citizens for Democracy, People's Union for Democratic Rights and other Human Rights Activists have been raising fingers in connection with anti-militant operations in Jammu and Kashmir, Punjab, Uttar Pradesh, North-East States and other parts of the country. During Emergency, tortures were reported from different States indicating police excesses on helpless civilians in utter disregard of law of the land. Many instances have been cited in the reports of Human Rights Activists and can be multiplied by adding more incidents that are taking place every day in our country and in other countries as well. Nobody will deny that such illegal and irregular acts at times fringing barbarism should not be stopped. No government worth its name will hesitate in meeting out most stringent punishment possible to the perpetrators of crime. In India also we do not have dismal record of punishing the violators of civil liberties as projected by the activists. Supreme Court has emerged as a champion for victims and heard cases by removing away the procedural cobwebs but the fact remains that tendency to violate civil liberties on slightest provocation by security forces on their own or at the behest of bureaucrats and political heavyweights is on the increase unabated. This tendency to flout norms both social and legal deserves thorough examination and bold corrective steps.

From the reports that appeared in newspapers it appears that the incidents of human rights violations reported by international press are based on newspapers only and in some of the cases they have not bothered to look into the judicial or administrative pronouncements. Some of the instances which figure in the national press prominently later on turn out to be false and exaggerated stories. It is really amazing that the crusaders also appear to play for the galleries and do not have patience to wait for the truth to come out after enquiry or court verdict. The agencies reporting on such incidents should keep in mind that not only the so-called victims but also so-called accused have some inalienable rights and they should not be condemned even before enquiry.

Those who are agitating for the denial of civil liberties to the members of extremist groups have never reported anything about those who suffered at the instance of these groups. It is not to justify atrocities on anyone but to point out the political considerations at the back of such reporting which turns Nelson's eye on the doings of those who have no regard for any law, leave aside Declaration of Human Rights.

The Human Rights activists became louder in 1970s when force was increasingly used to quell Nexalite activities in West Bengal and again in Andhra Pradesh. The events during Internal emergency also raised eyebrows against repression. The movement spearheaded by Shri Jai Prakash Narain gained momentum during Emergency when unbridled power in the hands of government was used against the political activities as if they were hardened criminals. During these years the people were reminded of days of Independence movement when British agents in India used all that was in their armoury to crush the movement and eliminate the agitators. Besides the violation of human rights in dealing with law and order problems at times groups of people also violated human rights of groups such as the reactionary action directed against Sikhs in 1984 after the assassination of Mrs. Gandhi and again the killing by Bodos and Nagas in the North-East, to mention a few. Still another category of oppression includes the police excesses in dealing with crime or law and order problems, the use of third degree methods, false incrimination and elimination in false encounters. Of the above three categories of human rights, violations is the immediate concern to deal with police excesses or the violation of human rights in enforcing Law of the Land.

"The ambition of the greatest man of our generation has been to wipe every tear from every eye. They may be beyond, but as long as there are tears and sufferings, so long our work will not be over. And so we have to labour and to work hard to give reality to our dreams", thus spoke Pandit Nehru on the eve of Independence Day on 14th August 1947. "To make this dream a reality we should do our utmost, without being deterred by disappointments. We do not always undertake things in the hope of succeeding. It is better to fail in a right cause that will ultimately triumph than succeed in a wrong cause that will ultimately fail. Truth alone trimphs not untruth-*Satyameva Jayate, Nanritam*. Above exhortations and ideals notwithstanding we in our country have not even started to have the way to attain the goal set by great men like Mahatma Gandhi, Pandit Nehru and Dr. S. Radhakrishnan.

Third Degree Methods

The most widely labelled allegation against police is the use of third degree methods against the suspects. The physical torture has been accepted as norm to extort confession from the suspect in shortest possible time. The so-called 'experts of interrogation' invent new methods to shatter the suspect without leaving behind any traces of torture on his person to defy the most thorough medical examination. Each and every policeman knows that the Constitution of India in its Article 20(3) forbids ill-treatment of persons in police custody. The Section 29 of Police Act, 1861 and Sections 330 and 331 IPC also prohibits physical torture. Every one in society is very vocal in criticising police on this issue. Severe punishment, social stigma and image distortion of the department besides utter discomfiture on the family of Police Officer and the suspect has not been able to deter policemen to resort to third degree as an instrument of investigation. Why?

Pressures on Investigating Officer

If we delve deep into the psychology of policemen then it would appear that he is under great mental strain to prevent crime, detect all crimes and secure 100 per cent conviction from the courts who feel that all policemen are liars and deserve almost same treatment, if not worse as the accused they are prosecuting, in their courts. If the policeman fails in prevention there is hue and cry and bad publicity shakes the confidence of the officers responsible. If the case has not been worked out speedily then departmental pressure mounts and threatens the policemen with change in placement as supervisory officers want only those men to be in the charge of the police-stations who are efficient. The successive failure in courts spoils the record statistically speaking and invites chiding from above and displeasure from the government. All these factors and chain reaction make the Police Officer jittery who adopts shortcuts and third degree method, he is told by the experienced ones, is the only solution to extort confession which will lead to the clues which may be supposedly useful in investigation.

Distrust in Police

The time at the disposal of Police Investigating Officer is very short, i.e., 24 hours which introduces an element of urgency which is exhibited by the innovative methods of interrogation which more often than not lead to custodial deaths. The grant of remand from courts is cumbersome and can be granted only after production of case diaries and evidence to suggest that further remand is necessary for investigation. All this has to be done within 24 hours along with raids, arrests and recovery of property or physical evidence. These are some of the reasons why a Police Investigating Officer risks his life, and career and that of his family members, besides earning social stigma and bad name for the department.

Dichotomy between Theory and Practice

There is dichotomy between theory and practice of law enforcement by the police. The policemen, officer in the government and even the practitioners of noble profession of law will lecture on policemen and officers for hours about the violation of human rights but the same persons will goad at times blatantly to have a recourse to methods that are not provided in law. The government will issue circulars after circulars about proper registration of cases, polite behaviour of policemen, impartial investigation and humane and strictly legal action but no executive of Government could muster up enough courage to face the reality and the consequences thereof which becomes obvious at the time of serious law and order problems such as Telangana movement, agitations during internal emergency, pro-Mandal and anti-Mandal riot and Ram Janam Bhumi agitations, which reminds of Harold Laski when he wrote, "I know of no instance in history in which men in possession of power have voluntarily abdicated its privileges. They say that reason and justice prevail but they mean their reason and their justice." So long as we have tacit approval of Senior Police Officers, politicians and above all public, this practice is going to stay despite all exhortations, protestations and judicial pronouncements.

Interpretation of Law by Courts

The confession made by the suspect before the police officer is not admissible but Section 27 Indian Evidence Act makes an exception to this rule. The provisions of Indian Evidence Act on one hand discredit the police officers in general and on the other encourage them to collect evidence to make it admissible Section 27 Indian Evidence Act. The courts in their anxiety to protect the rights of the accused demand a very high standard of foolproof evidence and not the best available evidence. This distrust on police by law and the courts of law leads to padding and collection of evidence. In this connection the views of Justice V.R. Krishna Iyer are noteworthy: "Judicial quest for perfect proof often accounts for police presentation of foolproof concoction. Why fake up? Because the court ask for manufacture to make truth look true. No. We must be realistic.. While it is necessary that proof beyond reasonable doubt should be produced in all criminal cases, it is unnecessary it should be perfect. If a case is proved too perfectly, it is argued that it is artificial if a case has some flaws, inevitable because human beings are prone to err, it is argued that it is too imperfect. One wonders whether in the meticulous hypersensitivity to eliminate a rare innocent from being punished, many qualitymen must be callously allowed to escape. If we want to eradicate concoction and padding then courts must be reminded of the advice of J. Bentham, "To acquit a criminal is to commit by his hand all the offence of which he is afterwards guilty. The difficulty of proceedings against offences is great cause of feebleness in the executive power of justice and of impunity to crime.

Interference in the Judicial Process

During pre-independence days police functioned as an agency totally subservient to the then Executive and main objective was to protect the interest of British Crown. After independence and adoption of new Constitution to establish Democratic Republic a change became perceptible under the guidance of patriotic, dedicated and enlightened political leadership. The vacuum in power structure created by withdrawals of Britishers was filled adequately by the political heavy weights who preserved the age-old traditions of service and also commanded respect in public because of their adherence to higher values of life. As the years rolled by the deterioration in national life was quite perceptible in new generation of whole time politicians who earned their livelihood from politics. Those who were out of power wanted to acquire power by any means and those who were in power wanted to retain it by all means which included acquisition of assets, granting of favours to near and dear ones and all the dirty tricks of present-day politics. With the above objective in view, bureaucracy was subverted and next in line came police and efforts were also made, time and again to lure judiciary. Police had to suffer infiltration as well as interference from political leadership in the name of public interest which was the first casualty.

The infiltration in police gave birth to a new politically-oriented work culture which eroded the regular chain of command and also compromised the declared objectives of the organization besides denying opportunity to meritorious men and women. Interference in day-to-day working paved the way for innovating new method to squeeze money from the industrial houses, suppress the political opponents and in unethical hands these powers violated human rights with impunity. The threat of transfer and suspension has become a potent weapon in the hand of politician to bend down the police to his will.

Police Sub-culture

If one sees in a very objective manner career span of an officer in police department and studies attendant attitudinal changes in him, certain traits would be easily discernible so as to term them universal barring a few honourable exceptions. With the passage of time, these common traits form a subculture. The most important trait right from the constable to the top of the department is self-righteousness and intransigence while they are on duty. This brings them in confrontation with others including politicians, bureaucrats, judiciary, media and other organized sectors where he finds himself alone and without support which is closely related to lack of credibility and unfavourable image in society. This further makes police officers more defensing to the point of being evasive and secretive which is an important trait of police subculture and also an important factor in breding corruption and attendant ills in the department.

The difference between law and practice (covert support from public, politician and even press) lack of resources at his disposal to perform his duties properly and frequent suspensions and transfers make him cynical and unsocial, further complicating police-public relations. More often than not, the law and order problems leave one or two police transfers or suspensions at the end. The police officer is readily available as a scapegoat to save political leadership or high-up in bureaucracy.

The department as a whole suffers from stagnation syndrome which makes the officers and men highly competitive in their anxiety to rise in the department. They become overjealous to show result without caring means such officers and men are easy prey to the politicians who are always in search of their 'own men' in the police which paves the way for violation of all norms.

Remedies

Police has to perform number of functions: some are purely judicial, while others are administrative or service-oriented functions. In judicial functions there should not be any outside interference to keep them impartial and strictly in accordance with law. In administrative functions functional autonomy should be respected subject to general control of government. The interference without responsibility is dangerous and such behind the scene manipulations result in barbarous acts at the instance of those who had higher stakes and will take us back to Emergency days.

The judicial interpretation of law also needs some guidance from highest court so that accused persons are not let off on procedural grounds.

Political infiltration of the Police Department is to be taken care of and recruitment to all rank has to be through independent agency not directly under the control of government which at times tends to grant favours to their supporters and discriminates against other sections of society.

The training with special emphasis on Rule of Law with repeated in-service courses, conducted by dedicated experienced and successful policemen who practiced Rule of Law, will go a long way in guiding youngmen entering the service which will be a well spring of new work culture.

Once the people are convinced of the idea that Rule of Law is to be maintained and every human being deserves dignity then not only Police and Judiciary but all agencies will naturally combine and will herald the dawn of new era, where justice will prevail because it is only justice that prevails: *Yato dharmah tato jayah.*

2

Indian Police after 50 Years of Independence

The concept of justice and the system to adjudicate against the violation of cannons of law are the foundation stones of progressive civilization. Right from the ancient tribal societies to the present days' complex social organism, the keepers of the peace, that is the Police have played a crucial role in maintaining peace and orderliness in society.

With the march of civilization it was felt that the defence against the enemies from without and violators of the crime within the community itself require different treatment and the single force could not have been able to cope with a dual task hence peace keeping force was envisaged. The rights and duties, accountability and privileges, strength and weaponry all depended upon the imagination of the particular community but universally this institution was created to bring peace and orderliness in society and therefore gradually collaborate procedure was evolved for its functioning depending upon the level of progress of society.

In India the old system of administration which flourished in Mauryan era could not last long after the decline of Mauryan and Sung dynasties. The rise and fall of Guptas witnessed another system of administration which continued with minor changes here and there depending upon the genius of the rulers in first one thousand years of Christian era. Emergence of smaller states further created confusion and Indian jurisprudence could not grow in the manner the Western judisprudence grew, prospread and won acceptability in European countries with minor changes.

When Britishers came to India they found that the police was organized on the basis of land tenure and collective responsibility of village community in the rural areas and Kotwal (Kotpal or Durgpal of ancient India) system prevailed in important cities. Since there was no concept of state's intervention in the sphere of economic development, the keeping of peace and orderliness in society, quelling of rebellions against the rulers and providing basic security needs to the community were the main functions of the State. There was no elaborate system of policing, investigation, prosecution and punishment at the apex level and the village panchayats dealt with ordinary crime. East India Company acquired rights of Dewani in Bengal (including present Bangladesh, West Bengal, Orissa and Bihar) and then they started making changes in the police system prevailing in the country. Initially police functions were also entrusted to revenue functionaries later on in 1808 separate police functionary with the designation of Superintendent of Police, was appointed for Calcutta. Later on this system was extended to other territories acquired by the East India Company and later on by the British crown.

The British police system in India was evolved on the ruins of old Indian system. East India Company had three important settlements around Calcutta, Madras and Bombay which were first to be subjected to Anglo-Saxon law through retaining peculiarities of the old system.

From the above it would appear that police as an organization is a recent phenomenon though police functions served as anchor sheet for progress and development. The close study of the system also indicates that police system like any other organization reflects the genius of the community it intends to serve. The system of policing is nothing but reflection of the ingenuity of the community and its concept of justice. If society undergoes change the police system also adapts itself to the needs of time. Unfortunately in our country the foreign rulers evolved the system, made it applicable throughout the country, modelled it on the pattern of Western system but after independence, the change of governance, rulers, functions and policies of state required change in the police system which was never seriously contemplated. The top brass was changed but in lower and middle levels this change was imperceptible. The recruitment and the training pattern remained the same almost for quarter century after independence. The functions of the State changed and welfare State came into being but the police was not organized as welfare police. The police inherited same colonial outlook towards the public and was also prepared for the same as the public did not change its attitude towards the police.

Immediately after independence it was considered to be an achievement to retain the fundamentals of administration of the previous government but later on it became a drag on the body politic. The politicians whenever in tight corner threw the blame on police which had to bear the criticism. Efforts were made to control police by successive regimes with the result politicians, bureaucrats and judiciary all tried to subjugate police and no one was interested in reorganizing or remodelling the system. At present old police model with old concepts and susceptibility of being manipulated by interested parties has to defend itself against the criticism from every corner.

When the goals of society and law-enforcing agencies remain the same, there is no social conflict and police is supposed to handle crime and criminals in a straight and objective manner and without fear or favour. The legislatures have wider societal interest in mind and keepers of the peace have to deal with the persons with defiant behaviour in accordance with cannons of law. When few people act as think tanks and others blindly rely on their wisdom, then also there is no conflict so long as the thinkers are objective, impartial and the followers are simple and sincere. But in a modern complex society, a time may come when influencial persons or the trustees of the society start taking advantage of their position and exploit the situation to their personal advantage. Such situations lead to social conflicts which may be resolved either in a democratic way by due process of law or through violence and revolutions. Under the circumstances in an environment of social tensions, credibility gaps and lack of respect for law, it becomes extremely difficult for administration including police to function smoothly. Unfortunately we are living in the same vitiated atmosphere.

The Challenge

At the time of political independence we resolved to move in the direction of socialism, secularism, egalitarianism and decentralization of power so that common man can come to the mainstream. Initially it appeared that we are moving in correct direction but within first two decades it became apparent that our cherished dreams will remain unfulfilled and people felt frustrated with the slow pace of development and also the widening gap between haves and have-nots. The guarantees given in the form of fundamental rights and goals set in the form of Directive Principles of State Policy were also threatened by the political parties in power. The silent and non-violent revolution gave us political freedom but the vision of Gandhi, Nehru, Patel and other political luminaries of pre-independence days' was found missing from the political rulers which resulted into the distortion and we moved away from our cherished goals.

Political distortions resulted into social discord, extremism on the frontiers, near political chaos and economic anarchy in some of the states. The police organization was supposed to cope with such situations with archaic out-moded pre-independence legislation and feudal departmental setup and leadership with colonial work culture in background. The new legislation which came into being to control violence and separatism further alienated police from society, as a result the credibility of the police organization in the masses also suffered steep decline.

Degeneration of Institutions

The democracy depends on democratic institutions and philosophy. Whatever institutions were borrowed from United Kingdom and other Western Democracies were not given proper respect and proper environment which caused their degeneration and decline. The institutions of parliamentary democracy such as legislatures (Central as well as State) have become malignant and are being used to project inter-party and intra-party conflicts instead of resolving problems of the community. The conflict and tension of the society instead of being resolved in the legislature are being accentuated. The entry of persons with criminal bend of mind is certainly going to damage the credibility of Parliament and lower its prestige in public eyes.

The institutions of democracy can function smoothly when they compliment each other but in our country more than once it appeared that they have lost sense of direction and started operating in a culture of conflict and confrontation instead of complimentarity. It has been noticed that the democratic institutions instead of strengthening each other have trespassed into the territory of others and at times even tried to undermine authority of others. Such distortions and confrontations cause unexpected tension for police leadership and blurs its vision.

Economic Distortions

During the span of 53 years, emphasis has been changed more than once. With the result, neither we could achieve economic prosperity nor we could bring about egalitarianism. The fruits of development were not equally distributed. The deprived sections despite all thinking and political slogans were not benefitted and the army of unemployed youths has grown beyond the feeding capacity of productive segment of society. Everyone knows that such conditions generate crime and interaction with electronic media (both national and global) provides them new ideas about organized crime and international adventurism. Such developments pose new problems for the community and its keepers of the peace.

Discipline

These democratic challenges and changes brought about with the change of political power were to be faced by organization burdened by colonial history. The very fact that at the dawn of independence we resolved to retain not only the old guards, rules but also old uniform and methods as well. Instead of changing the face of organization, political masters found them quite handy for their policies as well. So long as great men of vision and courage like Nehru and Patel controlled the destiny of nation, the going was good but with the exit of men of vision, integrity and commitment began the politicization of the system of governance including police. The mainstream politics has been reduced to a mechanism to capture power, at any cost and to cling to it at all cost. In this political system, politicization of police at the top level and undermining the authority of police leadership by encouraging indiscipline at the lower level, was shamelessly resorted to and professionalism and commitment to the public cause were the first casualty.

The ethos of service to community, commitment to the ideals and adherence to goals of the organization were replaced by commitment to political parties, politicians, careerism, casteism and total absence of 'espirite de corps'. The public view of police was even worse than colonial police in India at the height of freedom movement.

During the last 50 years of post-independence period all-round erosion of discipline was gradual but continuous. In police department the beginning was made immediately after independence when a large number of political workers were recruited in police at different ranks. These persons were no doubt nationalists but even after joining police they continued to live in their old sub-culture, i.e., the sub-culture of political workers having scant respect for establishment. These new members of the department were known to senior politicians and had regular communication with them which disturbed regular chain of command.

Failure to win elections for a very long time created an

impression in the opposition ranks that elections can be won only with the help of the administration including police. This impression motivated political parties to win support from government machinery and in case of failure, allegations were made against police. This frequently happened in second decade after independence and again during Emergency period. After 1977, things have become more confused. In some cases, police is targeted with political motives. In other cases, efforts were made to recruit policemen on grounds other than merit. Political ideology, caste and other parochial considerations played major role in matters of recruitment and placement. Now we have come to a stage when the public servants have started behaving like political functionaries. Political executive have also introduced from back door, a revised version of 'spoil system' prevalent in Western democracies. Every party tries to retain control over the administration during elections. Despite best efforts by Election Commission, the district administration remains under the control of officers known for their loyalty and not for their efficiency, integrity and impartiality.

Dilemmas Facing Police

Over the years credibility of police has taken a nose-dive, at the same time the expectations and demands on police have increased to the extent that police finds it difficult to cope with their normal duties of prevention and detection of crime. The functions related to security (both persons and places) have grown out of proportion, necessitating diversion of force from normal duties to vital areas. Despite disproportionate attention given to V.I.P. security, we have seen assassinations of Father of Nation Mahatma Gandhi, Prime Minister in office Indira Gandhi and ex-Prime Minister Rajiv Gandhi besides Chief Ministers and ministers.

The economic distortions in 70s- 80s gave rise to agitations based on economic problems, necessitating police action which alienated it further from the masses. The order became more important than the law enforcement. The prevention and detection of crime was given a back seat in police functioning causing loss of credibility of police as an organization. The lack of effectiveness of governance brought about a total anarchy in every walk of social life requiring police arrangements for conducting examinations, cultural programmes, holding meetings, yatras and religious congregations. This is really paradoxical to find that despite severe erosion in effectiveness and credibility of police, demands and expectations from police are rising, a problem which police leadership has to address itself to.

Socio-Economic Changes and Police

The aspirations of common man were whipped to very high pitch at the time of elections. Similarly the aspirations of those sections of society who were deprived for centuries were also aroused but the effort to meet these aspirations were not forthcoming in successive political regimes. The economic and social tensions as a result of gap in expectations and achievement brought police face to face with warring sections of the society. Further some of the policies of the government did not find approval of the masses but police was asked to implement such unpopular policies. As a matter of fact police was never consulted at the stage of formulating such policies. This trend is still continuing. During the elections thousands of people are arrested under the different 'preventive sections' and all such cases were either closed or died a natural death after elections. Similarly restrictions on the movement of people at the time of visits of political dignitaries is cause of annoyance to general public. Holding of rallies and dharnas disturb economic, social and academic life not only of the city but its hinter-land also. Some unscrupulous political functionaries even expect free transport, arrangement of fuel for vechicles, collection of crowd, etc. At times they are ordered to ignore violation of law with impunity on public places like Railway Stations, Bus Stations and hotels etc. 'Lawlessness on railways including ticketless travellings at the time of rallies has been viewed as right by the political parties and those public servants who dare to enforce law have to face physical assaults and also the harassment in the department 'in public interest'. Such happenings demoralise lower police functionaries and damage the image of police.

Police is not Alone to be Blamed

Police is not alone to be blamed for maintaining law. Police has to work within a parameter established by law of the land and strictly speaking police is to be treated as most important arm of the judicial system, the other functionaries of the system being courts, prosecutors and public. Unfortunately for every failure, police is blamed and the controlling agencies jerk away their responsibility. In such situations police finds itself on a very fragile pitch and always suffers. Police organization has remained static and no machinery could be evolved to have their purposeful interfare on terms of equality with other functionaries of judicial system, with the result it is made accountable even for the lapses of others.

Stagnant Organization

Police has to perform in a society which is undergoing constant change but with an organization which is stagnant and impervious to the problems of the masses whose protection from violators of law is their primary duty. Police organization in the whole country has remained the same for last 50 years or more. The basic pattern has not changed a bit. Whatever changes have been brought about are just like patch-work which instead of increasing cohesion, promote dissension and discordance in organization.

In the name of modernization, no doubt better facilities have been created. Transport and communication in the department has been improved. All this has been done in purely ad hoc manner without any planning. The force has been numerically increased. A perceptible tendency has been noticed in the increase of force to provide the job to a large number of people rather than for service of the community. Further there has been a steep increase in armed force (BSF, CRPF, RPF, and State Armed Police) while increase at the grassroot level of the civil police has been ignored.

The quantitative increase without any efforts to improve the quality of men has not done good to society. At the time of entry into the department the selection method has not been changed. The training pattern still remains the same. At slightly higher level even officers are not allowed to learn at the job by moving them almost continuously. The subject of internal security had been ignored to the extent that it was taken out from the agenda of planned development. Commissions for the improvement of policing in the states as well as at the national level were asked to submit their report regularly but nowhere in the country recommendations were implemented in spirit. The recommendations of National Police Commission have also been ignored definitely not on the grounds of merit.

We are on the threshold of 21st century which will have entirely different problems beyond comprehension of police in the most states of India. The information explosion, availability of firearms coupled with rapid social changes and interest shown by various secret agencies in our country will make things really difficult. The emergence of organized gangs of criminals and their links with international adventurism, brightest brains in the form of legal and financial advisors and assisted by technology both in form of weapons, transport and communication shall not be very easy to handle. In our country most of the states do not have the adequate funds to equip their police to meet such challenges while some states have financial resources but have no willpower to make their police modern and independent. We should prepare ourselves to face violence on a very big scale which may last a number of years but unfortunately we are not yet prepared to address ourselves to such problems let alone preparing to meet the challenges which are likely to be thrown up by growing technology in future.

Dehumanization of Police

During Emergency period it was alleged and was found

correct that police was used for political ends. In exchange for their loyalty some officers enjoyed absolute powers and to some extent administrative immunity. This fact coupled with general political environment made some men in khaki think themselves above law and this was beginning of a trend which still haunts police leadership. Once the process of brutalization starts, it is difficult to check the growth of this malignancy. Natural corollary to this process were political victimization, torture, illegal confinement and fake encounters. Besides tarnishing its image further, police also lost moral right to deal firmly with the criminals.

Criminalization of Police

When criminals have become cohorts of political heavyweights and police leadership is pressurized to deviate from lawful course and in some states even the honest officers are punished, then one can imagine the state of morale at the cutting edge level who has to risk his own life and life of his family members. Under the circumstances a demoralized lower functionary of police organization either surrenders to the criminal leader or in extreme cases commits suicide, leaves the job or kills his superior whom he considers his class enemy. Some policemen of weaker moral foundation, even join the gangs of criminals as regular members besides providing police protection in barter for political protection. This nexus between political leaders, bureaucrats and criminals has been highlighted by Vohra Committee Report. One can imagine about the enthusiasm of such policemen and officers when their cohorts occupy ministerial berths and that too all important portfolios connected with internal security. In these circumstances one can think of the plight of poor but honest and sincere law-abiding keepers of peace and order.

How to Meet the Challenge

Police as an organization has to imbibe professionalism and has to bring excellence in the field of prevention and detection of crime. This may need better facilities for training and sustained improvement in the intake and efforts to allow men in the job to achieve excellence. They have to be given reasonable freedom from wants by ensuring proper wages to lead a really dignifed and purposeful life for the growth of organization. It is essential that police as an organization should have autonomy and their voice should also be given proper respect in formulating policies which concern them.

Police organization must have fair and transparent grievance redressal machinery. It is common belief that police organization does not take complaints against policemen seriously and have a sub-culture of defending them. This alienates the organisation for people.

Subordinate ranks of police organization also feel that organizational grievance redressal system is also not effective and operational. This shortcoming is detrimental to cohesive functioning of organization.

Police must update their professional skills and scientific approach, should be adopted in prevention and detection of crime. Imaginative policing is needed in metropolitan cities by enlightened and better trained policemen. Police as an organization must adapt themselves to handle new gadget to cope with the modern criminal.

Justice C. R Krishna lyer says : "politicization is making rapid strides inside the police force and even communalization has infilterated into the police ranks. This is corrosive of discipline and eventually, of efficiency and reliability." The police has to bear pressure from executive and at times asked to 'bend the law' or even 'break the law' so as to favour political masters. Therefore, it is imperative to have some system to insulate police from direct political interference in implementing law.

According to Dr. G.R.S. Rao "the present image of police in public mind is very negative and it is characterized by attributes such as brutal, corrupt, immoral, insular, complacent, careerist, castiest, communal, fragmented, hierarchial absence of espirite-de-corps and devoid of ethical standards." To change this image of police reculturisation in thought, word and deed is very necessary if the police has to remain functionally relevant. Police needs integrity, independence, expertise and effectiveness, in dealing with law and order.

Police at present suffers alienation, therefore has to analyse and plan their strategy to involve "Masses and the classes" for which the organization will have to make massive efforts. Efforts are to be made to enlist the support of the community by improving their credibility and allowing more transparency in their system. Police functions are mostly confined reactive action pro-actively. Even government does not permit them to go to press or public to reduce alienation and promote pro-active welfare measures. In such situation perhaps people have to take up this issue by way of social movement. The PIL pending in Supreme Court for implementation of National Police Commissions recommendation may be viewed as a step in correct direction.

The Indian police suffers from very inception from certain statutory disabilities originating from distrust of police. These handicaps force the police to take recourse to unethical and highly questionable means which make them guilty in the eyes of people and reduce them to the status of culprits in the eyes of Human Rights organizations. Such disabilities have to be removed if we want straightforward and honest police.

The policemen on their part have to resolve only to act as per command of law because ultimately nothing but truth will prevail.

3

Anti-Corruption Law and Public Servants

Private gains from public offices have become a universal phenomenon. The acceptance of expensive gifts by the officials connected with Olympic games is recent example to prove universality of the malady of corruption. The allegations of match fixing by players in almost all the games, is a common feature in almost all the countries. The amassing of wealth and vulgar display of it is no more a peculiar trait of unscrupulous Asian statesmen. Further, it is not only the dictatorships that are suffering from this malaise, but even the most prosperous and smooth functioning Democracies world over are exhibiting symptoms of this affliction. It is not only lowly paid public servant who is immensed in graft, but even the heads of states and heads of political parties are smearing their faces with this muck. The scandalous commercial deals have become almost regular news items in the News-papers all over the globe but the developing countries of South and Southeast Asia, have acquired added significance in recent years.

In our national life, the erosion of moral values is painfully visible all over the country, in all sectors and at all levels. No area of our national life remains untouched by this moral degradation, but the deterioration in the standards of public servants is more perceptible in free India. A new political-administrative culture is emerging which is characterised by total lack of sensitivity towards common man, blatant and shameful display of power and wealth, high level of permissiveness and unholy alliance between ungrudging partners in the shady deals. The line between politics and crime is becoming unreal day by day.

Vohra Committee Report reiterated that a nexus has come into existence between criminals, politicians, bureaucrats and businessmen. This nexus has gathered tremendous financial resources and it has been allowed by various governments over the years to grow and to proliferate and therefore, it is now in a strong position says."

According to Transparency International's Survey, India is rated as 8th most corrupt nation of the world. (Bangladesh and Pakistan being rated as 4th and 5th). On 15th August 1997 the then Prime Minister I.K. Gujral gave a public call to combat corruption which was followed by sound deliberations by the agencies dealing with corruption. Shri Indrajit Gupta, the then Home Minister while inaugurating the Conference in Delhi on September. 4, 1997 most candidly admitted that this is quite a crucial moment, corruption is not a phenomenon, which can be overcome in one meeting or by making one speech. We are all conscious, but the point is that the system, in which we are working, is very much losing its credibility or has lost much credibility to the ordinary man, the public because of our failure to combat this menace of corruption. All People/every citizen are affected by it in greater or lesser degree and it is having a malignant effect throughout society.

The common man is disillusioned and in a democracy one can guess the consequences of cynicism and disillusionment. In the interest of nation and democratic form of government, we must unitedly root out malignancy from our social fabric.

Corruption Through the Ages

The defaleation of public money by the public servants worried a statesmen even in Mauryan period of our history and Kautalya, dealt with the subject very extensively in his famous *Arthashatra*. The literacy works produced during the period of mighty Guptas also hint at the extent of corruption in public life during the 'Golden Period' of our history. The period of disintegration affect the decline and fall of Gupta empire is known as the Dark Period of our history and abounds in references to not only monetary corruption but also general debasement and degeneration of a prosperous and enlightened pocket of human civilization. Mughal Emperor Shah Jehan was known for his high sense of justice. He introduced various populist measures to help common man in getting justice. He prescribed very severe punishment for corrupt officials. He ordained that the magistrates who failed to administer justice should be bitten by the snakes. He is said to have ordered one Mohd. Said, a Magistrate to be bitten by a cobra in presence of the Emperor himself. Shah Jehan remained in the court till Mohd. Said expired. The dead body of the Magistrate was left in front of his Court-room for two days. Other public servants, who failed to administer justice in accordance with tenets of law prevalent at that time were also severely punished by throwing them before the elephants. After the fall and disintegration of Mughal empire, there was chaos all around and Englishmen fished in troubled waters. Early period of British Indian history was known for its rampant corruption at high places and allegations against Warren Hastings were even discussed in British Parliament.

During the period of second World War, large sum of money was raised and spent on war preparations. New departments were opened, a large number of contractors were patronized for execution of government work connected with war efforts. Since the tasks were to be completed within quickest possible time, the adherence to financial rules and regulations was looked at times, thus, a situation was created which was promptly exploited by unscrupulous, greedy and anti-social persons (both officials and non-official) for their own enrichment at the expense of society and government. The then Government of India realised the enormity of the problem and created special staff in War Department in the year 1941 by an executive order of the Central government. The administration of this special staff was vested in a D.I.G. of Police with Headquarters at Lahore. Though the investigation of offences was to be carried out by the police staff under one D.I.G of Police yet the Superintendent of Special Staff was vested in War Department.

Since new department was created by executive order of Central government which was not in agreement with the provisions of the government of India Act, 1935, the powers and jurisdiction of the investigating officers were changed in Court of Law which necessitated promulgation of an Ordinance on July 12, 1943 (No. XXII of 1943) creating Special Police Force for the investigation of certain categories of offences, with all British India jurisdiction. Another ordinance was promulgated on September 25, 1946 before the lapse of the previous ordinance issued in 1943. This new Ordinance constituted a Special Police Force for Delhi Province (Chief Commissioner's Province). Section 2 of the Ordinance under reference created Special Police Establishment which formed the basis for Delhi Special Police Establishment Act of 1946 (XXV of 1946).

The Delhi Police Establishment Act was enacted in 1946 but necessary changes were introduced in the Act in 1950 under Clause 2 of Article 372 of the Constitution. Again in the year 1951, 1952, 1956 and 1964, certain amendments were introduced in the Act which were considered expedient in view of changing socio-political conditions in the country. The offences to be investigated by S.P.E. are given under Section 3 which says that "The Central Govt. may, by notification in the Official Gazatte, specify the offences or classes of offences which are to be investigated by the DSPE". In view of Section 3 the Central Government issued Notification on 31st October, 1952 which was later on superseded by Notification No. 7/5/55-ADV, dated 6th November, 1956 which inter-alia specified the offences for the purposes of Section 3 of the DSPE Act of 1946. Those offences included offences from the Indian Penal Code of 1860, Prevention of Corruption Act, 1947, Imports and Exports (Control) Act, 1947, Foreign Exchange Regulations Act 1947, Indian Post Offices Act, 1898, Companies Act 1956, Insurance Act, 1938, Indian Official Secrets Act, 1923; Essential Commodities Act, 1955; (Industries Development and Regulation) Act, 1951 and also the attempts, abetment, conspiracies in relation to or in connection with the offences notified in this connection. The offences of conspiracy attempt and abetment are dealt under Sections 120-B, 511 and 107 to 116 IPC.

The Prevention of Corruption Act, 1947 (No. 2) was enacted on 12th March, 1947 which inter alia provided for certain misconducts on the part of public servants but an important aspect of preventing the concealment and disposal of government property was still covered by the Criminal Law Amendment Ordinance, 1944, promulgated u/s 3 of the Emergency provisions (Emergency period 27.6.40 to 1.4.46) of India Burma (Emergency - Provisions) Act, 1940 omitting the limitation period of six months. The Criminal Law Amendment Act of 1944 was specially enacted to protect government money and property which was obtained by committing certain offences punishable under the IPC in the Ordinance, no specific provisions have been made with respect to public servants either protective or exclusively applicable to them.

The Prevention of Corruption Act, 1947 was enacted to make more effective provisions for the prevention of bribery and corruption, because, "the existing law has proved" inadequate for dealing with the problem which has arisen in recent years and the bill is intended to render the Criminal Law more effective in dealing with cases of bribery and corruption of public servants" (Govt. of India Gazette, 23rd November, 1946- (Part V). This Act made the offence u/s 165-A IPC as cognizable besides creating new offences and touching upon the older ones with more stringent punishment. This Act created presumptions in the Act itself to make the provisions more effective besides prescribing minimum punishment.

In brief, one can say that at the dawn of freedom we had DSPE Act for investigation and a number of Acts which dealt with the corruption of public servants employed by the Central Government. The Special Police Establishment, armed with the DSPE Act, the Criminal Law Amendment Act and Prevention of Corruption Act, 1947 failed to arrest corruption. After independence, the government in their wisdom appointed a committee under the Chairmanship of Dr. Bakshi Tek Chand in 1947 to give his recommendations about the working of SPE and also about the amendments in the prócedure if required to make the organization more effective. Bakshi Tek Chand made his recommendations which were considered by the government. Some amendments were made in the Criminal Law in the year 1952.

Birth of CBI

The Central Bureau of Investigation was constituted by Government of India by a Resolution (No. 4/31/61-1) dated 1st April, 1963 mentioning therein that, "The Government of India have had under consideration the establishment of a Central Bureau of Investigation for the investigation of crime at present handled by the Delhi Special Police Establishment including specially important cases under the Defence of India Act and Rules particularly of hoarding, blackmarketing and profiteering in essential commodities, which may have repercussions and ramifications in several states; the collection of intelligence relating to certain type of crimes, participation in the work of the National Central Bureau connected with the International Criminal Police Organization, maintenance of crime statistics and dissemination of information relating to crime and criminals; the study of specialised crime of particular interest to the Government of India or crimes having all-India or inter-State ramifications or of particular importance from the social point of view; the conduct of police research; and the co-ordination of laws relating to crime. "The CBI was set-up with Six Divisions, namely Investigation and Anti-Corruption Division (DSPE), Technical Division, Crime Records and Statistics Division, Research Division, Legal and General

Division and Administration Division. The charter of functions of CBI was appended to the resolution by way of an annexure. The Prevention of Corruption Act, 1947 was also amended.

In June 1962, some members of parliament were agitated over increasing incidents of corruption at high places which convinced Home Minister to set up a committee to review the problem of corruption and made recommendations regarding changes in law and procedure. Sri K. Santhanam, M.P. was made the Chairman of the Committee. The Committee submitted its final report on 31st March, 1964 suggesting for reacting changes in law and procedure.

After the establishment of CBI in 1963, the Anti-Corruption Laws came in greater focus and efforts made to make the law stringent and also effective. The day-today difficulties encountered by the investigation and well-to-do accused persons were also brought to the notice of the Vigilance Commission and the government which resulted into sweeping changes in the existing laws both in the substance as well as in procedure. The new Act, i.e. the Prevention of Corruption Act, 1988 was enforced on 9th September, 1988 with a view to consolidating and amending the law relating to prevention of corruption and for matters connected therewith". The Prevention of Corruption Act, 1988 incorporates the provision of IPC and the Criminal Law Amendment Ordinance, 1944. The 1988 Act also widens the definition of public servants and makes provision u/s 19(3) and 19(4) regarding sanction of prosecution in case of public servants which are considered very useful in ensuring expeditious finalization of the case.

The Public Servants

The Prevention of Corruption Act, 1947 (Section 3) depended on the definition of 'public servant' enumerated u/s 21 I.P.C. For the first time the word 'public servant finds definition in P.C. Act of 1988 in Section 2 alongwith public duty'.

The Indian Penal Code was first drafted by the 1st Law Commission constituted in 1834 on the initiative of Lord

Macaulay who moved House of Commons in 1833 to codify the Criminal Law. The draft code was submitted to the Governor-General of India in Council in the year 1837 by the Commission (Lord Macaulay, President Macleod Anderson and Milett being other Commissioners). The task before the Commission was enormous as it had to reconcile the existing law without offending different castes, communities and ethnic groups. Lord Macaulay observed while enumerating the task "I believe that no country ever stood so much in need of a Code of Law as India and I believe also that there never was a country in which the want might be so easily supplied. Our Principle is simply this—uniformity when you can have it, diversity when you much have it, but in all cases certainly." Macaulay Code could not be finalized as it was referred to the Law Advisers of the Crown then to another Commission which submitted its 2nd and final report in 1847. Again it was revised by Bethune and Peacock, the Law Members of the Council of Governor-General.

At the time of discussion on the draft of the code the objections were raised that the Section 21 is too comprehensive but it was over-ruled by Lord Macaulay who justified it. Later on we find that the same section could not cope with the needs of the progressive society and was required to be amended again and again. The Indian Penal Code was passed on 6th October, 1860 (though after revision draft code was submitted in the year 1847) a century before India earned freedom, which explains why the provisions made regarding 'public-servant' were found wanting and needed amendments time and again.

The 'public servants' as enumerated in Section 21 IPC are referred in the Penal Code in the context of offences committed by them (Chapter VI, Sections 128 and 129; Chapter VII-Offences relating to Army, Navy and Air Force; Chapter IX, Section 161—169 IPC) and also the offences with respect to them (Chapter VI, Sec. 124 IPC, Chapter IX, Sections 170-171: Chapter X, Sections 172—190 IPC, Chapter XVI Sections 332-333 IPC, Chapter XXI, Sections 500—502 IPC). The Anti-Corruption Laws are concerned with public servants in the context of offences committed by them, therefore, the Prevention of Corruption Act, 1988 has replaced Sections 161—165-A (Both inclusive) of IPC (Act 45 of 1860) and provisions have been incorporated in the new Act besides repealing Act 2 of 1947 (P.C. Act, 1947) and Criminal Law Amendment Act, 1952 (46 of 1952).

The provisions of Section 2(c) of the Prevention of Corruption Act, 1988 have been taken from Section 21 IPC and new provisions have been made to make it more exhaustive. The Section 21 IPC (1860) was clause 14 in the draft bill presented by Lord Macaulay. There were only 10 clauses and 1 explanation in the original Act in 1860. The 11th clause with Explanation 3 was added in 1920 (Indian Election Offences and Enquiries Act, 1920-Section 2). The 12th clause and Explanation 4 were added in the year 1958 (Criminal Law Amendment Act, 1950) which included "officers in the service or pay of local authority or corporations" etc. in the category of public servants. On the basis of Santhanam Committee Report the Anti-Corruption Laws (Amendment) Bill, 1964 was introduced in the Parliament and passed as Criminal Law (Amendment) Act, 1964 making changes in Clauses 3, 4, 8, 9, 12 while Clause 12 has been changed and divided into Clause 12(a) and 12 (b).

The PC Act of 1988 further widens the definition of 'public servant' and at present there are 12 clauses with 2 exlanations given in Section 2(c) of the Act. From the above discussion, it is seen that Clauses (i), (ii), (iii) of Section 2(c) of new PC Act correspond to Clause (12) of Section 21 IPC and Clauses (iv), (v), (vi), (vii), of Section 2 of new PC Act, correspond to Clauses (3), (4), (6), (11) of section 21 IPC. The Clauses (viii), (ix), (xi), (xii) of section 2 of PC Act, 1988 are new provisions. The new Act of 1988 resolves the controversy created by conflicting judgements of various High Courts and resultant uncertainty in the minds of the investigators and the courts with respect to offences of corruption and bribery. The Clause (b) has been incorporated in Sec. 2 which defines 'public duty' as 'duty in the discharge of which the State, the public or the community at large has an interest', apparently the emphasis has been shifted from appointment and renumeration, to public duty. The explanation under Clause (b) enumerates the word 'State' which includes "a Corporation established by or under a Central, Provincial or State Act or an authority or a body owned or controlled or aided by the government or a government Company as defined in Section 617 of Company Act, 1956 (1 of 1956)".

The Clauses 2 (c) i-ii read with explanation to 2(b) define public servants on the basis of pay or remuneration drawn from government or State funds. Even before the PC Act of 1988 it was held in G.A. Monterio *Vs.* State of Ajmer (1956 SCR 682) that true test to determine whether a person is a public servant, is whether he is in the service or pay of the government and whether he is entrusted with the performance of public duty and that if both these requirements are satisfied then the nature of office does not matter much.

The Clauses (iv) to (vi) of Section 2(c) of the P.C. Act refer to the officers of the Court. Only slight changes have been made in the Section 21 IPC. Similarly, the Clause (vii) of Section 2(c) of the Act does not need any elucidation.

Section 2(c), Clause (viii) is a new clause which added a new category to the public servants and provides a new concept to the definition by importing 'public duty' in Section 2(b). A Sarpanch of Gram Panchayat is a public servant within the meaning of this clause. It was held in Bhanwar Lal Mali *Vs.* State of Raj. 1994(3) Crimes 791 (Raj) that Sarpanch is public servant and prosecution sanction is required before launching prosecution. The question whether M.L.A. or M.P. can be held a public servant within the meaning of Section 2(c) (viii)was contested in courts prior to enactment of P.C. Act, 1988 and it was held in majority of cases that he is not a public servant within the purview of Section 21 I.P.C. Now, after the enactment of the P.C. Act, 1988 situation has changed drastically and interpretation is likely to be changed, however, in Habibulla Khan *Vs.* State of Orissa-1993 (Cr. L.J. 3604), it was held that, though an M.L.A. would within the fold of the definition of 'public servant' but he is not the type of public servant for whose prosecution, prior sanction is required. Now this matter has been decided by Supreme Court in famous J.M.M. Case on April 17, 1998. Five Judge Constitution Bench unanimously decided that M.Ps. are public servants as far as prosecution sanction is concerned Justice Bharucha suggested that Parliament can make law in this respect while Justice Agarwal suggested that till such time Parliament takes making law, Speaker and Chairman can accord sanction of prosecution. It was held in more than one cases that Hon'ble Ministers are public servenants within the meaning of Section 2 of the PC act 1988 despite a negative verdict in A.N. Patil Versus Maharashtra-1975, Supreme Court in M. Karunanidhi *Vs.* Union of India-1977 held that a Chief Minister as well as ministers are public servants and in this connection a reference was made to Article 164(5) of the Constitution of India.

The Clause (ix) of Section 2(c) of P.C. Act is a new clause introduced in the Act and needs a fresh look by the courts as previous case law did not recognise them public servants. Perhaps because of ambiguity a new clause has been introduced.

The Clauses (x) to (xii) are specific and these categories of public functionaries have been classed as public servants with all their privileges and liabilities.

The Explanations 1 and 2 have been appended to deal with controversial situations. Any person, who takes upon himself duties and responsibilities belonging to the position of a public servant must be regarded a public servant and the fact that he is not drawing salary or remuneration should not be allowed to change the position. An ex-public servant can also be prosecuted under P.C. Act as the crucial date for the purpose of attracting the provisions of P.C. Act is the date of commission of the offence and not the date of retirement, resignation, removal and dismissal of the public servant.

The Monumental Acts, namely, Indian Penal Code, Criminal Procedure Code and Indian Evidence Acts were enacted more than a century back entirely in a different socio-political environment but they continued to hold good even after independence because of the vision of those who drafted the enactments. The Indian Penal Code was first to be drafted but became law 26 years after its submission and final review by Bethune and Peacock, the law members of the Governor-General's Council. It goes without saying that the Commissions and other Committees constituted for the draft drew heavily on English Laws and prevalent Indian Law besides taking help of Livingstone's Louisiana Code and the Code Napolean. Despite the fact that men of eminence were associated with the framing of statute and they took help from all the sources and also that the Act was considered most upto date for almost 100 years, it needed changes specially with respect to anti-corruption measures and were duly effected.

The changes mainly aimed at making the law more effective and with this in view efforts have been made to raise presumptions in favour of prosecution. The changes were also incorporated to remove practical difficulties on the path of fair investigation. The powers and jurisdiction of investigating agencies were also enhanced. The concept of Welfare State changed the total scenario and government entered in the field of industry and commerce which resulted into flow of government money to the places and persons hitherto unknown. A class of new functionaries emerged who handle large amount of government money. The corruption became rampant in government servants and it reached very high places. All this and more gave rise to new concept of accountability and susceptibility of the highest person to corruption which necessitated changes in the definition of public servants from time to time. The public demand for Lok Ayukta both at State and National level and forceful advocacy of bringing Chief Ministers and Prime Minister under its purview represents the thinking of the people. Now the Lok Ayukta bill has been moved in the Parliament showing respect to public opinion, the government has proposed to bring the Prime Minister also under its purview.

संदर्भ

(क) यथा हनास्वादयितुं न शक्यं जिह्वातलस्थं मधु वा विषं वा।
अर्थस्तथा ह्यर्थचरेण राघः स्वल्पोप्यनास्वादयितुं न शक्यः।।

(ख) मत्स्या यथान्तः सलिले चरन्तो ज्ञातुं न शक्या सलिलं पिबन्त।
युक्तास्तथा कार्यविधौ नियुक्ता ज्ञातुं न शक्या धनमाददाना।।

(ग) अपि शक्या गतिज्ञातुं पततां खे पतत्त्रिणाम्।
न तु प्रच्छन्नभावानां युक्तानां चरतां गति।।

(घ) धर्मस्य प्रदेष्टा वा हैरण्यमदण्डयं क्षिपति, क्षेपद्विगुणमस्मै दण्डं दूदयात्। हीनातिरिक्ताष्टगुणं वा। शारीरदण्डं क्षिपति, शारीरमेव दण्डं भजेत। निष्क्रयद्विगुणं वा। यं वा भमर्थ नाशयत्यभूतमर्थ करोति, तदष्टगुणं दण्डं ददूयात्।

4

Police at the Crossroads

सर्वेषां स्वस्तिर भवतु, सर्वेषां शंतिभर्वतु ।
सर्वेषां पूर्णम भवतु, सर्वेषां मंगलम भवतु ।।
लोकः समस्तः सुखिनः भवंतु ।।

(ऋग्वेद-10/191)

The instinct of self-preservation must have brought homo-sapien erectus together at an early stage of world history. The sense of insecurity against other species, the feeling of helplessness against the elements of nature and apprehensions and suspicion against the fellow-beings must have taught them the first lesson of unity—a lesson learnt at the dawn of human civilization but forgotten again and again with disastrous consequences of human community as to the organic life on terrafirma.

A peep into the past will reveal that preservation is followed by procreation which ultimately results in formation of family units. When such family units unite then clan appears and then the tribe, the races and the nations that founded villages and towns, states and empires. At every stage it must have been felt that certain rules for governance of enforcing normative behaviour are essential and this was the beginning of rule of law. The community units must have recognised the need of setting up authority either preceding, accompanying or following the framing of rules.

The discovery of the fact that certain people will not adhere to some or all of the rules and instead prefer to have separate set of rules, must have given rise to plurality in the community life. To avoid clashes and consequential disintegration the institution of 'Danda' must have been recognised. The raison d'etre of 'Danda'is the recognition of the element of physical force as a means for compelling the observance of rules which marks the beginning of the system of justice and order in society. The system of punishment was used as a means to correct those who were on the wrong and at the same time it protected others who adhered to rules given by the community. The rules framed for the preservation and progress of society, the means evolved for ensuring adherence to rules so framed and objectivity of the person who were involved in the above process, reflect the level of social attainment and quality of social life on one hand and decide the quantum of influence exercised on the work cummunity and contemporary thought process on the other. "Without providing itself with effective means of secureng observance of its laws, no community succeeds in maintaining its existence for any appreciable length of time. The very existence of the community, state or empire depends on the effectiveness of its administration in ensuring observance of law, which it considers best in its own interest.

Quite early in human history, it was realized that observance of rules cannot be ensured without proper sanction. This sanction could be in the form of social disapproval, corporal punishment to apprehension of evil consequences in this life or beyond it. In the course of human history, various means were adopted to ensure the observance of rules in the interest of well being of the community, state, nation or the empire. The means employed for the above end in view depended on the ingenuity of the tribal leader or the arbiter or the leader of the community who secured observance by tribal patriotism or loyalty of his person; by popular disapproval of violators of tribal laws and breakers of custom and tradition; contact with supernatural influence which he possesses; fear of his own or the magical power of tribal religious leaders; giving material or spiritual reward for law-observance; instilling, for neglect of it, fear of punishment in the life of the next : but always, he depends on and is obliged to use, as ultimate sanction the physical or military force of the young men of the tribe. Ultimate dependence on the physical force for long period of time must have brought to the fore the disadvantages of the system necessitating the discovery of viable alternative in the form of some sort of policing.

The policing could be done either by the force exercised by the people indirectly through some persons selected for the purpose or it could be done by the force appointed by the ruler or the chief in authority. One flows from below upwards know as 'Kin Police' and the other one from above downwards and may be termed as gendarmerie of totalitarian police system. In the course of history the two systems can be seen at times to blend partially with one another, especially in early times and particularly, in the early history of city-states: and in some respects to have borrowed from each other in methods, in the later, but always distinctly differing stages of their evolution.[5]

The ruler appointed police was the general rule for the empires while in smaller democracies the community elected police was the norm. The empires of Sumer, Babylonia, Egypt, Persia, Rome, Byzantine and Islamic empires had ruler appointed police while in India both ancient and medieval, we had a mixture of two systems. The capital cities and other cities of importance had ruler appointed police with elaborate system to check espionage and sabotage while the rural areas continued to be governed by an elaborate but informal system of Panchayats at times organized on the pattern of castes or clans.

Freedom or Freedom from Crime

"Without liberty, law loses its nature and its name and

becomes oppression. Without law, liberty also loses its nature and name and becomes licentiousness."(James Wilson—1742—1798). When the community felt the need of parting with a portion of its freedom its exchange for peace and harmony in society, it developed an elaborate system of policing. Policing was evolved along with the evolution of community life and as the community life became more complex the system of policing and administration of justice also became equally intricate. The checks and balances were invented and various controls were introduced restraining hitherto free and unrestrained community life which made an eminent scholar voltaire say, "Man is born free but he is everywhere in chains." The legal system so evolved was initially the reflection of social life but later on it became a flexible instrument of social order (J. Homes). It creates new social values and gives new vision to the society and this paves the way for a new social order.

When the goals of society and the law enforcing wing including those who are entrusted with the job of framing laws are the same there is no social conflict and the problem of policing remains simple. Those who frame the laws think in terms of the wider interest of society and personal considerations take a back seat.[6] The people who indulge in deviant behaviour are treated as criminals in the eyes of law as well as in the eyes of society and such persons or groups are treated harshly.

When few people act as a think tank and others blindly rely on their wisdom and farsightedness then there is no conflict in the society so long as they are objective and impartial. But in every society a time may come when a few wise men take their followers for a ride or the gap between the thinkers and the followers widens. In such a situation the social tensions generate conflict in the different segments of the society. Policing becomes difficult in such circumstances in democratic countries. Such conflicts can be resolved in a democratic way while in a dictatorial set up violence remains the only alternative, as was witnessed in countries of eastern Europe. Under the circumstances mentioned above not only police but whole of the administrative machinery finds itself in a dilemma whether to enforce rule of law or should it join hands with those who feel that those who control administrative machinery are the usurpers. At certain point of time, a situation may arise when elected government may issue command to its own administrative arms to do certain things which are not lawful. In such circumstances it is the duty of administrative leadership to guide the organization in the correct direction otherwise the organization will lose credibility knocking off the very basis of its existence.

Functions of Police

The policemen tend to think that total responsibility for maintaining law and order rests with them and as such they feel fully justified to transgress the limits set by law in controlling crime by way of adopting preventive measures or questionable methods in eliciting information during investigation. In this connection, it should be quite clear to everybody that the instrument (law-making body) which created the police organization also created the body of law, therefore, both enjoy equal amount of sanctity and respect. Police on their part cannot think of enforcing law by breaking it and community cannot maintain peace and order by demoralizing and dehumanizing the police force. In maintaining law and order one should always keep in mind that the methods adopted to maintain order and prevent crime in the society should not be more oppressive and intolerable than the effect of crime itself.[7]

In brief one can say that police system does not only need to be efficient but also humane so that its operations do not alienate the people as has happened in certain regions afflicted by the extremism and separatism. It is true that "government cannot be exercised without coercion, but the coercion employed ought to be reduced to the lowest possible limit consistent with safety: the ideal police force being the one which affords a maximum of protection at the cost of a minimum of interference with the lawful liberty of the subject.

The real difficulty of police problem is, therefore, to fix the limits where non-interference should end and coercion should begin."[8]

Progress in the field of science and technology, revolution in sphere of transport and communication, collection of data in the sphere of electronics, change of perception in view of breakthrough in genetic sciences have brought about a vast change in the quality of life and social attitude. The administrative machinery is very slow to imbibe these changes in its system and so is the case with the judicial system including police. Further the ideas and attitudes travel fast while the systems take time in taking roots in new climate, therefore, the attitude of public and way of thinking of the masses gets new rays through all pervasive tele-media while the legal system including law and order machinery changes slowly with the result, in certain fields, it appears to be archaic. It also affects the effectiveness of the system, thus widening the gap between the system and those for whose benefit the system professes to exist.

In a country like ours, the spread of knowledge and resultant change in way of life and attitude differs from one region to another, from one ethnic group to another which gives rise to plurality of social values while law remains universal in application. In view of above at times it appears that enforcement of certain parts of social legislation should be selective which the law enforcing agencies cannot venture to do. This inability alienates the masses of the beneficiaries from the system, a situation which cannot be said to be conducive to the effectiveness of the police. The social legislations with respect to tribal areas can be cited as an example.

The Burden of History

In India, the British model which was an improvement over the French system introduced by Napolean era ... was transplanted in place of an indigenous in which administration was organized in groups of villages such as Sangrahan (10

Villages) Kharyatik (200 Villages) Dronmuk (400 Villages) and Sthaniaya (800 Villages). These units had their own police system and Paurjanopad had immense powers. Sthaniks were almost equivalent to present day Station House Officers. Gram Pradhan who was responsible for maintenance of law and order in his area had intimate knowledge about bad characters. With the arrival of Mughals this system was damaged. Some semblance was retained but after the arrival of Britishers, even this semblance was removed. New London Model Police could not get close to the masses resulting in alienation of public from police. During the days of Freedom Movement this chasm further widened which still affects police-public relations. Old mental reservations, secrecy and feeling of self-eminence affects the police attitude towards public. After 1947, we thought that we would not require police as Ram Rajya will prevail. The training in fire-arms was considered to be superfluous. Later on we were surrounded by very many problems necessitating police action. Under the circumstances we could not change our system, our attitude and even our equipment.

Police is not Alone

The criminal justice system includes besides police, the prosecution, the court and correctional service. At any given time any particular wing might appear important but it is certain that failure of one will definitely affect the working of the other partner of the judicial system. If those responsible for prosecution fail in their duties by betrayal, ignorance, the effect of best police investigation shall be reduced to nought. Similarly the efficiency and impartiality of the court is also a sine qua non for effectiveness of police. The correctional service, specially the four walls of prison, if not managed properly, are sure to affect police working. Police being the most visible and all pervasive wing of the systems, has to bear the brunt of the failure as the objective analysis was either never attempted or it was never allowed to be discussed publicly perhaps in order to cover up doings of those who publicly malign police after abusing the system blantantly. We have to muster up courage atleast to speak the truth and stand up against those who attempt to abuse the system to the detriment of society. If we do not accept the leadership at this time, perhaps others from below, will snatch the initiative.

In pre-independence days, the things of judicial system used to work in a very cohesive manner like well oiled machine but things are quite different after 53 years of Independence. Stung by the instinct of self-eminence, the members of different wings tend to appear taller than the system itself. Some coordinating body has to be thought of at the district level as well as the State and National level to overcome the difficulties mostly arising out of lack of co-operation.

Phenomenon of System Overloading

With the increase of legislative activities at the national and state level, the number of cases registered under various heads have gone up. A large number of cases are pending at the police station level, at the prosecution level and also in the courts. Pendency at the court level will increase the population of jails resulting in more expenditure deprivation, less attention and poor supervision which will in turn reduce effectiveness and increase frustration in police and give rise to criticism at every level. The overloading of the system can be reduced by taking certain categories of offences created under various social legislations out of police purview and given to Lok Adalats or Village Panchayats.

Checks and Controls

Police has to work under a legal framework. As regards the preventive, detective and investigative activities, the control has to be exercised by the courts, while for law and order and administrative activity they have to work under State executive, Financial control exercised by Legislative Assembly of people. At the time of allocation of funds, police has to compete with departments like Health Care, Education and irrigation and the result is too obvious to guess. With all these checks and controls police has to show results to the society. If something good happens, despite all these checks, controls and other impediments, then credit will be cornered by others but in case of failure the police officer is to be blaned. This declivity in assessment and appreciation has to be corrected in the public interest.

Conduct Rules

In the context of duality of goals and plurality of approach to given subject and innumerable pressures and pulls so natural to a democratic system, the system of police should have certain principles so fundamental to the systems that they serve as a beacon light in darkness and guide them on a path beneficial to them and the community they are supposed to serve.

In our country the situation has been further complicated by historical factors and traditional outlook of the public towards police. The concept of 'Kin Police' or 'Police in a Welfare State' is still in a very nebulous state. In this respect it is comparable to the British Police in 19th and early 20th century when persons like Henry Fielding, Patrick Colquhoun, Robert Peel, Charles Rowan and Richard Mayne gave it a direction and a philosophy. These principles are still relevant and have special significance in the present context in our country too. A summary review would be as follows:

1. "To prevent crime and disorder, as an alternative to their repression by military force and severity of legal punishment." This concept was most aggressively opposed in Britain but later in the New Science of Preventive Police, it was accepted by the majority of the people. The people realised that primary object of an efficient police force is the prevention of crime or the pro-active action to the exclusion of reactive action. In the commissioner's handbook, Rowan and Maync further clarified the stand by saying "It should be understood at the outset, that the object to be attained is the prevention of crime. To this great end every effort of the police is to be directed—Officers and Police Constables should endeavour to distinguish themselves

by such vigilance and activity as may render it impossible for any one to commit a crime within that portion of the town under their charge."

2. "To recognize always that the power of the police to fulfil their functions and duties is dependent on public approval of their existence, actions and behaviour, and on their ability to secure and maintain public respect." This principle recognizes the fact that the establishment could not function without obtaining public approval. It is, therefore, essential to the officials to acquire public approval. In this connection a long list of "Do's and Don'ts" have been prescribed in the pages of Police Manuals and in departmental circulars but early pronouncements of Charles Rowan and Richard Mayne still have relevance wherein they say. "He (The constable) must remember that there is no qualification so indispensible to a Police Officer as a perfect command to tempter, never suffering himself to be moved in the slightest degree by any language or threats that may be used."

3. "To recognize always that to secure and maintain the respect and approval of the public means also the securing of the willing co-operation is attained, the battle against crime is half won. The moment we attain this co-operation we are confident that once we act according to law nobody is going to raise an accusing finger towards police out of sheer prejudice".

4. "To recognize always that the extent to which the co-operation of the public can be secured diminishes proportionately the necessity of the use of physical force and compulsion for achieving police objectives." The use of coercive force to ensure adherence to law is the last resort, therefore, every effort to avoid it should be resorted to.

5. "To seek and preserve public favour, not by pondering to public opinion, but by constantly demonstrating absolutely impartial service to law, in complete

independence of police, and without regard to the justice or injustice of individual laws; by ready offering of individual service and friendship to all members of the public, without regard to their wealth or social standing; by ready exercise of courtesy and good humour; and by ready offering of individual sacrifice in protecting and preserving life. If we act according to the principle, then it will dispel all fears and remove all public ignorance about police, who are constantly fed on disinformation."

6. "To use physical force only when the exercise of persuasion, advice, and warning is found to be insufficient to obtain public co-operation to an extent necessary to restore order; and to use only the minimum degree of physical force which is necessary on any particular occasion for achieving a police objective." The adherence to above principles will definitely minimize the number of occasions when armed forces will be called upon to render help.
7. "To maintain at all times a relationship with the public that gives reality to the historic tradition that the police are the public and that the public are the police; the police being only members of the public who are paid to give full-time attention to duties which are incumbent on every citizen in the interests of community welfare and existence."
8. "To recognize always the need for strict adherence to police-executive functions, and to refrain from even seeming to usurp the powers of the judiciary of avenging individuals or the State and authoritatively judging guilt and punishing the guilty." By recognizing the above principles and strictly following it, the system can avoid so many changes of usurption of power and atrocities under influence of emotions.
9. "To recognize always that the test of police efficiency is the absence of crime and disorder and not the visible evidence of police action in dealing with them." This

principle is a natural corollary to the first principle which lays emphasis on the prevention of crime.

The basic principles of British Police as indicated by Rowen and Mayne about 250 years ago, still hold good, though some of them have been improved later on. In the present context when means of transport and communication have reduced the world as one global village, the organization set up enforce law in the society has also received pointed attention of the world body and the UN General Assembly adopted the code of conduct for Law Enforcement officials on 17th December, 1979 (Resolution 34/169). The General Assembly recognized that these are important principles and prerequisites of the humane performance of law enforcement functions and transmitted the same to member states for favourable consideration within the framework of national legislation of practice as body of principles for observance by law enforcement officials.[9] The police conduct rules in vogue also revised in the year 1985 by M.H.A. in the light of G.H. Code of Conduct for law enforcement officials.

Changing Pattern of Crime

The economic scenario is changing fast and the lifestyle of people is also undergoing change. The people who decide to live on predatory pursuits are also adapting themselves to ever changing socioeconomic pattern of their target groups resulting into emergence of well organized groups of criminals with very intelligent and well equipped members and efficient crime machine with inter-state and at times transnational linkage.

The emergence of criminal gangs having links with the so-called respectable sections of society was bad enough but now things have come to a stage when notorious criminals themselves have become notoriously respectable and the police men have to blow hot and cold at the same time. It has become very difficult to define criminals let alone identifying and chasing them to silence.

It is most important that when criminals are showing

ascendance the police is suffering from weak leadership. Absence of leadership or weak leadership in the police organization coupled with demoralized and divided policemen will not be able to fight the crime lords with economic and political power at their back.

Professionalism in Police

Policing may not be classed as profession in every strict classical sense but it definitely possesses some of the most important attributes of a profession. The importance of policing in keeping society free from perils of self-destruction demands that police organization should grow as a noble profession.

When we discuss police professionalism, we mean to refer pointedly the competence of the organization to meet the challenges thrown before the organization by the growing and changing society with its multiplied complexities of life. It also includes the capability of individuals as well as groups of men employed for the particular task.

Policemen, individually or in a group, must not only be competent enough to handle the problem at hand but he should also be properly equipped physically as well as mentaly to do so. The mental attributes are very important from the professional viewpoint as one unguarded utterance can shake the confidence of public in police which affects in large measure the effectiveness of police and reciprocal public cooperation.

The strength of character is no less important than the physical strength and endurance. The changing pattern of social values, does affect the objectivity and impartiality. Policeman should be able to see through the smoke screen of vested interest and tread on the correct path despite all allurements and threats. This is difficult to achieve without strong and inspiring leadership within the organization and without.

Training can no doubt do wonders but it has no magic band. To get good finished product one most have reasonably satisfactory raw material. Therefore the method of induction, insulation in selection process, training, placement and evaluation system has to be recast and constantly reviewed strictly on scientific plane.

Professionalism is the Only Answer

More communities have perished by their inability to enforce laws than have been destroyed by nature or hostile aggression. In the history of communities, absence or weakness of effective law-enforcement machinery can be seen to be, very frequently the true cause of failure in battle. The prevention and detection of crime is most basic to the administration of justice. This objective was never swayed away. It is unchanged, unchangable and remains evergreen.[10] The police organization which fails to perform its primary duties cannot win public approval which is essential for its effectiveness.

The concepts of policing, punishment and trial were evolved to allow each and every member of the society to enjoy their rights and save them from those who indulge in deviant behaviour. Therefore, in doing their duty, the police organization has to show objectivity and impartiality. The slightest deviation from the norms is bound to evoke reaction at times very sharp and even violent. Nowadays even the slightest lapse on the part of even the lowest functionary does not go unnoticed specially by media. The ignorance and lethargy is ridiculed in the press and indiscreet action is blown beyond proportion. The organization is condemned even before ascertaining full facts. Under the circumstances, the only alternative remains with us that we should develop a high degree of professional efficiency and decency in our conduct, maintain objectivity and impartiality.

REFERENCES

1. सर्वे दण्डजितो लोको दुर्लभो हि शुचिर्नर ।
दण्डस्य डि भयात्सव जगद्भोगाय कल्पते ।।
दृष्येयु सर्ववपशिच्भिधे रन्सर्वसेतवः ।
सर्वलोकप्रकोष्शय धवेद्दण्डस्य विभ्रमात् ।।

मनुस्मृति अध्याय-7, 22/24

2. अ. दण्डेन नीयते चेयकृ नयति या पुन ।
दण्डनीतिरिति ख्याता त्रल्लोकान भिनतते ।।

महाभारत शान्तिपर्व 56/78

ब. दुष्टस्य दण्डः सुजनस्यप पुजा न्यायेन कोशस्य च सप्रबृभि।

अत्रि श्लोक-28

स. दुष्ट दण्ड सताकृ धर्मरम च धनार्जनम्।
राष्ट्ररक्षा सतत्वकृ च व्यवहरेषु पच्चकम।
भुमिजानाकृ महायज्ञाः सर्वकल्भषनाक्षुनाः।।

वितरमा धर्मोत्तर-323/25-26

3. Charles Reith *The Blind Eye of History* p.15.
4. *Ibid* p.18.
5. *Ibid* p. 21.
6. प्रजा सुखे सुखी राजा तद्दुःखे यश्य दुःखित।

विष्णु धर्मसूत्र-श्लोक 3

7. ... but there is one limit which cannot be disregarded if police is to be blessing rather than a curse and that the plan adopted for the prevention of crime must never become more intolerable than the effects of the crime itself.

   Cap. W.I. Melville Lee - *A History of Police in England*. 1901-p. XIII.
8. Cap. W.I. Melville Lee - *A History of Police in England*. 1901, p. XII.
9. Code of Conduct for law enforcement officials : adopted by the U.N. General Assembly on 17th Dec., 1979 (Resolution No. 34, 169)

Article - 1

Law enforcement officials shall at all times fulfil the duty imposed upon them by law, by serving the community and by protecting all persons against illegal acts, consistent with high degree of responsibility required by their profession.

Article - 2

In the performance of their duty, in the law enforcement officials shall respect and protect human dignity and maintain and uphold the human rights of all persons.

Article - 3

Law enforcement officials may use force only when strictly necessary to the extent required for the performance of their duty.

Article - 4

'Matters of a confidential nature in the possession of law enforcement officials shall be kept confidential, unless the performance of duty of the needs of justice; strictly require otherwise.

Article - 5

No law enforcement official may inflict, instigate or tolerate any act of torture; or other cruel, inhuman or degrading treatment or punishment, nor may any law enforcement official invoke superior orders or exceptional circumstances such as state of war or a threat of war, a threat to national security, internal political instability or any other public emergency as a justification of torture or other inhuman or degrading treatment or punishment.

Article - 6

Law enforcement officials shall ensure full protection of health of persons in their custody and in particular, shall take immediate action to secure medical attention whenever required.

Article - 7

Law enforcement official shall not commit any act of corruption. They shall also rigorously oppose and combat all such acts.

Article - 8

Law enforcement officials shall respect the law and the present code. They shall also, to the best of their capability, prevent and rigorously oppose any violation of them.

Law enforcement officials who have reasons to believe that a violation of the present code has occurred or is about to occur shall report the matter to their superior authorities and, where necessary, to other appropriate authorities or organs vested with reviewing remedial powers.

10. R. Bhattacharya, *Police and the Criminal Justice Administration.*

5

Communal Riots in India

संगच्छध्वं संवदध्वं
संवो मनांसि जानताम्
समानी वः आकूति, समाना हृदयानि वः
समानमस्तु वो मन्से
यथा वः सुसहासति[1]

—*ऋग्वेद*

मा भ्राता भ्रातरं द्विक्षन्मा
स्वसारमुत स्वसा
सम्यच्चः सव्रता भूत्वा वाचं
वदत भद्रया[2]

—*अथर्ववेद*

Like-mindedness in living and thinking is *sine qua non* of national life and any discordance causes strain in the social fabric, manifested in the alienation of the group from the body politic and leading to tensions of various types in social life. When a man or a group of men feel a sense of deprivation, it begins to develop defence mechanism, and as a result fundamentalism is one of the ways a community may adopt against assimilation. The deprivation is the gap between value expectations of the group and the value capabilities. A feeling of deprivation may be the result of increase in value expectations or decrease in the value capability of the group or community. At times progressive decline in value capability or progressive increase in inspirations also results into frustration and motivates the group to stand against the establishment and also against other communities recognised as the tormentors.

The deprivation that fires the ambition in the communities leading to separatism may not be very real. This deprivation may be the result of decline in value capability or it may be the result of interpretation of historical events. Some groups or communities may identify themselves with certain races who dominated the course of history in the past. When descendants of some race compare their present value capability to that of others, they feel very much deprived and place all the blame on other classes or communities, whom they consider responsible for their decadence. This feeling of deprivation is further heightened by increased interaction with other ethnic groups which on the one hand strengthens the bonds of the group and also forces them to study relative achievements of other ethnic groups. This relative study makes them prone to relative deprivation and leads to identification of beneficiary, the frustration consequential to deprivation leads to confrontation. The mentality of confrontation blunts all sense of dialogue or social discussion and views every action with suspicion.

In our country the historical events encompassing a period of 1000 years have been quite complicated. The different groups of invaders came to India in waves, conquering a vast chunk of land and settling down. Some of these groups were assimilated and became a part of the mainstream, while others kept themselves aloof for various reasons and maintained their separate identity—the Mughals and Britishers being most important of them. These groups formed ethnic minorities. They maintained their language, tradition and separate religion. The followers of Vedic religion in their march inherited various points from the civilizations they came in contact with. Some of the religious fallacies were discarded after a long usage. Some of the reformers also tried to make amends in the practices followed by the religious groups while others propagated radical changes. This activity connected with reforms in religious practices gave birth to various sects which grew as branches of the main tree without confrontation as they drew their nutrients from the same soil. This was true of all the religions having roots in the country. Some of these sects retained their root connections and did not claim separate identity while others proclaimed separate identity. Once the State started protective discrimination, the confrontation became inevitable. Even in the early period of Indian history the State protection given to one religion resulted into skirmishes and bloodiest conflicts between Buddhists and Hindus. Even in the period of *Puranas* the battles between Vaishnavas and Shaivas were not uncommon.

The Freedom Movement against British rule was initially confined to those who were educated in England and America. With the passage of time masses were attracted towards the movement but they were to give some 'ideals' and 'heroes'. The Hindus who were numerically stronger brought their heroes in the front and scores of books were written on the life and deeds of those heroes who fought for the freedom against the invaders who were mostly the Muslims from the North-West. The bitter memories of battles of Panipat and Haldi Ghati were still fresh in the minds of society but the strong leadership kept them under control for some time. As soon as the leadership became restive to gain power, this cleaverage supported by other factors, social and political divided the country. The bitter memories of the past coupled with the wounds of partition, resulted into further alienation in the communities. The northern part of the country, which witnessed more such battles in the historical past and which also suffered at the time of partition, became more vulnerable to communal riots even after independence.

Once a group of a community feels deprived in the field of knowledge, wealth, political power, national importance and cultural suzerainty it faces the problem of preserving its identity. The liberal and progressive group tends to loosen its bonds with the backward segment and always remains prepared to get into the mainstream even at the cost of losing one's identity. The fundamentalists tend to maintain cohesion in the group at the cost of progress. In a way fundamentalism attempts to discipline enterprising segment of the group and sacrifices societal well-being for the short-term gains in political or economic areas. The rise of fundamentalism heralds the decline in the influence of liberal intellectuals and at the same time increases chances of group clashes which may be termed in the present context as communal clashes or riots. If extreme communialism takes over majority community, then state may ultimately go the German way, leading to persecution of millions of Jews. If fundamentalism captures the minds of minority communities, then it may lead to secession as happened in India, Cyprus and now in Yugoslavia.[3]

The historical events after the downfall of the Great Mughals unified different communities against the Britishers. Local Rajas and Nawabs were equally harassed by the Britishers. Therefore, unitedly they tried to prevent British East India Company to expand its wings. In 1857, the Hindus and the Muslims fought their First War of Independence together at all levels. The Britishers realized that united India will be a threat to their existence in this country of subcontinental size. The policy decisions taken in London all reflected the views of Sir Charles Wood, Secretary of State for India in the British Government : "We have maintained our power by playing off one part against the other, and we must continue to do so. Do what you can, therefore, to prevent all having a common feeling. It obviously is a cardinal point in India to keep races and classes so far away from each other as to obviate as far as possible the danger of combined action. Do the ordinary work of the North-West Provinces with North-Western troops. Punjab ditto, and then have your Punjab troops ready to beat the Eastern with, and your Eastern troops ready to beat the Sikhs with, if occasion should arise. The natural antagonism of the races is no inconsiderable element of our strength. If all India was to unite against us, how long could we maintain ourselves."[4] This policy brought desired effect and a number of communal riots took place starting from Varanasi, followed by riots of Bareilly (1871), Karnal (1877), Delhi (1886), Dera Ghazi Khan (1889), Selam (1889), Lahore (1893) and Calcutta (1897).

The above views reflect how the enlightened Britishers educated at Oxford and Cambridge under the shadow of European Renaissance, interpreted Liberty, Equality and Fraternity in a different way for India. The 'Divide and Rule Policy' forced creation of separate electorates for Muslims under Indian Councils Act of 1909—the first legislation to enunciate principle of election but also included the provisions for separate electorates for the Muslims. The year 1919 saw the Government of India Act which provided for separate electorates for the Sikhs in Punjab, the Indian Christians in Madras and the Anglo-Indians in Madras and Bengal. The Ramsay Macdonald's Communal Award also provided for Scheduled Castes and Scheduled Tribes, which was opposed by Mahatma Gandhi resulting into the modified Government of India Act of 1935. The first victory of the Muslim League, which was formed in Dacca in 1906, was the separate electorates for Muslims in 1909 Council of India Act. In pre-partition days strategy was designed to engineer a riot and then the government intervention and the separatist demand are put up to avoid such clashes in future, thereby further deepening the cleavage at the social level. Ultimately, the policy initiated by the British Government in India led to partition of the country and genocide of the magnitude unknown in the history of mankind. After independence, in our enthusiasm, we forgot to correct the historical declivity which was introduced by the rulers in 18th and 19th century.

The pluralistic society, with complex historical background and abysmal poverty, has generated tensions even after independence. The political developments have also encouraged political mobilisation of religious groups for political gains. Any concession granted to minority community is taken as appeasement of minority, while any measure distantly connected with religion is touched by Civil Law. The minority community feels threatened and this psychological cleavage is further widened by political propaganda of the vested interests.[5]

During partition, crores of refugees came from Pakistan and occupied new settlements in the cities and townships, outnumbering all other groups. The persons coming from Pakistan suffered inhuman treatment, massacre of their relatives, rape of their women and deprivation of all their belongings. The feelings of revenge against the Muslim minority were oozing out from the leaking wounds suffered in Pakistan which generated communal distrust and suspicion.

The Muslim leadership which was propagating 'Two Nation Theory' also left for Pakistan leaving behind a void in political fields. After the death of some of the renowned secular leaders, Muslim masses were rendered leaderless. It was very easy for the political leaders to organize these people on communal lines. The minority complex on the one hand generated apprehensions regarding losing identity and on the other, further alienated itself from the National mainstream. The National programme of family planning was opposed by some fundamentalists who had control over illiterate and poor sections of the society. This resulted into higher growth rate of population which further gave impetus to the propaganda that minority community will increase its population ratio vis-a-vis majority community. The percentage of Muslim population was 9.8 in 1951 which stood at 13.2 in 1981. This comparative increase and also the higher growth rate per thousand created apprehensions in the minds of majority community and provided fuel to communal fire.

The communal incidents were quite common even during pre-independence days but the incidents used to be localised and damage was also confined to the groups involved in the fighting. The riots took place only sparingly upto 1910 but later on both the frequency and fatality increased. The period from 1930 to 1946 witnessed numerous communal riots simultaneously starting from certain communally sensitive cities of Uttar Pradesh. The cities of Aligarh, Allahabad, Moradabad and certain towns of Rohilkhand were very sensitive in this respect. As an aftermath to partition the riots took place even in the rural areas. Immediately after independence, the Muslim community as a whole suffered the void in leadership and was shocked to bear the loss of influence in the social, cultural, economic and political spheres with the dawn of independence. There was no chance now for them of playing in the hands of the rulers. With the creation of Pakistan, the socially, politically and economically active Muslims left for Pakistan. Further the Muslim community as a whole suffered from the guilt of partition and the Hindus also considered them responsible for it. The refugees coming from Pakistan and Muslims going to Pakistan also suffered and the tales of their woes were in the air. Still communal atmosphere was surprisingly calm after 1950 and no major disturbance took place. In 1961, a major communal riot had broken out in Jabalpur with heavy casualties, in which even Army was called in aid of Civil Authorities. The riot was triggered by the love affair of a Muslim boy with a Hindu girl, and their parents were both in the same business. After this riot, Syed Mahmood felt so much aggrieved that he formed Majlis-e-Mushawarat—the first attempt in free India to organize Muslims. "It was the first attempt in the post-Independence India to bring together Muslims to pool their energies and intellectual powers not only to find solution to their problems but also to exert pressure on the political system for realising their demands. The Urdu Press by and large welcomed the move and published articles and editorials to this effect. But it also sent alarm signals to the Hindu Communalists and the right-wingers."[6]

The decade from 1961-71 was the very difficult period for the country as in this period India had to swallow defeat in the North-East and was forced to redefine its priorities. The conflict with Pakistan (in Kutchch in 1965), followed by Bangladesh War in 1971, also conditioned the mood of the majority community and in these wars the members of the Muslim community at the sensitive places were cause of concern. The rumour-mongers were at their job though without much success. The refugees coming from Bangladesh and also the trickle from Sind Province (West Pakistan) further added fuel to the fire. During this period the country suffered riots in Ranchi, Jamshedpur, Aligarh, Bhiwandi, Jalgaon and other towns. This was also the difficult period for the ruling Congress Party which suffered defeat in some of the States besides suffering the death of Pandit Nehru and Shastriji. The emergence of Smt. Indira Gandhi as the undisputed leader of the Congress Party inspired the party workers and a new equation was found out to bring back the party on a high pedestal of glory. The decisive victory on Bangladesh front further made her tallest of the national leaders. During this period the political parties, both regional and national, started a search for new strategies to dethrone the ruling party which was determined to retain control. In the aforesaid situation efforts were made to woo the electorates by raising populist slogans and religious minorities were also shown consideration with an eye on election. During this period Muslim Personal Law Board was formed to protect their Personal Law based on *Sheriat*. The Government assured the minorities that it had no intention of interfering with the Personal Law of the Muslims. It raised a controversy and the Hindus started demanding the uniform Civil Code as also the Indianisation of the Indian Muslims.

All this and other factors vitiated the general atmosphere in India. Then came Allahabad High Court decision against Smt. Indira Gandhi, followed by the imposition of Emergency. During this period, the political parties of every shade unitedly launched an agitation against the Government (s) under the leadership of late Shri Jai Prakash Narain. Even the political parties with declared religious bias changed their outlook and the Muslims openly voted for Janata Party even though Jan Sangh was one of its constituents.

After 1977 onwards, 'Shah Bano Case', 'Meenakshipuram Conversions' (Dalits to Islam), and the opening of Babri-Masjid claimed to be Ram Janam Bhumi, for the Hindus, brought fundamentalism of every shade on the surface. The policitical scene changed very quickly and the nation saw numerous rallies and violent agitations from 'Mandal' to 'Anti-Mandal' in the context of social justice. All this culminated into the fall of Shri V.P. Singh's Government after Shri L.K. Advani's 'Rath Yatra' and his arrest. The demolition of the disputed structure of Babri Masjid and its aftermath witnessed the bloodiest of the communal riots after partition. During this period the rift between the two communities was near complete but new equations were forged out at national as well as regional levels. New 'Brokers' of 'Vote Banks' have emerged and political leaders of every denomination lined up for their support unabashedly. The aggressiveness of the minorities even for the just cause is likely to be misconstrued and misrepresented. This gives rise to 'Competitive Communalism' and India is passing through this phase. The sanity has become rare even with responsible persons and a new era of 'Competitive Communalism' has emerged which is most disastrous for pluralistic society like ours.[7]

The communal clashes were confined to Hindus and Muslims only during the pre-independence period. Even after a lapse of quarter century in post-independence period the communal clashes involving other religions groups were unknown in the country. Thanks to the policies of the successive government and also the designs of our neighbour, we have seen command clashes of every denomination and description. We have seen clashes between Hindus and Sikhs, Hindus and Buddhists and now Hindu and Christians also. As if it was not had enough we have created caste hatred which resulted into clashes between Scheduled Castes and Upper castes, Upper castes and Backward classes, Backward classes and Scheduled Castes, Backward classes Tribals and non-tribals, Shias and Sunnis and Backward class and other Backward classes. The concept of minority community at national level has lost its meaning became members of majority community suffer from minority Psyche in the pockets having influence of minority community such as Pandits of Jammu and Kashmir and Hindus in certain pockets of western U.P. and Rohilkhand.

In Uttar Pradesh, the period between 1952 to 1970 was comparatively quieter but after that communal intolerance on the issues like cow protection. Urdu Movement increased and the incidents of communal frenzy were quite frequent. The decade between 1971 to 1980 witnessed some of the very serious riots, involving issues like Family Planning. The eighties equally witnessed some of the very serious riots connected with Ram Janam Bhumi-Babri Masjid issue and in the wake of Smt. Indira Gandhi's assassination anti-Sikh riots of Kanpur (1984). The Hindu-Muslim riots of Meerut (1987) and Budaun riots (1989) were very serious. The scenario in November 1990, was also quite grim. After 6th December 1992 demolition, the country was under the shadow of communal frenzy. It is really very distressing to note that the incidents from 1990 to 1993 crossed 1,000 mark per year while it used to be only 200 incidents in 7th decade. In the year 1993, over 2,000 people lost their lives in communal clashes and over 13,000 were injured.

After independence, India marched on the path of economic progress but the benefits of progress and economic development did not reach all the people, and thousands of pockets of under-privileged, uneducated, unemployed people sprang up in almost all the cities. Disparities have increased. We talked of socialism for forty years. We have people who have taken advantage of the socialist system to bring about prosperity but not general prosperity. They have to start from somewhere so they start with themselves. That is the kind of prosperity they want. This prosperity results into social tension. When a particular religious group suffers such economic backwardness more than other religious groups it widens the social cleavage.

The first few General Elections were fought on political agenda and caste and religion did not play any significant role in the selection of candidates but plurality in the political field and the near invincibility of Congress rule led some of the politicians to resort to religious and caste appeals, a fact which can be testified by the timing of communal riots in certain areas having predominantly Hindu or Muslim population.

After the outbreak of each riot there is an exchange of population in some of the cities whereby minority group leaves the locality and settles in areas where people of the same religion predominate. This tendency further heightens the divide, hinders interaction with each other and obstructs any kind of social understanding between the religious groups. One can find such localities in cities like Meerut and Kanpur. In such localities the bonds of religion are further strengthened by threads of neighbourhood and in the process excludes all opportunities of dialogue and resultant understanding.

The scenario is getting increasingly grim and communal atmosphere is vitiated in a large number of cities and even the rural areas have not been spared. It has also been noticed that attack by communal groups is very much planned and more and more fire-arms and explosives are being used as weapons of assault, which were earlier confined to knives, etc. for stabbing purposes. The study of riots that took place in the country in recent past reveals the following trends:

1. Riots are not local affairs now. The local incidents have representations in wider areas.
2. Riots are well-planned and propaganda after the riot is also well-planned and very extensive. Electronic media are also employed for dissemination of provocative information. There is a growing tendency to involve educated and half-educated youths in communal riots and resultant militant campaigns.
3. Even responsible circles have thrown caution to the wind and politicians and social leaders shamefully start taking sides even during riots. This tendency was unheard of during first 20-25 years after Independence.
4. Even the relief measures undertaken by various volunteer organizations are taken up at times on communal basis that shows the extent of degradation.
5. There is a growing tendency on the part of communal militants to attack the police and Government officers during riots which is reflected in the casuality list of the policemen during riots.

Communal Riots—Police Response

Considering the factors responsible for the creation of communal tension, the start of a communal riot is not within the control of the police, but the continuance of a riot definitely speaks of police unpreparedness and incompetence in dealing with riots. Normally, blame is thrown on political factors and the lack of intelligence in a very general and casual manner. No doubt the collection of information is a very important function of the police both at the level of the police-station and at the level of the District and State administration. Everybody knew that demolition of the structure at Ayodhya will have serious repercussions, still riots broke out all over India with disastrous consequences. Was it failure of Intelligence ? Was it due to lack of preparedness ? Did it reflect lack of commitment on the part of men who mattered The holocaust that took place at the time of demolition and afterwards could not be prevented because of epidermal secularism of men who could not hear the voice of their conscience, as a "Man's conscience is the oracle of God"(Byron).

From the study of various riots it becomes clear that in certain cases riots are the direct result of some local events which were not attended properly in the beginning. Later on when the local community got involved in this the riots escalated. In such cases lack of Intelligence and prompt and effective action on the part of the Police and Magistracy are the main causes for escalation. When a criminal act, such as kidnapping of a girl belonging to minority community is reported in the police-station against a boy of majority community, one should feel sure that any slackness or partiality in investigation will lead to communal trouble. Similarly, any sacrilegious act will definitely have repercussions if prompt action is not taken in the matter. In such cases the police cannot absolve itself from the responsibility for escalation of an ordinary communal situation into a full-fledged riot.

In certain cases certain emotive issue are taken up by the political parties and social environment gets vitiated because of communal propaganda, all around. It is true that the police cannot change the social environment but in such cases preventive action and utmost preparedness are the least one can expect from the police. Any dereliction in this leads to riotous situation and any ineptness or partiality in dealing with Law and Order situation leads to escalation of riots in other areas.

The loss of credibility of the Police and the Magistracy is the most important hurdle in bringing normalcy. The loss of such credibility reflects the effectiveness of leadership and also the support they get from public in general. If police leadership wavers because of political interference or personal prejudices and fails to implement Rule of Law, the communal riot cannot be stopped—the large amount of force and the material resources notwithstanding.

Similarly, quantum and timing of force to be used is very important. In certain cases it is reported that local administration's indecisiveness in imposing ban orders encouraged the rioters. Similarly, Administrator's lack of decision regarding use of force allows rioters to play havoc with government and public property.

In certain cases nervous action on the part of the government in transferring officers also leads to continuance of riot while in other cases when fury of the community is directed against a particular officer, transfer of the officer brings immediate peace in the township. In controlling riots no hard and fast rules can be made but a conscious decision considering all the facts and pros and cons of a particular step should be taken promptly and effectively.

The role of media is very important in riotous situation. If exaggerated news are disseminated then atmosphere is built for communal tension. If communal elements gain control of the Press, especially local and yellow periodicals and journals, then it is difficult to control emotions. In situation like this even the uncommitted member of the community becomes active and can perpetrate crime.

In such a situation it is not only the police which is to act but the whole community and all the limbs of the government to respond immediately and in well-knit programme of action.

In this connection it is to be noted that even in the face of most serious communal riots, the process of investigation should continue, as it helps in normalising the situation and only strict and proper legal action under proper law can deter the rioters. Everyone knows that preventive action is only an *ad hoc* measure which can be forgotten after normalcy returns. It is really surprising that as soon as the riot situation tapers down, everybody including political executive pressurizes the police to withdraw the cases and the cases registered during communal clashes are not allowed to have proper adjudication which encourages the law-breakers. Similarly, the results of Judicial Enquiry are hardly published and recommendations are very rarely acted upon.

RECOMMENDATIONS

I. Recommendations with Respect to Administration

1. All communal disturbances should be thoroughly enquired into and enquiry reports published without delay to create confidence in the minds of the victims.
2. Religion should not be mixed with politics. Only those political parties which have a declared manifesto of socio-economic programmes should be recognised and those based purely on religion should be banned. Religious overtones and undertones should be avoided in State functions.
3. Migration of people to areas, where their community dominates, as a result of communal riots is an ominous development which produces a dangerous 'divide' between the communities and all efforts must be concentrated on stopping this polarization.
4. The fight against communalism should be a multi-agency effort. Once a year there should be an in-depth examination of the problem and Politicians, Judiciary, Teachers, Police and Armed Forces and in fact, all those agencies that can be expected to build up a popular response against communalism, must

participate in it. A multi-dimensional and integrated approach, in which resources of all agencies are harnessed to tackle the problem of communalism, is desirable.

II. Recommendations with Respect to Police

1. Strict, impartial and expeditious enforcement of law by the Law Enforcement Agencies alone can create the conducive atmosphere for the growth of secularism in India.
2. Wherever the Police and the Administration displayed anticipation and forethought action and the intelligence machinery had operated with competence, the communal forces could be kept under control. Proper training and reorientation courses are very essential in this direction.
3. Meticulous planning by the Police Authorities helps in obtaining positive results. They must anticipate a problem, react quickly to the earliest signals of the approaching trouble, plan for the contingency and immediately deploy the available force after due preparation. Any amount of resources would not yield the desired results without proper planning. A state of preparedness in matters of equipment, vehicles and other resources would help in avoiding failures in emergencies.
4. Effective action must be taken at the initial stages of a communal riot. Prohibitory orders under Section 144 Cr. P.C. must be promulgated and curfew clamped at the earliest inkling of trouble. Maximum use of force, is justifiable. The initial stage of a riot is the most important stage and any slackness, weakness or incompetence on the part of authorities at this time would have disatrous consequences.
5. Collection of intelligence plays a crucial role in warning the administration of the impending disaster. However, intelligence may not be restricted only to the reports

received from the Special Branch or the Intelligence Bureau. The basic unit for intelligence gathering is the police-station. The police-station staff is well conversant with the influencial local people who can prevent trouble. The resources, the quality of personnel and the public accountability of the police-station needs to be strengthened and upgraded. During communal riots, government must insist that all its agencies collect Intelligence and feed the Police and the Police in its turn, should not fight shy of sharing Intelligence with some influential members of the society, who may help in restoring peace.

6. Riot schemes should be periodically rehearsed and updated. Lists of anti-social elements, prominent citizens and peace committee members must be updated at regular intervals.
7. Special teams of Police Officers may be constituted for investigation of cases relating to communal riots and special courts entrusted with the trial of these cases to ensure their speedy disposal.
8. There should be intensive orientation training for Police Officers to deal with the communal problem. In pre-induction training also every officer should be made to develop secular outlook.
9. Communally sensitive police-station must be equipped fully and hand-picked officers, who have been properly trained and motivated be posted there.

III. Recommendations with Respect to Legal Measures

Law is outdated and there is a crying need to update the same. There should be a special enactment for controlling rumours and vicious propaganda. Whoever propagates hatred against others must be punished. We must display the necessary will to implement the law impartially and effectively. The cases should not be withdrawn on political reason. Further National debate is required to review various provisions regarding fundamental rights specially freedom of speech.

IV. Recommendations with Respect to Press and Media

1. Press and the Media must behave with restraint and maturity while dealing with emotive issues. The rumours regarding women being raped and children being assaulted published in some sections of the Press add fuel to the already inflamed sentiments. Biased reporting of events and tendentious propaganda based on unverified stories leads to catastrophic consequences.
2. Timely contradiction of rumours and provision of correct information by the administration and legal action against the mischief-mongers among the Press are measures that may lead to early control of riots, but the irony is that adequate legal provisions are available for action against such irresponsible elements but action is rarely taken.
3. The audio-visual Media including feature films should also project a secular outlook. The real message of religion must be conveyed to the people by the Media and the film world.

In the above context all political parties have to adopt a Code of Conduct for themselves so that narrow sectarian demands are not raised with an eye on election. Further, a National consensus has to be evolved so that certain matters are always viewed with utmost objectivity and no political considerations are allowed to cloud the political vision. The historians and intellectuals should also refrain from highlighting the points of difference between the communities, instead the points of similarity be emphasized to foster a new era of cooperation and brotherhood and make them understanding that 'By uniting we stand by dividing we fall" (John Dickinson).

REFERENCES

1. Move together, talk together and your perception should remain the same. You should act together think together and with this togetherness of heart all of us will remain happy.
2. Brother should not distance from brother, sister should not

distance from sister. All of us engaged in pursuit of one goal and one ideal should always communicate in respectful language.

3. Political mobilisation by religious fundamentalists are painted as the genuine assortion of national and sub-national identities. A majority community feels that the country really belongs to it exclusively and that the people belonging to other religions are aliens and have no right to thrive and prosper on the land where they are born. A minority community on the other hand feels threatened by the massive presene of the big brother and its feeling of psychological insecurity which finally leads to a search for a separate identity. And this is where a secessionist movement is born. [Shri Mohd. Shafi Qureshi, H.E. The Government of M.P. speech delivered on the occasion of 2nd National Seminar on Communal Riots (April 30-May 2, 1994).
4. Sir Charles Wood—Quoted on p. 13—*Forty Years of World's Largest Democracy.*
5. Shri Aghar Ali Engineer—*Demands of Ministry.*
6. From the address of Prime Minister Shri P.V. Narasimha Rao on January 30, 1993 (*The India Police Journal*, Vol. 40, 1994).
7. A minority—it may be ethnic or religious—has to adopt proper strategies for its own safety and security. If it adopts an aggressive stance, even for its legitimate demands, it ends up by further antagonising the majority community. Even the legitimate demands must be couched in a well-thought out manner. This is something which the new Muslim Leadership could not properly appreciate. (Shri Asghar Ali Engineer—*Economic and Political Weekly*—August 22, 1992).
8. Taken from the proceedings of 2nd National Seminar on Communal Riots.

6

Indian Police : A Study in Democratic Policing

The day man realised the significance of social and moral values, the anxiety to uphold these values was supreme in his mind. This process of realisation, enrichment and preservation of values brought various institutions into existence. The state with all its powers, functions and concepts of justice and welfare of masses, also came into being as a result of this quest for just societal order to ensure harmonious relations between the various parts of social organism. The ancient Indian concept of *Nyay* and *Dharma* found echo in the Platonic concept of justice as quoted above and still directs the thought process of those who provide value oriented anchorage to statecraft. Long back in early Roman history Cicero had also described justice as 'the disposition of the human mind to render to everyone his due'.

The ruler's mental attitude of fairness and concern for others is very important and a positive step towards achieving this goal of 'just societal order' but it is not sufficient enough to bring in the reign of justice without proper foundation of enactments, the system to enforce distributive, corrective and contractual justice and also the growth of normative behavioural pattern. Any system which aims at establishing ideal social order will have to develop a workable synthesis between various components depending upon the genius of the leaders of the society, system of governance, historical and economic background of the nation.

It is the notion of justice that brings with it the components of freedom, equality and security besides other values which may be considered of paramount importance for the creation of a just societal order. Justice requires that freedom, equality and security be accorded to all human beings to the greatest extent possible but always consistent with the common good.

Justice cannot be dispensed to the individuals without an orderly judicial system which will ensure in some measure consistency, coherence and objectivity into the uniform legal process which serves as corner stone for a fair and impartial judicial administration. For the progress of the human societies and the growth of human civilisation and cultures coupled with self-actualisation a substantial degree of the normative system and fair amount of its observance is an indispensable prerequisite.[1]

The degree of synthesis of orderliness in society with its rules, laws and fair amount of adherence to such rules on one hand and the concept of justice with its components of freedom, equality, security, public good and morality on the other directly affected the growth and sustenance of progressive societies. The concept of paramountcy of the state, primacy of the head of family and head of the clan also depended on the progressive level of the community and also the form of government. Similarly, effectiveness of various social, administrative and legal institutions also varied from place to place.

In a country like India, with long and rich history going back to more than five thousand years and witnessing the rule of hundreds of dynasties with diverse socio-ethnic back-ground the concepts of justice almost remained the same except in brief interludes but the effectiveness of socio-legal institutions varied from time to time, from place to place and from ruler to ruler. Ancient Indian *Ganarajyas* gave place to empires which fragmented again and again into smaller kingdoms ruled by kings having small armies and only a few villages to be governed. In such kingdoms the ruler who was considered fountainhead of justice also became supreme judge in temporal matters to be assisted by the *graminis* in the rural areas. The court had to dispense justice in cases of litigation between the parties and also the offences against the state such as armed rebellions or conspiracies against the king. The litigations between opposing parties were decided on the basis of principles of preponderance of evidence under elaborate procedure in vogue during greater part of ancient and early medieval periods of Indian history. The offences against the state were viewed very seriously and in most of the cases king himself took a decision. In such cases agency employed to collect facts and evidence was under the control of ruler himself or his most trusted minister who employed these spies or private informers for collection of intelligence and evidence and also for execution of the punishment. The spies so deployed were personally loyal to the handler and were very often used to execute political conspiracies as well. This function was considered to be very important and therefore the members of this organisation exerted considerable influence on administration. At times these spies were also employed to solve crimes against public at large which were considered to be crime against the state. The maintenance of order with the help of overt force was always enthrusted to Army. The maintenance of order and dispensation of justice in smaller villages was left to local organisation headed by *Graminis* etc. In India before the invasions of Arabs the police functions of the state were discharged partly by king appointed chain of spies and trusted armed men (European counterpart Gendermerie or totalitarian police) and partly by community police (kin police of medieval Europe).

The invaders, including Arabs, Turks and Mongols came from different socio-ethnic stock hence maintained separate identity and confined themselves to bigger clusters of human settlements. The administrative setup of bigger town was changed to suit the ruler of the time while in smaller towns and villages the system remained almost unchanged till the arrival of Europeans in the country. Europeans and specially the Britons when they acquired Dewani rights in Bengal started changing the system of maintenance of law and order as well. The French system of policing introduced by Napoleon in France was adopted by the Britishers with necessary changes to suit the needs of the time. In India, after successfully routing all opposition from fellow Europeans, they started experimenting with the system. In Sindh and later on in Punjab they had one model while in Bombay Presidency, the system adopted was entirely different. The system in Bengal and N.W. Provinces was happy synthesis of these models and was adopted for whole territory in course of time. The judicial system including policing was subjected to more experimentation and later on it was adopted for whole of the country including Indian Princely states with minor changes here and there.

Police System under Company Rule

The East India Company was being run on commercial basis and no wonder its prime objective was to earn money. The entire administrative system was only to guard the interest of the Company. Therefore, policing was to be inexpensive and effective in facilitating more effective exploitation of the natural resources and the masses. As such long range planning for better utilisation of natural resources and welfare of the masses was unknown to the company employees. In this situation one can very well visualise the attitude of not only police system but entire administrative machinery. For them maintenance of law and order was incidental and necessary only if it was essential to add to the income of the company. W. Hastings in 1772 paid special attention to the problem of dacoity (Regulation 35th) in the country side and on trade routes, but rural policing was still the responsibility of Zamindars. On 15th April 1785 the magistrates were given the powers to decide criminal cases hitherto enjoyed by Zamindars which further alienated the administration from public but the office of Judge Magistrate became very powerful.

The mismanagement of the affairs of the company and their cruel and immoral ways of dealing with the natives led to uprising in 1857 which marked the end of company's rule in the country and beginning of the rule of Crown of England and Ireland in the sub-continent.

Police after 1861

On 16 April 1855 the Torture Commission submitted its report suggesting wide ranging changes in police system because commission found, "Corruption and bribery regin paramount throughout the whole establishment; violence, tortune and cruelty are their chief instruments for detecting crime, implicating innocent and extorting money". The reports of 1st and 2nd Law Commissions were also available to the Government. Therefore, First Police Commission took only 22 days to submit draft of Indian Police Act which was later on passed on 16 March 1861. All this happened quickly and action was also taken swiftly to lay the foundation of present judicial system including police. Hence it may be mentioned that the then Governor General was not concerned about the welfare of the masses but his concern was to 'economise expenditure', and "increase efficiency in the existing police forces" as laid down in the notification dated 17 August 1860 issued at the time of appointing 1st Police Commission. The feudal administration in vogue during later Mughal period, therefore, slowly passed into a well oiled machinery to keep masses under control and also to deprive local feudal chieftains of their influence on the public and their say in the administration to ward off any possibility of uprising against the colonial government. This second half of 19th century was the period of consolidation of British Imperialism not only in India but all over the world but greater attention was paid to the colonies of Asia. During this period planned and sincere efforts were made to remove all impediments to the smooth adminstation but the interest of British Empire was supreme. The enlightened class was offered entry into elite services and other influential persons were given titles to ensure their loyalty to the crown and thus a new class of native supporters was created in the interest of the empire. Any liberal and right thinking person even among the Europeans was chastised and discouraged if he wanted to introduce reforms beneficial to masses at the cost of interest of the empire.

At the Dawn of Independence

At the dawn of Indian Independence, Police like any other branch of administration was loyal to the Government and had no responsibility towards the public at large, for them the day of independence was only the day of change of Government without any change in their uniform, mode of recruitment, curriculum of training, code of conduct, criminal law, disciplinary control and most importantly in their attitude towards public and towards government. Since there was no change in police-public relations, it was but imperative that public attitude towards police also remained unchanged thus a chasm between two attitudes was perpetuated. As if it was not enough, apathy of new rulers with the help of loyalist of previous regime perpetrated total indifference of successive governments towards police reforms.

Police of colonial India, created and trained to defend the interest of British Empire was now saddled to serve the democratic Republic of India. Those who fought the system were now destined to make policies and those who fought the fighters of freedom were supposed to implement the policies. Police as an organisation lacked this resilience and adaptability. The leaders of the organisation partly suffered from guilt of acting against national interest earlier and partly their view of discipline prevented them from telling the truth. The smoke screen between police leadership and political executive created a communication gap which was not to be bridged even after half century of independence. Even the legitimate grievances of police could never find the ears of the political masters let alone the sympathetic consideration. Similarly the executive orders though not strictly legal were often informally conveyed and police was supposed to obey habitually which created a darker image of police which suffered as a consequence in course of time. The police leadership which was in habit of obeying orders from above continued to obey such orders without getting an opportunity to apprise the real rulers the after effects of such blind compliance and even to verify the veracity of such orders what to say of questioning the legality and propriety of them.

New Challenges

The partition of the country created many a problem for the police. The population exodus on the basis of the religion without agreeing for exchange of population resulted in unprecedented violence in the form of massacres, arsons, looting and unauthorised occupation of immoveable property. The violence coupled with the problem of providing rehabilitation to millions crossing the border but unbearable strain on police system specially at the time when the system itself was under strain because of void created by exodus of officers to Pakistan and UK Police with depleted resources managed to do its best but the process itself left the organisation with ethnic bias within and suspicion in the minds of public. This ethnic imbalance proved disasterous later on when communal riots in the country became order of the day and minorities became suspicious of police raising all sorts of demands for the control of riots.

The Second World War and the partition devastated the economy of the country and necessitated economic reconstruction at vast scale which left little room for paying any attention to policing and as a result it was never given proper place on the agenda of the political parties. In course of time, this apathy demoralised the police, which degenerated the system in turn leading to indiscipline and unrest in most of the states. The men who mattered, instead of strengthening the organisational leadership weakened it in the name of reforms and imposing greater controls. The political parties who were waiting in the wings also tried to obtain political advantages of the situation which further damaged the credibility of the force and in some states gave it a biased character. The weak leadership, lack of objectivity in police and narrow considerations destroyed the integrity and cohesiveness of the force.

In the beginning there was one party rule in the country and the coordination between states and Centre was satisfactory but with the cracks in the monolithic political canopy, the political differences started showing up even in administrative matters. In some states the political instability paved way for 'committed bureaucracy' and 'committed police' followed by attempts by political cadres to subvert the police organisation. In such situations whole administrative machinery became partisan and objectivity and professionalism was given a silent burial by committed, motivated and ambitious officers. The difference between 'political executive' and 'executive' narrowed down to unidentifiable limits and police ceased to retain even the faintest consideration for the masses and gradually ceased to function as community police.

Socio-Political Challenges

The change in political leadership changed the social character of the ruling class. Initially the leaders were guided by Gandhian principles and were more concerned about the welfare of the masses and narrow considerations of region, caste and class never clouded their vision in taking administrative decisions but things changed and the new group of self seekers whole time political activists joined the race for chairs. This was the turning point which led the police to political mess.

The new generation of leadership was interested only in political power and after gaining access to the corridors of power to retain it by all means. In this process the Gandhian concept of 'fair means' was never allowed to blur their view of gaining power by all means including those which were questionable and harmful to the social fabric of the country. The numerous communal riots just before the general elections, sweeping declarations about the concessions to the religious minorities, decisions regarding creation of new states, grant of official status to languages and dialects are some of the examples of political malpractices the politicians indulged in just to gain political advantages even at the cost of social peace. The recommendations of Mandal Commission, its acceptance and implementation is all fresh in our minds and the political objectives have also become very clear now but it all dragged the country at least a few decades back on the path of economic well-being of all including Mandal beneficiaries. Similarly the temple issue, the debate, the demolition and its aftermath has not strengthened the bonds between the communities and definitely brought bad name to the country on international stage. The propaganda material emanating from the country, competitive mud slinging and violent fights between regional parties all proved our fragmented nationality and fragile nature of ethnic cohesion that affected our status among comity of nations.

The elections in a democratic country like India, which proclaimed its adherence to Gandhian principles have become more and more expensive. Those who had money spent it to influence the electorate and those who lacked in money, power banked on muscle power. In the beginning, money was collected by donations and industrial houses were rather too happy to give money but later on arm twisting was considered necessary which ultimately gave way to scandals after scandals in which entrepreneurs and politicians joined hands and siphoned public money with impunity and watch dog institutions like C.A.G., Vigilance Commission, Parliamentary Committees and investigating agencies were either gagged, passed by or won over to maintain silence. This process corrupted political and bureaucratic functionaries and also created an atmosphere in which corruption was granted respectability in society and was considered as normative behaviour.

Those political activists who depended on muscle power to collect crowd, maintain peace in public meetings (also disturbing meetings of political opponents) and influencing electorate, came closer to criminals. This closeness with the criminals has resulted into criminalisation of politics giving way to political violence and elimination of adversary by bullets if one fails in the fight of ballots. Now the politics in certain regions has been reduced to mafia activity and only hardened criminals can contest. These criminals get political support and political ideologues have to work over time to find out moral justification for giving political support, enacting laws and defeating legal process by administrative steps. Now quite a few political leaders of some consequence, have an organised machinery to collect money, conceal it and to support a private army of gangsters who can quell and create disturbances and silence the region into numbness if so desired. The words like 'corruption' and 'crime' have lost all relevance and have acquired new meaning in our country's political lexicon. Some of the taller leaders who still want to retain at least semblance of propriety and morality in political field as well have been reduced to figure heads or masks by those who are practitioner of 'real politik'.

The selection of candidates on the basis of narrow consideration of the caste and creed, use of money and muscle power in elections are considered normative action and public at large has also become immune to it which makes redemption more difficult.

Degeneration of Democratic Institutions

The democratic institutions are the pillars of democracy. If these institutions are allowed to grow and function properly then only democracy can survive and rule of law can be maintained. These institutions should be given proper environment to grow, i.e., they should be managed by persons with widest acceptability, once selected for the job they should be allowed to function properly without fear or favour. The political parties and people at large should show reverence to them naturally. In our country in recent years disrespect has been shown to the highest office and even to the judiciary by those who are responsible for the governance of the country. The occupants of high offices have also not crowned themselves with glory while taking decisions in matters of national importance. Casting as persions on the governors and other officials of the state without even an iota of truth has become order of the day and the public at large forgets it gleefully. We must realise that by disrespecting our institutions we are destroying the foundation of our democracy.

The persons occupying high offices should also realise that proper functioning of the government in democracy envisages a complementarity and not confrontation by the different institutions. In our country specially after the departure of tall leaders and statesmen from the national scene, we have been witnessing absence of this complementarity and national solidarity for more than two decades. This lack of national solidarity, unity of vision and cohesion in action and resultant degeneration of our institutions has disturbed social fabric and has put undue strain on law and order machinery which is still languishing in feudal attitude towards masses whom they profess to serve.

Distortions and Decline in Credibility

In the first session of Constituent Assembly Pt. Jawahar Lal Nehru, while moving the objectives resolution on 13 December 1946, declared that in our Constitution, "Shall be guaranteed and secured to all the people of India Justice, social, economic and political, equality of status, of opportunity and equality before the law, freedom of thought, expression, belief, faith, worship, vocation, association and action subject to law and public morality." After more than 50 years of above declaration can we say with confidence that we have attained the objectives? The public, though majority was illiterate too begin with, realises that we have lost the direction and so many distortions—economic, political and social have crept in our national life that make the realisation of goals difficult if not impossible in current social, economic, political and international scenario. Some of us have already voiced concern about the functioning of parliamentary democracy and have started debating possibility of other form of government. As far as illiterate, politically unbiased but truthful simple villager is concerned, he feels that to him the rule of foreigners was better in ways more than one. This being the level of credibility of government and standard of governance in free India one can realise the image of its governing hands including police, judiciary, bureaucracy and all democratic institutions on which rests the smooth functioning of democracy.

In our freedom struggle days, under the influence of Gandhiji we fought for the betterment of life of 'Daridra Narain'. Swadeshi movement aimed at self-reliant economy. In our Constitution also we declared to promote social justice and for that the political party in power adopted resolution to have socialistic pattern of society accompanied with rapid economic growth and fostering new enlightened scientific outlook in society. With march of time, we nationalised the financial institutions and established public sector undertakings to boost economic growth in core sectors. Now after years of experimentation we have liberalised our economy rejecting the old model and under international fiscal compulsions, have allowed the multinationals even in consumer sector. The political leaders of different hues differ as regards advisability of allowing multinationals to enter our economy in this way and compare it with sell out to East India Company that ultimately paved the way for British rule in India. The governmental agencies are publishing data to show gains of such collaborations and co-operation in economic field. The difference in the field of economic philosophy apart, people at large still feel deprived and number of people below poverty line is larger than the total population of most of the countries of the world (except China). The failure of economic experimentation and changes in policy have created chaotic conditions in economic field. The economic heights which we attained, have failed to make social impact as we have failed to maintain correst sight and certain sections feel deprived and disappointed with the system resulting into conflict situation at slightest provocation.

Negative Police Image

Police and as a matter of fact any social organisation, cannot function in vacuum. The social background, the forces conditioning the social reaction to problems, the socio-economic constraints all fashion the societal response in case of police-public interface. In India, despite credible performance and supreme sacrifices made by police in the early days of independence during large-scale migration of people; riots in the wake of creation of states on the basis of languages; anti-Hindi agitation in South; agitation in Kerala; liberation of Goa; emergence, growth and control of groups professing armed struggle to bring about economic changes, trade union activities specially in Railways and Post and Telegraph and also separatist movements in North-East, and tackling of dacoity menace in Uttar Pradesh, Madhya Pradesh, Gujarat and Rajasthan, the image of police remains very negative. In all these situations police at times had to act in a manner not liked by public or a section of it. The public view on a particular situation largely depends on the information given to them by local media and official sources. The public relied more on media than governmental sources, a legacy of foreign rule which made every nationalist against the establishment. Police being the most visible arm of the government had to earn this wrath of public more than any other organ of the government. Police in such cases, is made victim of the situation which is not their creation.

Police being the strong arm of the government has to use coercive power of the government. At times the policeman in his anxiety to maintain order and to prove his effectiveness and loyalty to his 'masters' (which is always suspected) acts in most unbecoming manner which is always disowned by the guiding hand. The deeds and misdeeds attributed to police during Railways strike are examples to prove the point. Similarly during Emergency, the police action against the national leaders, indiscriminate arrests, illegal detention and harassment of family members and supporters attributed to police in most cases was done in compliance to informal orders which police very meekly complied with without questioning the legality and propriety of the same. The findings of various commissions and committees are not made public as a rule to ward off searching queries and criticism and possibility of apportioning the blame with the result police got more than its share of the blame and was painted as the only devil in the society.

The policemen specially those who function at the cutting edge level are attributed with rudeness in behaviour and total indifference to the problems of the public specially of weaker sections of society. Police organisation as a whole, is always considered a secretive and rigid incapable of showing imaginative approach. Perhaps rudeness in behaviour is indicative of lack of proper training and a natural corollary of existing police sub culture. The rigidity in approach to a great extent is enshrined in the regimental training, living and accepted normative behaviour of armed contingent.

Indian police is considered as lazy, inefficient and ineffective and lower police functionaries are often painted as stupid fellows without any courtesy and manners. Such attributes have their roots in history when policemen were recruited as unskilled stoutmen fit only to wield lathis at command but such social prejudices continue even now and renewed by comic representations on silver screen.

Police is also considered as corrupt and immoral. Police department is blamed for increase in crime and also improper tackling of criminals. In this connection no one can deny the fact that corruption has permeated all ranks of police department. The fact that other functionaries of the government are also corrupt can in no way give solace to police managers. The senior police officers have been arrested for illicit trade of narcotics, for colluding with criminals and for conspiring with suppliers to siphon public money.

Indian police from Jammu and Kashmir to Kerala and Tamil Nadu is painted as crude and brutal and lacking all consideration for the victims of crimes. At times police is even blamed for siding with the criminals, a fact at times proved in court of law and bringing unsavory comments from the court. In some states the heads of the police departments have openly accepted unholy alliance with criminals. The report of Vohra Committee also pointedly castigated the politicians and police for having alliance with criminals. All these factors not only tarnish the image of police but they also alienate public from administrative machinery.

Another charge against police is that it acts in a partisan way and never functions as community police. The political party in power treats police as their private army and police willingly accepts it. This charge has been proved against police again and again but neither the leaders of the force nor political parties ever tried to find out causes for the disease. To insulate police from direct interference in their working as recommended by National Police Commission was never considered seriously.

The use of unethical means to carry out its legitimate functions is another charge against the police. This charge includes fabricating or padding of evidence. There is general impression that police, specially the investigating wing always tampers with evidence. The statements of witnesses recorded by police are always changed or witnesses are asked to depose before the court what they have never seen. The scene of crime is often changed to support the police case i.e. in accident cases the investigating officer even recorded the statements of senior magistrates as complainant in case diary without meeting or inquiring from them as required by law. Strange enough all this and even more is done in public interest or in the interest of police case but the net result of all this fabrication, padding, forgery and unethical methods is less than ten per cent conviction in courts with respect to heinous offences.

The short cut methods to work out the cases are other irritants in public minds. The deaths in police custody are rising in our country. The 'National Human Rights Commission' is flooded with complaints of custodial offences including deaths, rapes and illegal confinements. The enquiries conducted in such complaints by the Commission or by the state investigating agencies are found substantiated in a large number of cases. If one delves deep into the causes of such short cuts, one finds that in sizeable number the incidents were motivated by the vested interest or by corruption. In some cases, however, the poor police investigating officer is pressurised by press, public, senior police officers and also by executive including political executive to work out cases within given time, mostly announced at press conferences. The investigating officer has only limited time to interrogate the suspects as the courts are quite strict in granting police remand. The pressure and legal limitation force police investigating officer to resort to short-cut of torture, illegal detention and unethical interrogation tricks. The law commissions one after another totally ignored the ground conditions and obstinately adhered to norms set in Western countries without looking into the reality with regards to equipment, capability, character of police and courts and also the public morals. The commissions have also not considered the disqualifications with regards to police testimony and general lack of trust in police shown in the law of the land which is detrimental to police morale and leads to many unethical practices during the course of investigation. Of late, there have been some judgements which are almost impossible to follow in spirit and will certainly add to malpractices followed by police. Lack of interest by police leadership who tend to agree to carry out every order, prevented them from forcefully representing to government to go in appeal against such decisions which are likely to coax police to commit irregularity and at times fabrication.

Expectations from Police in Democratic Society

Police image in a society depends on the degree of equanimity it has with public expectations. For police this public is not a homogeneous entity. It is composed of many diverse and at times opposite interests. Consequently their expectations are also different and are likely to be changed in different situations. One tends to agree with Peter K. Manning, "The audience for the police is diverse : it should be considered many audiences. For the police must convince the politicians that they have used their allocated resources efficiently; they must persuade the criminals that they are effective crime fighters; they must assure the broader public that they are controlling crime."[2]

The change in situation can also change expectations from the police. A man who has suffered at the hands of dacoits, expects police to work speedily and act tough with the criminals. He also expects police to anyhow recover property but the legal advisers of the culprits insist and rightly so, to keep police within fore corners of law. In a situation of mass violence of communal nature things could be really difficult. The very nature of their work brings the policemen before the public more as adversary rather than as friend and most of the people feel that law enforcement is an undesirable intervention in their private affairs.

Besides maintaining order in society, the control of crime is another basic function of police. Public expectation goes beyond mere reactive action, i.e. public expects that the police by their vigilance and imaginative activity should render it impossible for anyone to commit a crime. This pro-active action will definitely interfere with the lives of many and will seriously affect the right of privacy. The restraint on the right of movement will jeopardise the fundamental right. In this field it is difficult to maintain a balance and society has to decide whether it wants absolute freedom or freedom from crime.

If despite their endeavours and best intention crime takes place, then public expects it to be worked out with utmost speed and the offenders must be produced before the court to face the consequences of their demeanour but all this has to be done after extending procedural safeguards to the persons responsible for crime and disorder. These contradictory expectations place an uneasing burden upon the police.

It is paradoxical but true that there has been gradual expansion in service oriented functions of police even in the face of declining credibility and poor image. In this connection one can cite examples with respect to envisaged role of police for the implementation of government policies, protection of wildlife even the conduct of fair examinations in colleges and universities. In a democratic society where sweeping social changes are envisaged to correct the prevailing distortions through the instrumentalities of state, police is expected to act as an agent of change. In formulation of these policies police has no say, not even prior knowledge till they get orders to implement.

It is again very surprising that most of the political leaders given a chance, will go on criticising police for hours together but they are the first to ask for police protective umbrella. Each and every mafia leader demonstrates his ability to manipulate political heavyweights by moving within police security ring followed by police vehicles with hooters and sirens. The political leaders with criminal links and lords of underworld having links with politicians represent the most vocal section of society that decries police achievements and damages its credibility most. Police as a social institution has to reconcile these contraditions.

This silent revolution in the areas of transport and communication, coupled with change in road topography, has changed the pattern of crime in society. With easy availability of improved fire power, explosion of information through media (including internet) without any moral strings, the men on prowl have become almost invincible for the police who are still equipped with discarded. 303 rifles (even muskets) and mounted on trucks (as small vehicles are considered luxury to them). But our society expects police to fight extremist outfits with lathies or muskets without infringing any procedural law even in the face of grave emergency.

Above all public expects police to act as impartial and independent social institution. In situations of agitations and demonstrations police should act as an arm of judicial system and not as arm of the government, and never as the arm of political party in power. Similarly in days of elections police should be very judicious, objective and firm. Nothing is more damaging to police image than lack of impartiality. "Few things in the world of the police service can damage the police image as much as police involvement in politics. Police in their professional capacity have to be political and impartial in their application of laws."[3] Public expects police to exercise discretion to consider individual circumstances in situations of their interface with public. Police is also expected to exercise their discretion in implementation of policies of the governments.

What Prevents Police to Come upto Expectations?

The negative image of police in public eyes, scores of judgement commenting adversely on police functioning, lack of public cooperation to police even in service oriented functions leave no one in doubt but to agree with the comments made by National Police Commission (1977-80). "The organisation is shaken by mounting criticism of its operational brutality and cancerous corruption. Clearly the police organisation as it stands today is unfit to discharge its duties".

(a) Redefining Role

The role of police during British regime was control and suppression. The interest of the crown was of the paramount importance. The acts and rules, checks, balances and controls, were all designed to protect interest of the crown. Police, a disciplined arm of the state was trained to obey the orders of their superiors in the style of Tennyson's charge of the Light Brigade. After independence things have changed drastically but the law, regulations and controls have not. The role of police has not been redefined. The interest of crown has been replaced by the interest of the state which in the hands of some unscrupulous political manipulators becomes the interest of political instead of interest of the masses. One tends to agree with the observations of National Police Commission, "The present culture of the police system appears to continue of what obtained under the British regime when the police functioned ruthlessly as an agent of sustaining the government in power. In public estimates the police appears as an agency more to implement and enforce the objectives of government in power, as distinct from enforcing law as such as independent impartial agency".

(b) Accountability

In a democratic society, every organ of the government is

accountable to public. Police accountability has not been defined. The mutual respect for other social institutions has no meaning now and there prevails anarchy in bureaucratic machinery having no regard for established conventions. In this confusion every one has to fend for himself and he considers himself accountable to one who can help him in times of need, maybe local leader, a minister or a gangster promising enough to become a minister or Chief Minister in course of time. This situation is not very conducive to responsive policing in a democrative society. The roles have to be defined and accountability has to be fixed if we intend to have responsible and responsive police service. Police have to perform basic functions of prevention and investigation of crime under judicial system while order part of their functions under magistrates, and they work under the government more or less directly for implementation of various social policies. For finances they have to depend on one agency while for their establishment on still other agencies. Their placement can be dictated by political functionaries. They don't have security of job or certainty of their tenure which develops into cynicism.

(c) Professional Standard

It is unanimously agreed that police need to update their professional skills so that they effectively control crime and on this depends their survival. If we glance through the pages of history it cannot but be admitted by every one that prevention and detection of crime was the sole objective of policing which remains unchanged, unchangeable and will always remain their *raison d'etre*. Police functions if they deflect from this fulcrum, can never come upto the expectations of public, but there is one limit which cannot be disregarded if police is to be a blessing rather than curse and that the plan adopted for the prevention of crime must never become more intolerable than the effects of the crime itself.

This contradiction can be managed by improving technical know-how and resources available to police. This updating of professional skills will include specialised knowledge, skills and expertise, higher functional standards, application of modern scientific methodology, functional autonomy and a sense of public accountability. The data regarding commission of crime, investigation and result of trial does emphatically prove that our police need this updating now and any further delay or indifference in this respect will cause harm to society besides eroding the institution of police. This weakness in terms of resources with the police came to surface when we had to face extremism on our borders in Punjab and Jammu and Kashmir. In Uttar Pradesh Terai also public had to suffer because of this apathy of government which instead of preparing police to face the challenge denied stoically the existence of extremists within the limits of state.

(d) Recognition as Agent of Change

In public expectation police has been recognised as agent of change. In a democratic society, progressive social legislation with a view to changing the quality of life have to be brought about through the instrumentation of the state. The police being visible arm of the state is one of the most important instruments to ensure compliance, may be with the help of coercion but "the coercion employed ought to be reduced to the lowest possible limits consistent with safety. The ideal police force being the one which affords a maximum of protection at the cost of a minimum of interference with the lawful liberty of the subject. The real difficulty of police is, therefore, to fix the limits where non-interference should end and coercion should begin."[5] In our country police organisation has not been allowed to play the constructive role in shaping and formulating the policies they are supposed to implement. At times modalities prescribed for implementation of these policies make police more vulnerable, in society and face alienation. If police organisation is also taken into confidence then police could avoid alienation which costs them dearly in term of public co-operation in law and order situation.

(e) Sub Culture

Policemen, when alienated from rest of the society develop

a subculture of their own. In our country, specially during British rule this was particularly true and was responsible to a great extent for the growth of police sub-culture. Some of the important attributes of this sub-culture include notion of self-righteousness, undue importance in the affairs of society, arrogance and lack of tolerance of criticism or suggestions even. This sub-culture is product of alienation and it perpetuates alienation. Police even after more than fifty years of independence continues to suffer from alienation and society suffers from the rudeness, rigidity, arrogance, insularity, secrecy and couldn't careless' mentality more so at the cutting edge level of police functionaries.

The use of violence against men and women in police custody is also part of this sub-culture. This violence justified by many police officers in the name of societal interest can go to any extent from ordinary physical violence to commission of rape, dismemberment of limbs and even killing of men in false encounters. The culture of violence not only violates the rights of the suspects, but also brutalises the perpetrators which is most harmful to society in general besides putting stigma on the image of organization. A policeman while indulging in 'third degree' methods reduces himself to the level of a criminal and even worse than the criminal in his custody. It should be remembered that violation of law even by policemen does not go unnoticed as ultimately it breeds contempt of law. In fact, "law observance by the police is thus the best form of law enforcement that one can conceive of in a country under the rule of law."[6]

The tendency to fabricate records and tampering of evidence to suit the prosecution case is another manifestation of this sub-culture. The Gandhian principle of fair means does not find favour with the officers and to them "the end justifies the means". This tendency being against law and morality further encourages non-compliance of law and negates fair investigation. It also develops a tendency to fabricate records which can be done even for reasons not so pious thus breeding corruption and concoction which ultimately adversely affects the credibility of the investigating agency. It sets in a chain of reaction, as unscrupulous victims, advocates and influential persons come forward with the demand that police should oblige them by fabricating records to help the victim or the accused and failure to do that is normally considered a dishonest act.

The police has elaborate system of grievance redressal but this is common belief, not without basis, that whenever there is a complaint against police functionaries, the department tries to cover it up. In every conference of senior officers there is serious discussion on concealment of crime. Elaborate schemes are prepared but during last 50 years this malady could not be controlled. Similarly the complaints of simple maltreatment of petty corruption are ignored in most of the cases that shows that police sub-culture envisages sufficient degree of tolerance in this respect. The incidents of petty corruption, maltreatment, rudeness are considered normative behaviour by a police functionary and people even in high places justify it by saying that, "a society gets the police it deserves", or in a mild term that "police is also a part of society", but no serious professional thought has been given to reform it and to give it a shape of movement to eradicate a social evil.

(f) Failure of Leadership

Police leadership has failed miserably to lead the organisation. It is common knowledge that such a huge force cannot function smoothly without sound leadership. The sound leadership means that the head of the force is a natural leader of the force, enjoying full confidence and respect of his subordinates and colleagues in other departments. There are so many attributes of good leadership, but the most important is the capability of guiding the department on the path of professionalism and maintaining credibility and confidence. When top leaders succumb to the political pressure at the cost of national and organisational interest then subordinate formations start forging their equations in political circles giving rise to a sense of despondency among honest and straightforward men and officers. In this uncertain organisational environment the lower functionaries start to fend for themselves and can go even to the extent of favouring gang leaders what to say of shady politicians.

(g) Recruitment, Training, Placement and Intra-departmental Grievances

The intake of human raw material is not on sound basis. The job analysis should be carried out and then a sound method should be evolved to recruit men of requisite qualities of head and heart. Undue emphasis has been laid on physical attributes neglecting qualities of mind specially the capability of handling tension. The corruption and favouritism in making recruitment are well-known which further deteriorate the general standard of the organisation. Caste, creed, regionalism and all social evils were represented in the force even during foreign rule but its unity was never threatened. Now the police stands fragmented, on the lines of caste, creed and political ideologies. Training is most neglected. Training depends on human raw material to be trained, the standard of instructors, the material component of training such as training aids, libraries etc., and the training curriculum. The recruitment has been discussed earlier and even National Police Commission has found it far from the ground realities. In most of the states, the conditions in training centres, schools and academies, are appalling. Only 'inconvenient', 'unpliable' and 'condemned' officers are considered fit for training institutions. The 'successful', 'tactful' and 'go-getters' always escape 'agonies' of being posted to training institutions. The senior police officers and politically influential persons always consider training institutes as dumping ground with the result efficient and competent officers shirk from such postings to avoid stigma to their career. Under the circumstances good instructors who are competent and willing do not go to training centres. If by chance any willing, competent, self-motivated person fired with nationalist zeal happens to find way to such institutions he is made victim of police sub-culture and more often than not he is termed as 'visionary', 'theoretical' and ahead of his time and never taken seriously.

As regards the material component, training is always last on the agenda because good or bad results surface after a long time. The managers of the force, having tenure of one or two years, always believe in adhocism and investment giving results after decades does not fit in their priorities.

Gore Committee Report was the first serious attempt to improve training. That report has also celebrated its silver jubilee but its implementation is still neglected by the states. The emergence of organised gangs of criminals, armed with sophisticated fire-arms and employing experts for their operation add a new dimension to our fight against crime. One must realise that under fast changing scenario this Bible of police training needs revisions. At the national level a training policy has to be formulated. Some states have come up with their training policy while others still consider it fit to be postponed for better days. Proposals for improving the training never finds access to the room of senior police-officers and senior bureaucrats and normally end at the table of expert section-officers who know the trick of killing the proposal by making some enquiries.

Not only the basic training, but inservice training is also neglected. In most of the seminars and training courses one finds only those officers who can be easily 'spared' by the administration. Even amongst the 'most trained' officers there are two sets of officers, one who can be spared only for so-called prestigious courses abroad while another set is kept in reserve for training courses run in moffussil towns only. This neglect and dishonest implementation of policies of the government adversely affects the morale of the force and corrodes the system.

We have discussed grievance redressal machinery of the department with respect to public grievances but equally important is grievance redressal of the members of the department. Police department is organised on the pattern of armed forces and therefore it suffers from lack of internal autonomy. Too much centralisation of power stifles initiative and stunts the growth of personality which in turn stagnates the organisation and also diminishes the chances of its redemption by organisational instrumentalities. The difference in opinion with respect to policies, planning and implementation when suppressed leads dissensions and vested interests further accentuate it leading to harassment and victimisation. If machinery for the redressal of grievances is smooth, the organisation does not suffer violent tremors like mass agitation and uprising. Unfortunately police as an organisation, does not have impartial and efficient system of grievance redressal. Therefore, department suffers from lack of vertical interaction and the consequences thereof.

Remedial Measures

If democracy has to survive then democratic institutions have to grow and prosper in a democratic environment. Police a social institution, as it operates today is not able to cope with the requirements of the complex society and also growing complexities of social life. Police have to change and sensitise to the growing needs of democratic conduct if it has to remain relevant to growing progressive society. Already, people have started looking regretfully back to old times of comparative peace and honest administration and a peculiar cynicism has overtaken the enlightened segment of society as wrote Nani Palkiwala, in one of his books, "The quality of our public life has reached the nadir. Politics has become tattered and tainted with crime. The moral standard of our politicians, policemen and criminals are indistinguishable from one another. India today is a living example of the fact that cynicism corrupts and absolute cynicism corrupts absolutely".

First of all the legislations and the rule of governance have to be changed right from preamble to the saving clause of the Act to define in clear term the role of police and its accountability. What functions of the police will remain under the supervision and guidance of the government, political executive or party in power for the time being, should be stated clearly to avoid undue interference in the judicial part of police functions. Further the implications of words like 'supervision' and 'guidance' should be amply explained to prevent any abuse of power. The accountability should be defined and modes to implement it should not be left to the surmise of the usurpers and other vested interests. Such structural changes can be effected by initiating national debate and then taking a conscious decision.

Recruitment and training should be given their due place in the organisational plan of the police. Due care and caution has to be exercised at the time of recruitment to prevent the politicians from swarming the ranks of police as has been done in some states under well rehearsed schemes. This infiltration subverts the role of independent and impartial force in time of turmoil. Independent recruitment boards with adequate checks and balances can be established. The training of human raw material should be so organised that they do not starve of resources both financial and human. Like education, training should be given proper place in the career graph and can be linked with career prospects in the organisation.

Upgradation of police skills with a view to improving police performance in discharge of their core functions like prevention, detection of crime and creating healthy security environment is another important field, requiring immediate attention. This upgradation will result in speedy response to community need, and foster competent handling of the situations avoiding unnecessary interference of confrontation which is ultimately bound to improve police image. It must be realised that, "The capacity to sustain supportive environment for police work must be a critical quality of the police function in democracies. The upgradation should be first attempted in areas in which community life is generally and directly affected. The process of upgradation should be a continuous process. This needs regular research and planning in every functional unit. To implement the schemes involving upgraded skills will require upgradation of training facilities and creating an innovative and scientific temper in police. Supportive legislation and enlightened judicial appreciation are other requirements for making modernisation fruitful and productive. The organisational improvements such as transparent system for placement and promotion, performance appraisal, and creating facilities for continuous consistent improvement in the quality of human component is another field where delay is unpardonable because no extra resources are required for them. The functional division of the manpower in consonance with the recommendations of several commissions in order and investigation wings can be attempted without any delay. Rationalisation and reorganisation of prosecution branch, so that the police investigator gets legal help when he needs it most, is a crying need in the present context. Reorganisation of panels of lawyers and of their selection, and ensuring their objectivity is also essential for the control of crime and protection of human rights.

The police organisation needs changes to facilitate intra-departmental as well as inter-departmental interaction which is most neglected at the moment. The lack of vertical interaction in the department is single most important factor to affect the quality and credibility of leadership adversely. It also acts as stumbling block in the growth of leadership at secondary and tertiary level which puts department at a disadvantage in situations of social turmoil. Lack of interaction with other government functionaries except magistrates, creates a negative image among the government functionaries of other departments. The departmental culture prevailing these days, results into regimental functioning where one or two persons think and others must obey and any attempt to think at variance is considered as deviant behaviour and always frowned upon. This culture has to be changed and open, vertically and laterally communicative atmosphere has to be created to spring up leaders and not mere commanders. Functional autonomy of the department should be ensured by insulating it from direct political interference. National Police Commission have very emphatically recommended measures to make police department impartial and accountable to law and not to function as arm of the party in power. Political interference at every level, placement on grounds of political expediency frequent transfers, harassment, humiliation on political and personal considerations compels an average policeman to succumb to pressure and act in accordance with the wishes of political masters. National Police Commission's recommendations are very reasonable, forthright and the only remedy to solve the problem of functional aberration of police.[8]

In the past, to mend the working of police to make it more humane, sensitive and well suited to the democratic working is tried but all such attempts have proved to be only the patch-work. Now time has come when attempt at the reform of the whole system shall be done starting from prevention of crime, investigation, prosecution to jail reforms and rehabilitation. Similarly in the field of maintenance of order, fighting terrorism and other fields we must revise our strategies our tools and our philosophy in handling such situation.

We have in India the privilege of having very old system of policing. We have as a nation, suffered quite a lot at the hands of police and the matter was examined in details by the commissions. During British regime also we had two royal police commissions besides law commissions to enquire into whole gamut of police working. Even after independence, police commissions have made certain recommendations of far-reaching consequences but strange enough we have not debated the recommendations, let alone implement them. It appears that over years we have developed "an indigenous art of non-reform that has left the police system substantially unaffected and largely uninfluenced by the culture, ethos and temper of the modern society". Now if we want to take police reforms seriously, then recommendations have to be implemented sincerely and without wasting time in lamenting failures of police. The blatant indifference shown by those who are responsible for improving police, despite all hue and cry made by the police organisations, indicates action by the victims of the indifference, i.e., public at large with the support of appropriate legal and political bodies beside seeking redressal from court of law.

In a country of the size of India it is imperative to integrate police with people. As is well known that order can be maintained in a society when most of the people naturally obey law and only handful of people are to be tackled by police to combat crime and maintain sustainable public security and order. People, press, politician and police should be made to realise that police is the core force and the people are the supporting force. Therefore, police should also be made responsible to develop people's capacity to be a supporting force by organising them well and providing integrated training and counselling. The integration of police with people will create a positive and dynamic environment in society quite conducive to stable public peace and security.

REFERENCES

1. "While order..... focuses on the formal structure of the social and legal system, justice looks to the content of legal norms and institutional arrangements, their effect upon human beings and their worth in terms of their contribution to human happiness and the building of civilisations". Edgar Bodenheimer Jurisprudence. *The Philosophy and Method of the Law* ... p. 196).
2. Peter K. Manning : *The Police : Mandate Strategies and Appearances 1971.*
3. R. Haldane :Improving the Police Image... *Indian Police Journal,* Jan. March, 1980.
4. Capt. W.L. Melvilla Lee : *A History of Police in England.*
5. Charles Reith : *The Blind Eye of History.*
6. R. Deb : *Police and Law Enforcement* 1988.
7. M. Taylor : Constraints to Community Oriented Policing : *The Police Journal* Vol. LXV No. 2, 1992.
8. "The quality of police determines the quality of society and of governance, competence, integrity, professionalism and commitment to Rule of Law and public service have to be the hallmark of policing. Bangalore Declaration, on Police Autonomy and Accountability adopted at XXIV Criminological Congress 1996.

7

Independent India and its Keepers of Peace

The progress of life from a single cell has been saga of creativity, indomitable courage and undying desire for progress and sublimation, a precondition to progress both material and intellectual which needs peace and freedom from wants. The communities which could ensure peace and freedom including freedom from wants to its constituents could rise to the highest ladder of civilization. The communities who subjugated large parts of the world with their aggressive designs without creating institutions which could ensure peace and peaceful co-existence with others perished without leaving any evidence of their achievements. The nomadic hordes emanating like locust swarms from Central Asia can be cited as an example. The civilization of China, India, Egypt, Mesopotamia, Greece and Rome created institutions to ensure peace and created conditions in which human mind could reach a stage of sublimation and attain enlightenment leaving behind an indelible mark in human history.

The concept of justice and the system to adjudicate against the violation of cannons of law are the foundation stones of progressive civilization. Right from the ancient tribal societies to the present day complex social organism, the keepers of the peace, that is the police have played a crucial role in maintaining peace and orderliness in society. The moment need for peace was felt by the community, the rules for governance or procedure for enforcing normative behaviour must have been conceptualised which ultimately resulted into the organization for enforcing the will of the community on different groups of men and also to handle the enemies from within and without.

Later on with the march of civilization it, was felt that the defence against the enemies from outside and violators of the crime within the community itself require different treatment and the single force could not have been able to cope with a dual task, hence peace-keeping force was envisaged. The rights and duties, accountability and weaponry all depended upon the imagination of the particular community but universally this institution was created to bring peace and orderliness in society and therefore gradually elaborate procedure was evolved for its functioning depending upon the level of progress of society.

In India the old system of administration which flourished in Mauryan era could not last long after the declice of Mauryan and Sung dynasties. The rise and fall of Guptas witnessed another system of administration which continued with changes here and there depending upon the genius of the rulers in first one thousand years of Christian era. Emergence of smaller states further created confusion and Indian jurisprudence could not grow in the manner the Western jurisprudence grew, prospered and won acceptability in European countries with minor changes.

The early Indian law books provided for separate civil and criminal law but there is no specific mention of any organization on the pattern of modern police. There is mention of rural police functionaries even in Kautilya's *Arthshastra*. The capital town used to have Kotpals. With the arrivals of Mughals the urban policing was further streamlined though rural policing was not given the attention it deserved because the Mughals and their noblemen mostly settled in comparatively bigger centres of population. Therefore, more attention was paid on policing of important cities. When Britishers came to India they found that the police was organized on the basis of land tenure and collective responsibility of village community in the rural areas and Kotwal (Kotpal or Durgpal of ancient India) system prevailed in important cities. Since there was no concept of State intervention in the sphere of economic development, the keeping of peace and orderliness in society, quelling of rebellions against the rulers and providing basic security needs to the community were the main functions of the State. There was no elaborate system of policing, investigation, prosecution and punishment at the apex level and the village panchayats dealt with ordinary crime. East India Company acquired rights of Dewani in Bengal (including present West Bengal, Orissa, Bihar and present Bangladesh). Then they started making changes in the police system prevailing in the country. Initially police functions were also entrusted to revenue police functionaries. Later in 1808 separate police functionary with the designation of Superintendent of Police, was appointed for Calcutta. Later on this system was extended to other territories acquired by the East India Company and later on by the British crown.

The British police system in India was evolved on the ruins of old system. East India Company had three important settlements around Calcutta, Madras and Bombay which were first to be subjected to Anglo-Saxon law through retaining peculiarities of the system.

From the above it would appear that police as an organization is a recent phenomenon though police functions served as anchor sheet for progress and development. The close study of the system also indicates that police system like any other organization reflects the genius of the community it intends to serve. The system of policing in France and Germany is different from the system that prevailed in United Kingdom. The system prevailing in South-East Asia is different from the system prevailing in United States of America. The system of policing is nothing but reflection of the ingenuity of the community and its concept of justice. If society undergoes change, the police system also adapts itself to the needs of the time. Unfortunately in our country the foreign rulers evolved the system; made it applicable throughout the country modelled it on the pattern of western system but after independence, the change of governance, the change of rulers and change in the functions and policies of state required change in police system which was never seriously contemplated. The top brass was changed but in lower and middle levels this change was imperceptible. The recruitment and the training pattern remained the same almost for quarter century after independence. The functions of the State changed and welfare State came into being but the police was not organized as welfare police. The police inherited same colonial outlook towards the public and was also prepared for the same as the public did not change its attitude towards the police.

Immediately after independence it was considered to be an achievement to retain the fundamentals of administration of the previous government but later on it became a drag on the body politic. The politicians, whenever in tight corner, threw the blame on police which had to bear the criticism. Efforts were made to control police by successive regimes with the result politicians, bureaucrats and judiciary all tried to subjugate police and no one was interested in reorganizing or remodelling the system. At present old police model with old concepts and susceptibility of being manipulated by interested parties has to defend itself against the criticism from every corner.

When the goals of society and law-enforcing agencies remain the same, there is no social conflict and police is supposed to handle crime and criminals in a straight and objective manner and without fear or favour. The legislature have wider societal interest in mind and keepers of the peace have to deal with the persons with deviant behaviour in accordance with cannons of law. When few people act as thinkers and others blindly rely on their wisdom, then also there is no conflict so long as the thinkers are objective, impartial and the followers are simple and sincere. But in a modern complex society, a time may came when influential persons or the trustees of the society start taking advantage of their positions and exploit the situation for their personal advantage. Such situations lead to social conflicts which may be resolved either in a democratic way by due process of law or through violence and revolutions. Under the circumstances in an environment of social tensions, credibility gaps and lack of respect for law, it becomes extremely difficult for administration including police to function smoothly.

Challenge

At the time of political independence we resolved to move in the direction of socialism, secularism, egalitarianism and decentralisation of power so that common man can come to the mainstream. Initially it appeared that we are moving in correct direction but within first two decades it became apparent that our cherished dreams will remain unfulfilled and people felt frustrated with the slow pace of development and also the widening gap between haves and havenots. The guarantees given in the form of fundamental rights and goals set in the form of directive principles of State policy were also threatened by the political parties in power. The silent and non-violent revolution gave us political freedom but the vision of Gandhi, Nehru, Patel and other political luminaries of pre-independence days was found missing from the political rulers which resulted into the distortion and we moved away from our cherished goals. Political distortions resulted into social discord, extremism on the frontiers and near political chaos and economic anarchy in some of the states. The police organization was supposed to cope with such situations with archaic, out-moded pre-independence legislation and feudal departmental setup and leadership with colonial work culture in background. The new legislation which came into being to control violence and separatism further alienated police from society as a result the credibility of the police organization in the masses also suffered steep decline.

Degeneration of Institutions

The democracy depends on democratic institutions and democratic philosophy. Whatever institutions we borrowed from United Kingdom and other Western Democracies were not given proper respect and proper environment which caused their degeneration and decline. The institutions of parliamentary democracy such as legislature (Central as well as States) have become malignant and are being used to project inter-party and intra-party conflict instead of resolving problems of the community. The conflict and tension of the society instead of being resolved in the legislatures are being accentuated. The reported deeds and misdeeds of parliamentarians as highlighted by the media tend to lower the prestige of this temple of democracy further.

The institutions of democracy can function smoothly when they complement each other but in our country more than once it appeared that they have lost sense of direction and started operating in a culture of conflict and confrontation instead of complimentarity. It has been noticed that the democratic institutions instead of strengthening each other have trespassed into the territory of others and at times even tried to undermine authority of others. Such distortions and confrontations cause unexpected tension for police leadership and blur their vision.

Economic Distortions

During the short span of fifty years we have changed our emphasis more than once. With the result neither we could achieve economic prosperity nor we could bring about egalitarianism. The fruits of development were not equally distributed. The deprived sections despite all loud thinking and political slogans were not benefited and the army of unemployed youth have overgrown beyond the feeding capacity of productive segments of society. Even one knows that such conditions generate crime and interaction with electronic media (both national and global) provides them new ideas about organized crime and international adventurism. Such developments pose new problems for the community and its keepers of the peace.

Discipline

These democratic challenges and changes brought about with the change of political power were to be faced by organization burdened by colonial history. The very fact that at the dawn of independence we resolved to retain not only the old guards, and rules but also old uniform and methods as well. Instead of changing the face of organization, political masters found them quite handy for their policies as well. So long as great men of vision and courage like Nehru and Patel, controlled the destiny of nation the going was good but with the exit of men of vision, integrity and commitment began the politicization of the system of governance including police. The mainstream politics has been reduced to a mechanism to capture power. Politicization of police at the top level and undermining the authority of police leadership by encouraging indiscipline at the lower level, was resorted to and professionalism and commitment to the public cause were the first casualty.

The ethos of service to community, commitment to the ideals and adherence to goals of the organization were replaced by commitment to political parties and political persons, careerism, castism and total absence of 'espirite de-corp'. The public view of police was even worse than colonial police in India at the height of freedom movement.

During the last fifty years of post-independence period all round erosion of discipline was gradual but continuous. In police department the beginning was made immediately after independence, when a large number of political workers were recruited in police at different ranks. These persons were no doubt nationalists but even after joining police they continued to live in their old sub-culture i.e. the sub-culture of political workers having scant respect for establishment. These new members of the department known to senior political leaders and had regular communication with them which disturbed regular chain of command. With the decline and fall of Indian National Congress in some of the states created impression in the opposition ranks that elections can be won with the help of the administration including police. This impression motivated political parties to win support from government machinery and in case of failure allegations were made against police. This frequently happened in second decade after independence and again during Emergency period. After 1977, things have become more confused. In some cases police is targeted with political motives. In other cases efforts were made to recruit policemen on grounds other than merit. Political ideology, caste and other parochial considerations played major role in matters of recruitment and placement. Now we have come to a stage when the public servants have started behaving like political functionaries. Political executives have also introduced, from back door a revised version of 'spoil system' prevalent in Western Democracies.

Dilemmas Facing Police

Over the years credibility of police has taken a nose-dive, at the same time the expectations and demands on police have increased to the extent that police finds it difficult to cope with their normal duties of prevention and detection of crime. The functions related to security (both persons and places) have grown out of proportion, necessitating diversion of force from normal duties to vital areas.

The economic distortions in 70s-80s gave rise to agitations based on economic problems, necessitating police action which alienated it from the masses. The order became more important than the law enforcement. The prevention and detection of crime was given a back seat in police functioning causing loss of credibility of police as an organisation. The lack of effectiveness of governance brought about a total anarchy in every walk of social life requiring police arrangements for conducting examination, cultural programmes, meetings, *sammelans*, *yatras* and religious congregations. This is really paradoxical to find that despite severe erosion in effectiveness and credibility, police demands and expectations from police are rising, a problem which police leadership has to address itself to.

Socio-Economic Changes and Police

The aspirations of common man were whipped to very high pitch at the time of elections. Similarly the aspirations of those sections of society who were deprived for centuries were also aroused but the efforts to meet these aspirations were not forthcoming in successive political regimes. The economic and social tensions as a result of gap in expectations and achievement brought police face to face with warring sections of the society. Further some of the policies of the government did not find approval of the masses but police was asked to implement unpopular policies. As a matter of fact, police was never consulted at the stage of formulating such policies. This trend is still continuing. During the elections thousands of people are arrested under the different 'preventive sections' and all such cases were either closed or died a natural death after elections. Similarly restrictions on the movement of people at the time of visits of political dignitaries is cause of annoyance to general public. Holding of rallies and *dharnas* disturbs economic, social and academic life not only of the city but its hinterland also. Some unscrupulous political functionaries even expect free transport, arrangement of fuel for vehicles, collection of crowd etc. At times they are ordered to ignore violation of law with impunity on public places like railway stations, bus stands and hotels etc. Lawlessness of railways including ticketless travelling at the time of rallies has been viewed as right by the political parties and those public servants who dare to enforce law have to face physical assaults and also the harassment in the department in public interest. Such happenings demoralise lower police functionaries and damage the image of police.

Police is not Alone

Police is not alone to be blamed for maintaining law. Police has to work within a parameter established by law of the land and strictly speaking police is to be treated as most important arm of the judicial system, the other functionaries of the system being courts, prosecutors and public. Unfortunately for every failure, police is blamed and the controlling agencies jerk away their responsibility. In such situations police finds it on a very fragile pitch and always suffers. Police organization has remained static and no machinery could be evolved to have their purposeful interface of terms on equality with other functionaries of judicial system, with the result it is made accountable even for the lapses of others.

Stagnant Organization

Police has to perform in a society which is undergoing constant change but with an organization which is stagnant and impervious to the problems of the masses whose protection from violators of law is their primary duty. Police organization in the whole of the country has remained the same for more than fifity years. The basic pattern has not changed a bit. Whatever changes have been brought about are just like patchwork which instead of increasing cohesion, promote dissension and discordance in the organization.

In the name of modernization, no doubt better facilities have been created. Transport and communication in the department has been improved. All this has been done in purely ad hoc manner without any planning. The force has been numerically increased. A perceptible tendency has been noticed in the increase of force to provide the job to a large number of people rather than for service of the community. Further there has been steep increase in armed force (BSF, CRPF, RPF and State Armed Police) while increase at the grassroot level of the civil police has been ignored.

The quantitative increase without any efforts to improve the quality of men has not done good to the society. At the time of entry into the department the selection method has not been changed. The training pattern still remains the same. At slightly higher level even officers are not allowed to learn at the job by moving them almost continuously. The subject of internal security had been ignored to the extent that it was taken out from the agenda of planned development. Commissions for the improvement of policing in the states as well as at the national level were asked to submit their report regularly but nowhere in the country recommendation were implemented. The recommendation of National Police Commission have also been ignored definitely not on the grounds of merit.

We are in the 21st century which has entirely different problems beyond comprehension of police in most of the states in India. The information explosion, availability of firearms coupled with rapid changes and interest shown by various sections in our country will make things really difficult. The emergence of organized gangs criminals and their links with international adventurism, brightest brains in the form of legal and financial advisors and assisted by technology both in form of weapons, transport and communication shall not be very easy to handle. In our country most of the states do not have adequate funds to equip their police to meet such challenges while some states have financial resources but have no will power to make their police modern and independent. We should prepare ourselves to face violence on a very big scale which may last a number of years but unfortunately we are not yet prepared to address ourselves to such problems let alone preparing to meet the challenges which are likely to be thrown up by growing technology in future.

Dehumanization of Police

During Emergency period it was alleged and was found correct that police was used for political ends. In exchange for their loyalty some officers enjoyed absolute powers and to some extent administrative immunity. This factor coupled with general political environment made some men in khaki think themselves above law and this was beginning of a trend which still haunts police leadership.

Criminalization of Police

When criminals have become cohorts of powerful heavyweights and police leadership is pressurized to deviate from lawful course and in some states even the honest officers are punished, then one can imagine the state of morale of the policeman at the cutting edge level who has to risk his own life and life of his family members. Some police men of weaker moral foundation, even join the gangs of criminals as regular members besides providing police protection in barter for political pretection. This nexus between political leaders, police and criminals has been highlighted by Vohra Committee report. One can imagine the enthusiasm of such policemen and officers when their cohorts occupy ministerial berths and that too all important portfolis connected with internal security. In these circumstances one can think of the plight of poor but honest and sincere law-abiding keepers of peace and order.

How to Meet the Challenge

Police as an organization has to imbibe professionalism and has to bring excellence in the field of prevention and detection of crime. This may need better facilities for training and sustained improvement in the intake and efforts to allow men in the job to achieve excellence. They have to be given reasonable freedom from wants by ensuring proper wages to lead a really dignifed and purposeful life for the growth of organization. It is essential that police as an organization should have autonomy and their voice should also be given proper respect in formulating policies which concern them.

"Politicization is making rapid strides inside the police force and even communication has infiltrated into the police ranks. This is corrosive of discipline and eventually, of efficiency and reliability." (Justice V.R. Krishna lyer) The people have to bear pressure from executive and at times asked to 'bend to law' or even 'break the law' so as to favour political masters. Therefore, it is imperative to have some system to insulate police from direct political interference in implementing law.

"The present image of police in public mind is very negative and it is characterized by attributes such as brutal, corrupt, immoral, insular, complacent, careerist, casteit, communal, fragmented, hierarchical absence of espirite-de-corps and devoid ethical standards." (Dr. G.R.S. Rao) To change this image of police reculturisation in thought, word and deed is very necessary if the police has to remain functionally relevant. Police needs integrity. Independence, expertise and effectiveness in dealing with law and order.

The police at present suffers alienation, therefore it has analyse and plan a strategy to involve "masses and the classes" for which the organization will have to make massive efforts.

The Indian police suffers from very inception from certain statutory disabilities originating from distrust of police. These handicaps force policemen to take recourse to unethical and highly questionable means which make them guilty in the eyes of people and reduce them to the status of culprits in the eyes of Human Rights Organizations. Such disabilities have to be removed if we want straightforward and honest police. The policemen on their part have to resolve only to act as per command of law.

8

Terrorism: Tenets and Tactics

संगच्छध्वं संवद्ध्वं
संवो मनांसि जानताम्।
समानो वःआकूति, समाना हृदयानि वः
समानास्तु वो मानो
यथा वः सुसहासित।

ऋग्वेद *(10/191)*

Togetherness in living and thinking is sine qua non of happy community life and any deviation means strain in social fabric manifested in many ways. When a man or a group of men feel lack of integration with the rest of society, it suffers deprivation or a gap between value expectations of the group and the value capabilities. Such a man or a group, "if he does not come to terms with his own self, if has not an integrated view of life, he will become ruthless, destructive even insane. He will be a lost spirit."[1] This is the case with most of the terrorist groups which are operating in different parts of the world.

The feeling of deprivation may be the result of increase in value expectations, or decrease in the value capability of the group. At times progressive decline in value capability or progressive increase in aspirations also results into frustration and motivates the group to stand against the establishment which is considered responsible for the malaise in society. T.R. Gurr[2] has divided such deprivation in three categories : Decremental deprivation, aspirational deprivation and progressive deprivation. 'Decremental deprivation' results when value capability of a group or groups decline appreciably due to certain factors such as wars, famines and other calamities. Such calamities weaken the government and emblodens the rebel groups. 'Aspirational Deprivation' is the result of increase in the expectation levels while the value capability remains constant or declines. This may be due to propaganda engineered by the group theorists or the result of general education and comparison with other groups. After French revolution in Europe and after Second World War in Africa and Asia, there was general increase in the level of political aspirations which gave birth to dozens of independent states. Progressive deprivation is felt when value capabilities of a group come to a plateau after a period of steep ascent of value capability aspirations or expectations. The military take over of the democratic governments in Africa and Asia can be cited as examples.

The deprivation which motivates a group to take up course of terrorism may not be very real always. This deprivation may be the result of the interpretation of historical events. Some groups may identify themselves with certain races who dominated the course of history in the past and when descendants of the same racial stock compare their present value capability with others, they feel very much deprived, which results into frustration and deviant course of action to regain past glory.

The progress made in the fields of transport and communication has reduced to a great extent the barriers of time and space thus succeeded in breaking the isolation of ethnic groups. The increased inter-action within the same ethnic group strengthens the bonds of group while the explosion of information gives them a fair idea of the achievements, in the fields of knowledge, power, wealth and social status of other ethnic groups. Thus modernization has laid the stage for analysing and interpreting the value capabilities of different groups which gives birth to relative deprivation in the ethnic groups and sub-groups.

Once a group feels deprived in the field of knowledge, wealth, political power and national importance, it faces problem of preserving its identity which gives impetus to ethnic fundamentalism. The progressive and forward looking segments of the group tend to loosen their bonds with the backward segment. The fundamentalism tends to maintain cohesion in the group at the cost of progress. In a way fundamentalism is a denfence mechanism of the ethnic group which attempts to discipline enterprising segment of the group and sacrifices societal well being in the long run. The rise of fundamentalism in different ethnic groups increases chances of group clashes and the weakened groups may resort to terrorism.

Terrorism may be the outcome of group deliberations, planning and evaluation of a strategy to attain certain political, social, economic and cultural goals or it may be the result of individual adventure by a person, fired by a certain idealism attempting to apply correctives to the existing system.

Historical Perspective

Terrorism a term little known before French Revolution (1793-98) has assumed a special significance in present context. Terrorism might be a new entrant to our lexicon yet it was known to the kings and the subjects, the rulers and the ruled, political thinkers and followers alike during most part of our written history. *Ramayan* and *Mahabharat, the oldest of the epics, are replete with the names* of tyrants who were overthrown by the heroes by adopting unorthodox methods such as terrorising the servants of the rulers and striking panic in the minds of the public. The rulers also adopted the terrorist methods to keep the rebels under constant fear. Kautilya's *Arthashastra*, a treatise on statecraft prescribes strategy to unearth and demolish enemies within and without by striking terror in the minds of public to discourage them to rise against the king which may be termed as 'Enforcement Terror'.

In Greece also, the tyrants were looked down upon for their autocratic rule. Assassination of Julius Caesar by Brutus in conspiracy with others may be treated as act of gaining power from an autocraft.

From 11th century onwards the followers of Hassan-Ibn-Sabehat employed the services of assassins to liquidate religious and political opponents as they were not in a position to challenge the authority of the rulers openly. This group, though liquidated by Mongols later, left behind a tradition of winning popular support through propaganda and oath of secrecy which is followed by most of the terrorist even today.

French Revolution marked the beginning of contemporary terrorism. The objectives of Jacobin terror was to recreate France as Republican Frame and the enemies of the Republic were to be demolished to safeguard the revolution. The revolutionary government in France in 1793 set up a committee for public safety which decided to strike terror in the minds of enemies of the Republic to ensure success of revolution. Robespierre was of the strong view that when threat to revolution was extreme then the reaction or remedies to meet the threat should also be extreme and violence was legitimate weapon under the circumstances.

Terrorism and the Left

Traditionally speaking Marxism-Leninism considered terrorism or violence as the legitimate weapon to foster mass struggle under the control of revolutionary party. Terrorism as a weapon to eliminate the enemies of the revolution was very extensively used during the period 1878-81 and again in the beginning of the current century. The terrorist campaign of Nardonaya Volya, was shortlived and was different from Anarchism and Nihilism prevalent in Europe at that time. The influence of writings of Mikhail Bakunin, Serge Nechayev, Feter Kroptokin and Morozov was tremendous on the later days revolutionaries. In the early phase of terrorism, the campaign of Nardonaya Volya could win only thin support from the masses but after the birth of Social Revolutionary Party in 1900 and slight change in the philosophy could broaden the base of the party." In the early years both Marx and Engels held the view that violence was an engine of social change and it was 'Therapeutic in character'. It would 'psychologically renovate' the working class and make them fit to rule."[3] Both Marx and Engles did not like the idea of killing innocent persons unconnected with the enemies of the revolution. Lenin also did not like the idea of anarchist terror and considered it counter productive.

Frantz Fanon had significant impact on contemporary revolutionary ideology. Fanon considers that violence is useful and productive as it leaves positive impact on individuals. He argues that violence is a cleaning force and it makes the individual fearless. The people, who have attained freedom after violent struggle, remain jealous of results and keenly guard against recapture of power by vested interest or so-called liberators. The violent struggle also causes positive impact on community as it raises the level of national consciousness. The practice of violence binds the oppressed people in one composite self-conscious group. Fanon's arguments in favour of violence has promoted present day terrorists in ruthless killing of innocent persons. D.V. Segne and J.H. Alder hold the view that unconditional support to violence by Fanon and others have prompted the governments to take sympathetic view towards the terrorists and resultant lenient punishment to the extremists.

Terrorism and Strategy

Terrorism is "A term used to describe the method or the theory behind the method whereby an organized group or party seeks to achieve its avowed aims chiefly through the systemic use of violance.[4] From the above definition it is clear that terrorism aims to target state and relies on 'random or extortionate violence' causing harm to unarmed civilians, or non-combatants. Terrorism, is a part of strategy for usurping political power and it has following components.[5]

(a) Terrorism is manifested in acts of socially and politically unacceptable violence.

(b) There is a consistent pattern of symbolic or representative selection of the victim or objects of acts of terrorism.

(c) The revolutionary movement deliberately intends these actions to create a psychological effect on specific groups and thereby to change their political behaviour and attitudes.

The long-term objective of every terrorist movement is to overthrow the target government or established order and to establish itself. The short-term objectives or methodology varies from group to group and undergoes change with the stage of revolution and socio-economic conditions of the target group.

The short-term objectives of terrorist movement could be: (1) Public support or polarization, (2) Attack on law enforcement agencies, (3) publicity, (4) propagation of moral justification, (5) shaking public confidence in establishment by showing incapacity of the regime to provide security (6) tactical objectives or operational steps, (7) Aggravate relations between states so as to prevent a lot of political events harmful to terrorists.

Public Support or Polarization

Every tyrant knows that without support of sizeable population, order cannot be maintained in society. In 1971, this fact was amply proved by the birth of new State of Bangladesh. The terrorist outfit also seeks to enlarge its support base which is so essential for survival and operational needs. The mass support of the target population could be won by projecting the terrorist group as the only saviour of the ideology of the adherents. In areas where different ethnic groups live in close spatial proximity this could be achieved by generating ethnic tensions and inviting reprisals from other side. At times wanton killings of innocent children, women, old and infirm, ignites attack on the ethnic groups supposedly responsible for killing and leads to polarization which ensures support of fence sitters and compels even the secular minded people to think about their stand.

Law Enforcement—Key target of Terrorist Movement

In the eyes of a terrorist, the law enforcement officer is a class enemy and possesses no dignity as a human being therefore elimination is the only way. The police officer is just a 'pig' for them that indicates the amount of hatred the terrorists have for police. 'The only good pig is a dead pig', considers a Black Panther Party leader. The law enforcement machinery includes all members of the government working to maintain order in the society.

The attack on law enforcement is directed against all those who are on protective duties and also those who are likely to join them after training or education. These groups are targeted by propaganda machinery and every effort is made to indoctrinate them to thwart regular supply of recruits so as to change the ethnic or class composition of law enforcement machinery which further helps in polarization.

The terrorists and their allies do not spare sweeping derogatory charges without evidence to convince citizens that police is corrupt and brutal in approach and does not deserve any support. This step on one hand shakes the confidence of public in law enforcement machinery and on the other hand it gives moral justification for taking violent steps against them.

For terrorists everything is justified so long as it will harass, embarrass, defame, incapacitate and harm law enforcement machinery. The tactics employed with above end in view, include bombing of Police Stations, officers, and vehicles, laying ambushes after alluring the officers (by calling for police assistance or by killing innocent persons and throwing dead bodies on highway to be brought to the notice of police by innocent informers), sniper attacks after breaking the mode of communication, theft of weapons from government arsenals, or private gun shops issuing threatening letters to officers of law enforcement and their families, kidnapping of the police officers and their family members and other such unlawful acts. To embarrass police the political wings or sympathizers start issuing statements with respect to imaginary stories of police harassment and brutalities. The rallies and demonstrations are organized to convince the public about the brutalities of law enforcement.

Publicity

The terrorist wants publicity and best publicity is the story of their deeds which is very popular with the media-men. The stories in local papers are exaggerated beyond proportion to make the criminals as heroes and to denounce the police. At times leaflets and letters are left at the place of crime to justify the crime. In their anxiety to unearth 'real story' the crime narrations are made more theatrical with the support of such leaflets and at times fake letters under the garb of 'investigative journalism'. The voice of honest journalism is muffled by threats of dire consequences either to the journalist or to the owner of the press with disastrous effects.

"For the media, terrorism is theatre, they tend to present the terrorist side for the drama it presents, it becomes a form of mass entertainment. The advent of electronic media has greatly facilitated the attainment of this objective of terrorists. The quest of scoop can cause the media people to go to a great lengths. A reporter-photographer team from DER SPIEGEL accompanied Post of Balder-Meinhof group of a raid on Hamburg and an American documentary team was able to film an IRA bombing mission. This extensive media coverage enhances their sting capabilities."[6] The publicity for terrorist acts is addressed to native audience to project the image of the organization and to win mass support. It further terrorises the target group and induces polarization. The consistent favourable publicity in the press attracts young men as recruits to the organization besides giving further motivation to the members of the organization. The value capability of the organization also increases. The terrorist publicity is also aimed for international community of nations for securing support of some of the nations, insuring financial and weaponry supply from same and also to assure the friends and collaborators in other countries, that their agents are doing well which increases their effectiveness in the countries of their domicile.

Moral Justification

Every terrorist organization tends to show to the ethnic or socio-economic group which it pretends to work for that all its actions are directed towards furtherance of common cause. Whenever any of the member of the outfit is eliminated due to internal bickering then they issue statements to give moral justification for the same. Such statements are intended to win support of righteous people and also paint, the members as the reformers or crusaders for the lofty ideals. The propaganda to that effect makes all those killed in action as martyrs and boosts the morale of those who survive to keep the struggle alive.

Public Confidence

The assassination of political leaders who have been provided security by the government, shakes the confidence of people and makes them apprehensive which sets a chain reaction. More and more demand on police, for personal security of leaders leaves very little resources for the security of common people which further alienates them from public. Similarly the bombing of guarded buildings, kidnapping of important and very important persons way-laying of police contingent demonstrate the striking power of the organization and lack of effectiveness of enforcement agencies to provide security cover to public in general. This feeling in public mind conditions their reaction in the face of terrorist threat which makes their task easier as chances of resistance diminish considerably.

Tactical Objectives

Every group selects its tactical objective as per needs of the organization. For finances, some groups resort to raids on the Banks and government treasuries while others indulge in kidnapping for obtaining ransom. Similarly the kidnapping of important persons, for whose release government will be exposed to pressure, is resorted to secure release of important members of the organization while some organizations opt for jail break with or without connivance of the enforcement agencies.

Indiscriminate killing is also resorted to obtain tactical advantage for the movement. The arbitrariness in selection of targets, unpredictability of attack and incomprehensiveness of the magnitude of threat strikes terror in the minds of the target groups which numbs them to inaction depriving law enforcement agencies of public support so vital in dealing with terrorism.

International Relations

The terrorist organizations never allow the peace process to progress. Whenever there is thaw in terrorist activity and government or governments try to seize the opportunity to negotiate peace, the terrorists tend to create situations not conducive to peace talks. In certain areas democratic process such as elections etc. were not allowed to take place while in other cases delegates to the negotiation table were kidnapped or murdered to block the negotiations. This might appear just a coincidence but the strategists of the organization see through it and dub it as distraction which dampens the spirit of revolution hence such processes are never allowed to succeed. Terrorists take advantage of the intricacies of international law and try to aggravate relations of states because it helps them in escaping the rigors of law of the affected state.

Governmental Response

The tenets of terror are clear manifestations of despair, destructiveness, unpredictability, arbitrariness and all that which is negation of constitutional democracy. For the terrorists no holds are barred, no targets are immune and no one is fortunate to have status of non-combatant innocent. The terrorists have no parliament to seek directions from, no courts to adjudicate upon their doings, no code of conduct to govern them and no moral code to show path in the moments of utter despair and darkness and still society has every right to protect itself from them, and that too within the framework of democracy, with all its commitments to international declarations of Human Rights, under the watchful eyes of that temple of democracy known as Parliament, and in conformity with the law of the land. The task is stupendous but there are no short cuts.

In democratic setup public is the ultimate arbiter and also the worst sufferer in low intensity conflict like the one we are facing in Kashmir therefore it needs to be educated about the nature of terrorism and magnitude of threat in its wake. Genarally the establishment tends to screen the terrorist activities so that it does not have demoralizing effect on public and sympathetic reaction in other parts of country. Such screening or blackout of the activities gives rise to spread of rumours which is very demoralising and adversely affects the credibility of establishment hence counter-productive. The people must know the facts and all the facts of threat including governmental response to the threat barring operational details which have to be kept secret. The political leaders and non-governmental organization can be motivated to prepare public to face the reality. Once the public is taken into confidence the propaganda and smear campaign engineered by terrorists will not have desired impact on public mind, besides the prior knowledge and proper threat perception will mentally prepare them to face the threat and worst to bear the shock. This openness will to a large extent, diminish chances of alienation of public and people can join the resistance efforts.

No organization can wage sustained low intensity war without men, material (including weaponry) and money. Men, should be committed, trained and mobile. Generally speaking, men are available initially but new recruits are difficult to get due to reverses at the hands of government forces. Regular availability of human resource depends on the image of the organization, degree of risk involved, and chances of success in the context of short-term as well as long-term goals of the organization. Any government which aims at fighting terrorism successfully has to check completely the supply of human raw material to low intensity war-machine, while strict checking at the international borders can check movement from outside but to check indigenous supply of human raw material needs very good long-term psycho-social engineering to the potential supporters of the movement. This could be achieved by offering appropriate jobs to potential recruits and also by increasing risk factors in case they drift to extremist current. In this connection establishment has to prove its credentials also as 'government that cares', in offering help to those who have suffered at the hands of terrorists.

The supply of weaponry and periodical replenishment of stock is very important to sustain long-term operations. Again checking at the borders can be very useful for inward flow of modern and sophisticated weapons while constant vigil is essential to check indigenous supply. Indigenous supply is normally procured from police and army sources by deceit and depredations. Safety and security of private shops and individual licensed weapons depends on internal security environment. The law enforcement agencies have to devise ways and means to check this supply if they really want to stamp out the terrorism.

Money supply to terrorist outfit is also very essential and for the most part underground organization depend on subterranean sources of money. Besides clandestine help from supporters within and without, they indulge in criminal activity such as smuggling of contraband, articles including narcotic-drugs and exciseable articles, bank robberies and ransom money by kidnapping. This can be curbed by stepping up regular policing.

We must keep in mind that once we allow supremacy to lawlessness over the law of the land, cordan breakers of law on any pretext and declare amnesty in the midst of operations then we willingly creep into the trap of a no-win situation. Law of the land is the collective will of the nation and should not be compromised on one pretext or, the other. This applies to both the sides and 'enforcement terror' or 'state terror' should not be resorted to on any consideration. The failure of law enforcement is the failure of entire judicial system and failure of judicial system is failure of state in its avowed objective of dispensing justice.

It is common knowledge that democracies or the open societies are more prone to birth of terrorist movements as compared to states having dictatorial forms of government. In democratic governments, the reaction to a problem is very slow and at times lukewarm which helps the terrorist organization to grow and organize itself before government machinery goals up to face the challenge. It is suggested that on important problems the government should evolve a national policy after obtaining consensus of all political parties so that change of government does not affect the operations adversely. The decisions on vital matters connected with operations should be taken up quickly and should avoid dilatory democratic practices.

The manifest response of the state is seen in the form of law enforcement operations conducted by police, para-military forces and at times by army but people generally forget that terrorism is not an ordinary law and order problem hence it is not addressed to police and para-military forces only. All government agencies and forces interested in societal well-being, have to share the burden of preparing background for launching such operations. The destruction caused by operations should be matched by reconstruction work so as to reduce inconvenience to the minimum so that people do not feel to have been punished for the acts of the terrorists. The lateral damage caused to public property or property of individuals should be repaired and if possible compensated at the earliest. The forces entrusted with the job of launching operations should also have separate wings to organize services for the help of society in general which will help the integration with the people they have to work with.

Law Enforcement Operations against the Terrorists

The operations against terrorists consist mainly of collection of intelligence and counter-intelligence, protective arrangements for the targets, additional actual operations against the militants.

The importance of intelligence cannot be overemphasized in the context of counter-operations against underground operations of the terrorists. The counter-intelligence measures are equally important specially with respect to movement of force and plan of operations. In this connection subversion and in-filtration need special attention of the planners of the operations to avoid chances of heavy loses and resultant demoralization.

The protective arrangements have to be planned after analysing carefully the operation pattern of the terrorists. The protective arrangements consist of making police arrangements, training of non-governmental organizations and individuals in selective cases. By swift and dependable communication one can economise on excessive deployment of force. The listing of likely targets and periodic revision of the list is very essential for providing protective umbrella.

The operations against terrorists are difficult and need careful planning, preparations and swift follow up action. The planning of operations of the magnitude we require in our country need resources in fair quantum. The resources in this context include men, armament and money besides commitment of the government and morale of the public. The law enforcement forces require intensive pre-induction training which includes the psychological conditioning, orientation, language, cooperation and tactical training.

The anti-terrorist operations are quite different from ordinary military or police operations. In low intensity conflicts the targets are not well defined, therefore operations need to be revised every now and then, requiring immediate decision which normally baffles the executive force. To keep law enforcement agencies cohesive and effective it is essential to expose them to psychological pre-conditioning. The forces are to be briefed about the nature of conflict and the difference in the nature of operational enemy. The psychology of terrorist should be understood properly. He should not be considered as enemy in the ordinary sense of the term. He is brother or son of our own neighbour. He can again come to our neighbourhood after throwing away or concealing arms to strike again at soft targets at will. His knowledge of the terrain is as good as of local police if not better. When anyone in the unit or sub-unit is attacked then normally feeling of anguish followed by feeling of revenge takes over the unit which becomes counter-productive in such operations. The vindictive approach should be scrupulously avoided because. "The greatest tool of psy-ops. is the impeccable behaviour of troops their ability to mingle with the population to make it readily feel that S.F. are its own. This will counter the militant's campaign of discrediting the S.F."[8]

As discussed in foregoing paragraphs, that to label unwarranted and imaginary allegations against law enforcement agencies is one of the objectives of terrorists therefore those involved in counter-offensive should be forewarned to prepare themselves for such attack. The government should also be advised to prepare for such criticism so that there is no panic reaction which will demoralise the force and will lend credence to the allegations as well.

The government allocates the funds therefore they want results quick and tangible. The legislative machinery also jealously guards the governmental expenditure and the executive, both political and bureaucratic, needs tangible results to be announced to maintain its credibility. In anti-terrorist operations the results are very slow to come about and are not always tangible. The enforcement agencies should brief all concerned and media should also be educated about the operations and its evaluation in terms of both tangible and intangible results.

The operations are at times quite frustrating. The large contingent camping in unfavourable conditions may not encounter success for years and slight lowering of guards may result in casualty giving a feeling of omnipresence of the adversary which may lead to vindictive action. The psychological pre-induction training will give them pre-conditioning so essential for the task.

The troops involved in anti-terrorist operations should be trained to act in very small groups and should have a very high degree of adaptability. The troops be trained to work on minimum provisions. The tactical training to troops should be tailored for the task and terrain involved.

The terrorist activity is the latest in arsenal of revolution and brings in its wake serious problems for the community therefore it needs proper planned action to defeat the terrorists in their game. Constant research and training is very important to update the law enforcement agencies. The psychological pre-conditioning of troops, the leaders of the force, political activists and the public is essential for successful anti-terrorist operations. The media-management is integral part of the operations and needs be handled at the highest level. The adequate legal provisions be made to punish the wrong doers but law enforcement should be very impartial, just and truthful.

REFERENCES

1. S. Radhakrishnan, Inaugural address - Meerut College Diamond Jubilee Celebrations, 20th Dec. 1953, Occasional Speeches and Writings, p. 75.
2. Ted Robert Gurr, 'Why Men Revel', 1971.
3. Sankar Sen, Terrorism—A Historical Perspective, N.P.A. Magazine No. 2, 1989.
4. The Encyclopaedia of Social Science.
5. Naunihal Singh, *The World of Terrorism*, 1989 pp. 2-3 from Martha Genshaw Hatchinson 'The Concept of Revolutionary Terrorism'.
6. Dr. V.Verma, Terrorism—Source Material for U.P. Academy of Administration, Nainital, Training Programme on Police and Terrorism'.
7. Lt. Col. S.A. Hasnain, 'Security Forces and Low Intensity Conflict. A Matrix for an Improved Response', N.P.A. Magazine Vol. 45, No. 1, 1993.
8. *Ibid.*

9

Motivating the Police

One of the major objectives of an organisation, such as the CBI, is evaluating and analysing attitudes of its force—the police, towards society and towards the organisation at large. The efforts of organisational leaders should, therefore, be directed towards creating condusive working conditions for its employees in order to meet his psychological and physiological needs. The greatest challenge facing the supervisory cadre is to strike a balance between individual employee's aspirations and the organisational objectives, and to provide maximum job satisfaction to its workforce.

Getting People to Work, the Way You Want them to Work,
When You Want them to Work, is Indeed a Challenge

Donald F. Favrean and Joseph E. Cillespie[1]

"....the great man is the man who distinguishes himself on the battlefield of life with an undaunted determination to fight for his ideals in the face of difficulties and absurdities that lay his weaker brethren low. The weaker ones, the hedonistic comfort-seekers and stoical preachers of acquiescence, fail to meet the demands of human existence. The purpose of human drama, for man, is identically the great effort he can make and the personal power he can manifest in the pursuit of the ideals he sets for himself. The extent to which a man makes the heroic effort in struggling for his ideals is the direct measure of that man's worth as a man[2]. Willian C. Charron.

In an organization, specially one like the police, where human raw material has the greatest input, achievement of goals; is squarely dependent on the attitude of the policemen towards the organisation. One of the challenges facing the organisational leaders is to bring about an effective compatability between individual goals of the employee and the organisational objectives, so as to resolve conflicts of ideologies, if any.

The government fixes primary goals for the police, such as maintenance of law and order, prevention and detection of crime etc. These are stepping stones which leads towards the fulfilment of the vital objectives of the organisation which are preventive action against the known criminals or night patrolling to prevent recurrence of crime.These subsidiary or secondary goals also fulfill the gaps left behind the legislative body in the legislation and as such, they constitute one of the important duties of the supervisory leadership. From the above, the position regarding goals of the organization by and large remains clear from the very inception except when it undergoes transformation when conditioned by socio-political growth. The position regarding the goals or the needs of individuals serving the organisation is not so simple because "We are complex. We are a complicated, searching, wanting and knowing human form of life. Variety is our byword.[3]

"An Individual is motivated to the greatest extent, in terms of performance defined by an organisation, when the manager in the organisation creates conditions of work in which all the needs of the employee are satisfied.[4]

Since man is a 'wanting human form of life', the full satisfaction of his individual as well as socio-cultural needs is the goal in the back of his mind when he joins any organization. It is not, however, essential that all the needs have same priority for him. More often than not, the employees needs also grow with the fulfilment of his basic needs.

"Man is a wanting animal and rarely reaches a state of complete satisfaction except for a short time. As one desire is satisfied, another crops up to take its place. When this is satisfied, still, another comes into the foreground etc. It is a characteristic of the human being throughout his whole life that he is practically always desiring something."[5]

Since human beings are complex forms of life, and many variables and responses creep in human behaviour, the process of formulating a policy for motivating them is also complex needing flexibility and constant review.

An Effective Compatability

The energy provided by physical and intellectual capacity of the person is the motivating force which aims at fulfilling a need or desire. If there is any incongruency between the needs of the individual and the requirement of the organization, then the individuals shall not be able to get job satisfaction. This state of affairs, if allowed to continue over a long time, will give way to demoralization, frustration, physiological failure and conflict amongst the employees which will in turn reduce effectiveness and usefulness of the organization. *Therefore, adaptive organisations should increase motivation and thereby effectiveness because they create conditions under which the individual can gain increased satisfaction with the task itself. Thus, there should be a harmony between the educated individuals need for tasks that are meaningful, satisfying, and creative and an adaptive organizational structure.*"[6]

The action that energizes, activates and directs an organism towards a goal is motivation. The study of man and his behaviour has been pursued by the behavioural scientists from different angles. Some scientists believe that man's behaviour is conditioned by responses. Others believe that such simplistic approach reduces human dignity and consider behaviourists as threat to human race and in turn they propounded humanistic approach to study of man.

Maslow's Need Hierarchy

Abraham H. Maslow (1908-70) conducted an indepth research at Maxwell Air Force Base, Alabama, USA. On the basis of his research, he postulated that the factors which make production oriented people function in a particular fashion can also be applied with respect to persons whose performance has not been upto acceptable level to achieve better results. Maslow demonstrated by his research findings that every man has a need system ranging from very basic and primary needs, such as air, food, water, sex and shelter which are essential for survival to the needs related to safety, i.e. protection against danger, threat, deprivation and torture. After safety has been secured, there comes the need for affiliation or belongingness to the organization or the peer groups. All the three type of needs—survival needs, safety needs, and needs for belongingness—can be termed as physiological needs. Up the ladder come, the needs related to ego—self esteem, self respect, power, prestige, recognition and status. Lastly at the end of the continuum comes self-realisation—self-fulfilment, creativity or self-actualization. The last two types, of needs may be grouped as social and human needs respectively. The quest for self-actualization continues till the individual is doing what he individually is fitted for.

"What a man can be, He must be. He must be true to his own nature. This need we may call self-actualization."[7]

Maslow's Hierarchy of Needs*

Needs for self-Actualization	The need to be creative, innovative and challenged in the work environment.
Needs for ego-status	The need for self-competence, recognition, status, prestige, etc.
Needs for Be-Longingness	The need for job affiliation, team membership, etc.

*Adopted from Maslow's Hierarchy of needs.

Needs for safety	The need to feel secure and protected in the job environment.
Basic Needs	The need for food, air, water, work conditions, comfort, etc.

Physiological Versus Psychological Needs

Since physiological needs are very essential for survival of the organism, these are shared with other living beings unlike the higher needs. The other needs include the desire for power, confidence and general advancement which should be followed by recognition and prestige. For example, a police officer while on duty in uniform commands respect in public. If someone hurls insulting remarks on him, he may react very sharply to it if he has an image to protect, while a person who may not have that courage to face the situation will run away from the scene. On the other hand a balanced officer who has an image but at the same time enough confidence in himself will neither shy away nor over-react to the situation but will take a calculated risk and try to handle the situation. An Officer with a hurt ego may not be able to give his best despite full satisfaction of his physiological needs. Lack of cooperation at higher level of bureaucratic ladder is more often than not the direct result of ego problem.

Self-actualization (coined by Kurl Goldstein) may be described as full use of the talents, and potentialities of a man. This kind of self-estimate is usually high; therefore, at higher levels there is a general feeling that one's talents are not fully utilized by the department. In a police department where there is not much variety of work and less space at the top, an officer who has been doing creditably well during his early years, often gets a feeling of frustration in the later years. At this stage placement according to merit becomes important —not only to satisfy his ego but also for the blossoming of the latent qualities in him.

David C. Mc Clalland[8] and J. Atkinson[9] have further analysed the motives behind employees responses in an organization and have come to conclusion that most of the employees are motivated to work for any organization for personal satisfaction and recognition. Their ultimate goal is to influence and control the functioning of the organization. In this connection, it may be borne in mind that different employees have different needs in any given situation.

The employee who needs affiliation, wants others to like him and develops friendly relations with others. An individual who wants achievement, will aspire to get tasks involving risk and would like to influence others and try to occupy positions from where they can influence persons and policies and thereby control the organization.

I. Mc Gregor : Theory 'X' and theory 'Y' Analysing Attitudes to Work

Theory 'X'

1. First assumption of the theory is that average human being has an inherent dislike of work and will avoid it if he can. The managers of different organizations can advance evidence to prove this.

2. According to the second assumption, most people have to be coerced, controlled, directed or threatened with punishment to get adequate effort towards the achievement of organizational goals. The dislike of work is so strong that in case of some, even the promise of rewards is not enough to motivate them. People will expect regards even for average routine work. Only the threat of punishment or the punishment for not doing the work can coerce them to do their jobs.

3. Third assumption regarding 'mediocrity of masses' is that average human being prefers to be directed, wishes to avoid responsibility, has relatively little ambition and wants security above all.

Theory 'Y'

1. This assumption paints average man as one who likes to work for his own satisfaction or for fear of deprivation.

2. External control and threat of punishment are not only means for bringing about effort towards organizational objectives. Man will exercise self-direction and self-control in the service or objectives to which he is committed.

3. Commitment to objectives is a function of rewards associated with their achievement. The most significant of such rewards e.g. the satisfaction of ego, and self-actualization needs, can be direct products of efforts directed towards organizational objectives.

4. The average human being learns, under proper conditions not only to accept but to seek responsibility.

5. The capacity to exercise a high degree of imagination, ingenuity and creativity in the solution of organizational problems is widely distributed in the population.

6. Under the conditions of modern industrial life, the intellectual potentialities of the average human being are only partially utilised.

The two theories propounded by Mc Gregor[10] give the basic assumptions about human behaviour on which one can construct the office of organizational actions and decisions. Some supervisory managers have found that most of the industrial units in private sector are still basing their decisions on the assumptions of theory 'X'. Some managers find ample evidence that theory 'X' assumptions still hold good in most of the government departments and doubt the feasibility of applying assumption of theory 'Y' in departments like police and other paramilitary organizations where great risk is inherent in the job performance.

II. V.H. Vroom[11] : Expectancy Theory

Vroom has postulated his Expectancy Theory on the assumption that people work hard because they feel that working hard pays in life.

An individual strives harder to perform if he sees that some relationship exists between performance and benefits or rewards, such as promotion after passing certain examination. Lastly, the rewards or the benefits should be attractive enough to motivate the employee. If these conditions are created, then effort is more likely to occur.

III. Herzberg[12] : Job Enrichment Theory

Herzberg after conducting painstaking research into the factors causing satisfaction and dissatisfaction among the employees came to the conclusion that the factors which produced job satisfaction are entirely different from the factors which result into dissatisfaction.

Further developing on his theory, Herzberg identified Positive Job Events such as achievement, recognition, work, responsibility, advancement and growth. All above factors are intrinsic to the job and motivate the employee resulting in job satisfaction. He also identified Nagative Job Events which are likely to result into dissatisfaction. Such factors which are likely to result into dissatisfaction are extrinsic to the job and include company policy and administration, supervision, relationship with supervisor, salary, relationship with peers personal life, relationship with subordinates, status and security.

The Negative Job Events have been termed as KITA and may be likened to an 'attempt by management to install an internal generator in the employee'. Similarly, it is possible to have, positive KITA which may include system, incentive programme, performance linked promotion etc. Herzberg's postulate highlights that Positive Job Events or intrinsic job values are more important than extrinsic factors and therefore, attempts should be made to enrich the job content to have more satisfaction among the ranks.

Problems of Motivation

The employees in an organization can be divided into three categories in view of their level of performance with respect to the organization: (a) unacceptable in terms of performance, (b) acceptable, and (c) high performance. The unacceptable group of employees, is that segment of work-force whose usefulness to the organization is doubtful but it is not essential that such employees should necessarily be fired. The aim of the supervisory manager should be to reduce the number of employees in high performance category. In government departments mostly people are satisfied with middle category. The ideal situation could be to motivate unacceptable and acceptable categories so as to bring them in high performance categories by using motivational methods.

Certain assumptions[13] have been postulated for evolving new motivational techniques :

1. Man is highly variable, besides being complex. His needs and motives change from time to time and from situation to situation.

2. Man is capable of learning new motives through his experience.

3. Man's motives in different organizations may differ.

4. Man may become involved with organizations on the basis of many kinds of motive.

5. Man can respond to many different kinds of managerial strategies, meaning thereby, that 'there is no one correct managerial strategy that will work for all men at all times'.

From the above assumptions, one can very well conclude that the supervisor has to be always very searching in order to find out motives and responses of his men. If the needs and goals are different, then every individual or class of individual will need different treatment.

The task of police supervisors is made difficult by the fact that most of the motivational factors are beyond their control. The extrinsic factors such as salary, status, security of job, work conditions, policy of the government are not under the control of police managers. Only those motivational factors which are intrinsic to the job (achievement, recognition, work, responsibility, advancement and growth) can be manipulated to the advantage of the department. This process of making the job more satisfying to the employees may be loosely termed as job enrichment. Normally police managers are comparatively free in this field and they can definitely support their subordinates in their fulfilment of industrial needs, while performing their duties as sincere police officers.

Theories for Job Enrichment[14] : Traditional Theory

If justice is allowed to pervade the pivotal goals set by an organization, then morality will reign supreme in the administrative arena. The worker will take interest in his work if the work is 'psychologically acceptable' to the individual, and if it allows him to develop his faculties besides giving him freedom to change to a great extent, the work environment. According to the Traditional Theory:

1. Authority should be 'one way' from superior to subordinates.

2. Supervision should be detailed and span of control very narrow.

3. Organization should respect physiological properties of the individual.

4. Work should be routinized at the lowest level and organized in terms of functions at higher level.

Job Design Flexibility

This theory envisages that job should be designed to suit the potentialities of man. In the field of research and higher pursuits, one can strictly adhere to the above postulate but in department, like the police, such designing is not always feasible but still within the given parameters, the job can be reasonably altered to suit the potentialities of the individual, failing which placement could be organized in reasonable manner.

Job Enlargement (Horizontal and Vertical Job Requirement)

Enlarging the job by including a variety of functions to be done by the individual increases the number of motor or doing potentialities used and can be termed as horizontal job enlargement. Enlarging a job vertically on the other hand means that the individual feels more job autonomy and control over factors which reduces his dependence on superiors. Job enlargement has got its limitations; therefore, it can be attempted only after careful study, situational analysis, proper training and after developing proper supervisory habits.

Job enlargement in police is possible according to James Q. Wilson:

"Enlarging the Job of a Patrolman is Currently Much in Vogue for Reasons of Both Morale and Effectiveness. Reversing the Past Tendency to Take Away from the Patrolman Various Tasks and Give them to Specialised Units (Detectives, Juvenile Officers, Community Relation Specialists, Narcotics Investigators) should have, in View of many the Effect of Making the Patrolman's Tasks Personally, More Satisfying and Organizationally more Effective."[15] Thus, Job Enlargement Appears to be Quite a Useful Technique for the Police Department.

Participative Supervision

"Participative Supervision Strives to Accomplish Organization Objectives by Developing its Human Resources. It is Based on a Climate of Trust and Freedom of Action that Stimulates Individual and Group Growth."[16]

Participative supervision creates mutual understanding and respect and it increases psychological commitment to objectives, 'collective sense of purpose and involvement', high performance standards, self-discipline, self-motivation, enjoyment of job, and greater adaptability to the job. It further promotes belongingness, brotherhood, self-expression, creativity and openness.

Participative supervision depends on the interaction of people at different levels. The following reactions are likely to increase feeling of trust, caring and empathy.[17]

1. Level with one Another. Levelling means saying what you think is significant, with intention of helping the other person to learn from the experience.

2. Focus on Behavioural Trends and Not the Person. Giving emphasis to what a person does rather than what you imagine

he is.

Analytical Approach

3. Describing the Behaviour Rather than Judging it as Good-Bad, Right-Wrong.

4. Think Flexibly Rather than Rigidly.

5. Share Ideas and Information, not Advice.

6. Explore Alternatives Rather than Answers.

7. Be Aware of what is Going on in the "Here and Now", not "There and then". Information is more meaningful when relayed soon after the fact.

8. Ask Questions which help clarify understanding.

9. Seek to Be honest, Caring, and Non-Manipulative with People.

Job Satisfaction and Morale

Job satisfaction and morale have similar connotation, except that job satisfaction is an individual feeling while morale is a group phenomenon. "Job satisfaction is the degree of liking a person has for his work role. Morale is the degree of liking that a group has for its particular work assignment.....An Individual's Position on a job satisfaction continuum is determined primarily by the amount of value fulfilment provided by the work role".[18]

Job satisfaction determinants include occupational status and intensity of need fulfilment. Occupational status plays a very important role in affecting job satisfaction. Professionalization increases chances of intrinsic job satisfaction. As far as need fulfilment is concerned, it is dependant on various items, such as salary, security, prestige, job uncertainty, working conditions, distance of work place, number of years on the job, number of friends on the job, rating by immediate superior and other such factors depending on individual attitude towards the work.

The important determinants of the morale includes general

attitude to the organization, attitude toward supervision, job satisfaction, consideration of supervision towards the worker, pride in organization, pride in uniform, satisfaction with salary, attitude toward formal communication system of the organization, intrinsic job satisfaction, attitude towards co-workers and chances of self-advancement and self-realization.

Techniques of Motivation

Motivating a policeman is a complex problem. A policeman has to work in a variety of work situations and during his tenure of service he has to interact with people from different walks of life. Every experience leaves an imprint on his mind which affects his responses to a given situation. It is, therefore, very difficult to give generalised simplistic solutions to the problem. Those who are responsible to the community and the government for high performance of the organisation have to have diagnostic flexibility in their approach to cope with unforeseen situations and also immense capability for resolution of conflicts.

The motivating techniques have been evolved by a number of social scientists after painstaking research. Thomas C. Clary has given his views on motivation through positive strokng while Herzberg has dwelt upon at length on the factors causing dissatisfaction and satisfaction. Vroom on the other hand has given another variable of expectation to the problem. Despite various approaches to the problem, certain techniques to motivate are common to all the scientists and surprisingly enough majority of them have been used even by the conventionalists.

Stimulus for Better Results

The managerial cadre should provide humane conditions of work. The pay packet and fringe benefits should be adequate so that employees are able to meet their needs. Proper sanitary conditions in work place and provisions of accommodation for policemen to lead a healthy family life, are required. Lack of which will lead to dissatisfaction. It may be mentioned here that out of a total of 14 serious agitations (5 in pre-independence period and 9 in post-independence period) 7 had sevice conditions as import component in the demands of police agitations.[19]

Security of job is a very important factor which affects the morale of the men and precisely for this reason people are still attracted by government jobs as compared to jobs in private sector. In some of the companies in western countries they do not dismiss any employees but undertake programmes to improve performance.[20] The security cover extended to the families in case of loss of bread winner, is an important step towards achieving this exercise. In case of defence forces, a certain percentage of job is fixed for the wards of retired employees which always all apprehensions about the future of their family in case of loss of bread winner. This provision motivates the employee and fosters a sense of belongingness not only in men but also in their family members. The close and continuous contact also broadens the communication channel which can be made use of in difficult situations.

Satisfying the social needs of men, specially after long hours of strenuous work is essential for physical and mental health. Socialization includes many facts of human activity. It includes horizontal interaction with colleagues and vertical interaction with supervisors. During the course of horizontal interaction conflicts may crop up which should be resolved with utmost promptness in the interest of morale of the police organization. Vertical interaction brings into focus human qualities of managerial cadre such as interest in well being of subordinates, sincerity, friendliness, approachability and patience in listening to the grievances and criticisms. Both vertical and horizontal communications are essential but we do not have any system by which this could be established. At present we have systems such as Orderly Room, Sampark Sabha/Durbar or Sainik Sammelan, besides interviews. Occasionally we also hold 'Bara Khana' for such informal interaction. All these methods are useful if taken up seriously but mostly officers treat them in a very routine way and more harm is done to the morale by this attitude, 'Suggestion box system' could also be introduced in police. The suggestions which are accepted should be properly rewarded and recognized which will instill confidence in men and encourage them to think about the organization.

A sense of belongingness comes only when the person concerned gets affection and recognition. Recognition and appreciation are very important for those who have to undergo great stress, physical and emotional risk endangering their life. ("A PAT ON THE BACK IS ONLY A FEW VERTEBRAE REMOVED FROM A KICK IN THE PANTS, BUT IS MILES AHEAD IN RESULTS").[21] If an individual is treated with dignity, he is likely to return it with interest in the shape of respect, sincerity and increased performance.

Individuals when given responsible jobs become responsible. If a senior person in the department is not given the job of responsibility commensurate with his seniority, capability and past experience, then he feels frustrated. Fyoder Dostovesky mentioned that *"if one wanted to crush, to annihilate a man utterly......One need only give him work of an absolutely, completely useless* and *irrational character."*[22]

Gone are the days when majority of policemen used to be only literate and were not able to understand intricacies of administration or administrative intrigues. Everybody in the present situations understands his right and is capable of staking his claim through various acceptable or unacceptable means. The workman's awareness and approachability of political matters has added another dimension to the problem. Under the circumstances, it is imperative to have clear cut and understandable policies of placement, promotions, allotment of houses, grant of leave, sanction of loans and subsidies, and also that absolute fairness is observed in implementation of these policies. If an individual feels victimised, then his style of functioning is distorted, self-confidence suffers, and he feels estranged from the department. It is, therefore, absolutely necessary to have fairness in service matters and no exceptions be made, except on well-known grounds.

Every organization expects a particular level of

performances as well as conduct from the employees and in turn employees also expect something from the organization. In government departments these points are regulated by government orders and code of conduct for government servants but still some gaps remain to be fulfilled by organizational leadership. These values or norms may not be stressed overtly always but are brought home by way of organizational socialization which creates the set of values or a new sub-culture. The cultural traits or the norms or the values system of the department could be divided in two categories : 1. Pivotal values and 2. Peripheral values. Those who neglect even pivotal values are the rebels. Those who accept the pivotal norms but neglect peripheral norms in the interest of organizational functioning and are prone to introduce innovative methods are the thinkers or creative individuals. Those who accept pivotal and peripheral norms rigidly are the organizational persons and they resist every change for a progressive organization. The second category of employees at a lower level of management hierarchy can be tolerated but at the higher level it has to be discouraged.

Every human being has a very high estimation of himself. Throughout his life, he yearns for fulfilment of ego needs. He has yearning to influence others and thereby to command power over others or obtain control of organisation. Since there is little room at the top, it is not possible for everybody to reach that height. Hence, this need can be satisfied by participative supervision. Besides satisfied by participative supervision. Besides satisfying ego needs, this will also elicit co-operation of others. Individuals in useful interaction will also contribute in decision making. "Use the brains of your people more. Compare them to a car with six cylinders. Most people are actually working on only three. What an appalling waste! With a little encouragement and guidance, they could be working all the six cylinders. And look how much this can help all-round".[23]

REFERENCES

1. Donald F. Favrean and Joseph E. Gillespis, "Modern Police Administration" 1978, p. 85.
2. Willian C. Charron, "An exposition and analysis of William James Views on the Nature of Man", (Unpublished Doctor's dissertation Marguette University 1966—quoted in 'The Humanistic View of Man' by Jai Deep Singh, 1979.
3. Paul M. Whisenand 'Police Supervision :Theory and Practice', 1976, p. 359.
4. Jack L. Kuykendall and Peter C. Unsinger, 'Community Police Administration' 1979, p. 48.
5. Abraham H. Maslow, *'Motivation and Personality'* 2nd Edn. 1970, p. IX.
6. Warren G. Bennis and Philip E. Slatar 'The Temporary Society' 1968, p. 74.
7. Abraham H. Maslow, 'Motivation and Personality', p. 46.
8. David C. Mc Clelland, *'Assessing Human Motivation'* 1971.
9. J. Atkinson, *'An Introduction to Motivation*, 1958.
10. Douglas Mc Gregor (1906-67) served as President of Antioch College before joining Massachusetts Institute of Technology. At Antioch College, he tested his theory 'X' and theory 'Y'. His work 'The Human Side of Enterprise' was published in 1960.
11. V.M. Vroom and E.L. Deci, 'Management and Motivation', 1970.
12. Frederick Herzberg (a) 'One more time. How do you motivate employees' Harvard Business Review Jan.-Feb. 1968. (b) Work and Nature of Man, 1966.
13. Edgar H. Schein, 'Organizational Psychology', 1965.
14. From Paul M. Whisenand, 'Police Supervision—Theory and Practice' 2nd Edn. 1976 pp. 369-80.
15. James Q. Wilson, 'The Future Policeman' in future Roles of Criminal Justice Personnel Position Papers—The American Justice Institute.
16. Paul M. Whisenand, 'Police Supervision : Theory and Practice' 2nd Edn. 1976, p. 375.
17. *Ibid.*, p. 378.
18. *Ibid.*, p. 380.
19. Ram Anuj, Decline in Standards of Discipline in Police, its cause and remedies XXIV All India Police Science Congress papers, pp. 105-107.
20. "The classic example of the use of good human relations and fringe benefits to provide an atmosphere where workers are

fully motivated is the International Business Machine Corporation. I.B.M. seldom dismisses workers. Their jobs are almost guaranteed and they are secure in their employment". C. Northcote Parkinson and M.K Rustomji "Realities in Management", 1981 pp. 114-15.

21. Dr. Laurence J. Peter, *'The Peter Prescription'*, 1973.
22. Fyoder Dostoevesky, *'The Horn of the Dead'*, 1959 quoted in 'Modern Police Administration' by Donald F. Farrean and Joseph E. Gillespie, 1978 p. 85.
23. C. Northcote Parkinson and M.K Rustomji, '134 Tips for the go ahead Manager', 1987, p. 27.

10

Supervisory Leadership and Police Organization

Evolution of Welfare State is the most significant achievement in the field of political development. Historically speaking the functions of the State as defined even during the period of monarchies included welfare of the subject as prime objective.[1] Of the welfare activities of the State, the most important function is to create a social order which is conductive to all progressive social activities and here comes in the organization of police.[2]

Like any other organisation, police organisation is also a social unit deliberately structured to seek specific goals and possessing characteristic division of labour, authority, power and other responsibilities rationally planned to achieve goals set for it. The rules and norms together with centres of power set limits to its activities as well as the conduct of the individual members and also motivates the organisation and direct its way to achieve its goals in planned way.

No organisation can be perfect in all respects and for all time to come and this is more true with respect to organisations like police who have to tailor their activities in accordance with changing social fabric, who have to deal with people having different social background and who have to interact with scores of departments having different goals to achieve. The complexities of governing system, geographical distances, ethnographical differences and international problems arising out of interaction between different states expose such inadequacies and incompleteness of the organisation. The leadership is one way of overcoming such problems and offsetting such inadequacies by filling the voids in the organisational designs and this becomes very essential for the smooth running of the system. The smooth running of the organisation is not enough. It must run to achieve its goals and here comes the need of direction and supervision.[3] The direction of the organisation is determined by the centres of power which control the organisation. In an organisation like police and others involved in enforcement of law, the job behaviour is conditioned by role determinants as well as the personality of the leader who performs the role of the supervisor.

Leadership and Authority

Leadership is an "art of influencing, directing, guiding and controlling others in such a way as to obtain their willing obedience, confidence, respect and loyal co-operation in the accomplishment of an objective. It is the human factor which binds the group together and motivates it towards goals".[4] The right of command by virtue of authority is one thing while ability to command with or wihthout authority is quality of leadership. The rights assigned to an individual in a particular position in an organisational hierarchy give him authority to control, direct and motivate people who have been placed under him but leaders motivate their followers who willingly obey and lend loyal co-operations.[5]

The supervisor is normally very well identified in an organisation and finds prominent mention in organisational charts but he may or may not be a leader. A leader may not have any authority to control fellow workers but he has power to command, control and direct his followers. One has 'right' over his followers while others has the authority to supervise and control. A supervisor, when he possesses or acquires the art of influencing others co-ordinating their efforts and directing them to declared goals in such a way as to entice them to willing obedience, mutual confidence and respect, he becomes a leader and can ensure highest performances with minimum conflict and maximum satisfaction to the beneficiaries.[6]

Types of Supervisory Leaders

Every organisation consists of different types of persons with different perception and value systems. Similarly different supervisors exercise their powers in a characteristic way which is influenced by their own perception, view of life, value system, priorities and their understanding of their fellow workers. Extraneous factors such as peculiar situations, resources at command, demands of various types of pressures also affect styles of functioning.

N.F. Iannone has suggested following three types of leaders.[7]

1. **Autocract** : This type of leader does not allow his subordinates to take part in decision making. He directs, commands and controls his men in a very authoritative manner. This type of leader is a driver 'who uses his authority lavishly demanding complete and unquestioning obedience from his inferiors'.

2. **Democratic Leader** : This type of leader is used to democratic way of decision making. The leader treats his men as associates in a joint venture, and thus infuses in them sense of belongingness, achievement and increases their commitment to the goals of the organisation.

3. **Free-Rein Leader** : This type of leader minimises his role and allows others to grow but at times neglects his duty of motivating the fellow workers who suffer lack of direction and guidance.

James Q. Wilson while analysing police behaviour recognised the categories i.e. 'Watchman', 'legalistic' and 'service oriented'.[8] These categories clearly reflect the attitude of the policemen towards the role of police in contemporary society. Adrian Kinnane suggested five styles of policing.[9]

1. **Safe** : This style of functioning of officer reflects his anxiety to complete his service without any major setbacks. The officers in this category follow departmental regulations and try to keep trust of the fellow officers. The safe officer carries out his basic duties and responsibilities with minimum fuss and emotionality. At times this style of functioning was found to have defensice origins for an attempt to adaptto pressures felt from inside or outside department. This type of leaders are sincere and hard working but they will never seek new responsibility or that extra work which earns commendations. His heart is not really in the job but in the stability and financial security that the job brings.

2. **Producing Style of Functioning** : The officer of this category takes up this work in a very legalistic way and does not allow any ambiguity or discretion to creep in. 'He is most at home in a statistically-oriented department and seeks the relative clarity of numerical performance standards'. Such officers consider themselves as real workers and lack adaptiveness and sensitivity so necessary to rise in modern bureaucratic ladder. These officers at times risk positive police-public relations in their jurisdiction and create situations which will take days to be resolved. These officers lack the ability to discriminate between the situations that demand immediate and effective action and those which one should ignore.

3. **Crime Fighter Style of Police Functioning** : This style of functioning is not concerned with goals but aims at image building and more or less conforms to T.V. image of a policeman. This type of officer is always prepared to take more than usual risk. 'Over the long haul, such an adaptation can deaden sensitivities, increase cynicism and produce a crime fighter who characterologically resembles more and more the criminal he is supposed to be fighting.[10] This is the popular image of police officer and ordinary policeman also likes such people.

Such supervisors can go far if they continue to grow mentally also. Department needs such officers specially when the organization is under pressure from public or Government but soon such officers become frustrated when they don't get any other reward except routine departmental promotion.

4. **Avoiders in Police :** Avoiders always try to evade work. They are always satisfied with minimum possible work. Their energy is mostly wasted in finding the ways and means to avoid work rather than to perform it. Such people are mostly frustrated and cynical in nature. The avoiders usually survive and reach highest spot if they continue to pull enough load and supervisors ignore such persons out of sympathy. Such supervisors always compare them with others in crime fighter category and get frustrated very soon. This style appears to be a response to stress and disappointment. This response is really a mask for personal failure or difficulties.

5. **Street Cop Style of Policing :** Such police officers are adventurous and feel happy in doing active physical work. They are not contemplative and mostly by their misplaced aggression create more problems than they intend to solve.

It is difficult to find any pure style of functioning in Police Organisation, and most of the officers exhibit one or two traits of every style of policing. Officers at times change their style in order to adapt to changed situation.

Lawrence M. Miller postulates that every corporation has a life cycle and leadership also conforms to the various stages of corporate life cycle.[11] At each state and for each leadership style, the difficulties develop and leaders creatively apply themselves and solve the problems benefiting units and also motivating the fellow workers. The leadership component not only sets the pace of progress of the unit but also makes the workers more confident and contented. This process also creates a bunch of good second category leaders who can take over the organisation and lead it to onward march thus ensuring security of the system for a long time to come. The moment leadership relaxes or starts enjoying the fruits of earlier gains in utter disregard of welfare of the men and health of the unit, the decline sets in. "The weight of administration tends to grow unless deliberately checked by leadership. Unchecked administration inevitably leads to bureaucratisation and decline of creativity. The original purpose of administration was first to provide for the integration and co-ordination of diverse elements, within the organisation and second to serve the operations by providing score keeping mechanism. In periods of decline that purpose gets lost. The synergist understands the purpose of administration. He knows systems and structure and structure were designated to serve customers".[12]

The styles of policing reflect the personality of the officer and his response to a given situation. There can be as many styles of policing as the officers. As two persons cannot be identical similarly two persons cannot be totally different. One style of policing will have so many traits of other styles thus one can say that there cannot be many pure examples of any particular style of policing.

The leadership style also undergoes evolutionary changes with the passage of time. Most of the beginners who start with sincerity have very aggressive style but with the maturity of understanding in life and experience (sweet and sour) one mellows down. The extent and speed of tempering depends on the overall personality of the person. There are certain members of supervisory corp who never grow while others may attain maturity even without experience. Those who start as crusaders normally end up as decent penpushers but at times older cops also retain youthful over enthusiasm and vigour.

The style of policing is influenced, to a large extent by the situations one has to face. The responses of supervisory leaders may be different to a given situation when we examine in detail but the intensity of situational pressure dictates a particular type of response from most of the supervisors.

"Leadership fails more often through default than through error. Often when it is most needed, it is not present". When leadership fails certain symptoms appear on the surface. Indiscipline and lack of effectiveness are the effects which manifest on the surface. The fellow officers start working for personal gains completely ignoring the goals of the organization. "The appearance of selfishness, suspicion, envy, failure to give credit, hypercriticism, and arbitrariness will usually denote weaknesses if not down failure of an individual as a leader". The failure in leadership will result into decline in effectiveness, poor image in society, low morale and lack of *espirit de corp*. The incidents of indiscipline, misbehaviour, absenteeism, outside interference, will increase.

REFERENCES

1. (a) "Thus conducting himself (and) over intent on (discharging) royal duties, a king shall order all his officials to work (for the good of his subjects), (Manusmriti Book IX Verse 324)
   (b) "In the happiness of his subjects lies his happiness, in their welfare his welfare, whatever pleases him (personally) he shall not consider as good but whatever nakes his subjects happy, he shall consider good". (Arthashastra Book Chapter IXX, 39)
2. "A king of pure soul and devoted to the duty of protections his subjects acquired fame and immorality both here and hereafter by acting righteously. (Shanti Parva-Chapter LXXXV Verse-2).
3. "An organisation is a structure through which people work as a group. Whenever two or more persons are associated in doing something, there is some sort of organisation. It presupposes an orderly arrangement between individuals and groups, but a mechanical accomplishment of organisational objectives. Direction and control must be provided so that the necessary co-ordination of human effort can be achieved". (N.F. Iannone 'Supervision of Police Personnel', p.11).
4. *Ibid.*, p. 28.
5. "The leader stimulates, motivates and inspires the group to follow willingly, even eagerly. The authority pushes and drives his men, who yield and obey because they fear the consequences of disobedience.".
   (W.E. Parker and R.W. Kleemeier 'Human relations Supervision, Leadership in Management' p. 412).
6. "Any reasonably intelligent person with enough forcefulness to develop his ability to inspire others to follow him can earn leadership status. He may never be recognised on the organisation charts, he may never be awarded stripes or bars,

but he nevertheless is a leader if others are desireous of following him. The true leader—the ideal for the organization—is the leader recognised as such formally and granted leadership authority not only by his organization but by his subordinates. The grant of authority by the latter is the only real source of authority." (N.F. Iannone "Supervision of Police Personnel", p. 30)

7. N.F. Iannone, "Supervision of Police Personnel", pp. 30-31.
8. James Q. Wilson, "Varieties of Police behaviour".
9. Adrian Kinnane, "Policing", pp. 75-101.
10. Adrian Kinnane, "Policing", p. 85.
11. Extract from the Book Reviews by Sh. Hari C. Arora. (New York, Clarkson, N. Potter Inc. 1989).

    "The author has identified seven stages of corporate life and seven leadership styles that dominate during each stage as follows :

    1. Prophet (inspiration and innovation) is the visionary who creates the breakthrough and the human energy to propel the company forward.
    2. Barbarian is the leader of crisis and conquest who commands the corporation on the march of rapid growth.
    3. The Builder and Explorer are developers of specialised skills and structure required for growth, who shift from command to collaboration.
    4. Administrator is the creater of the integrated system and structure, who shifts the focus from expansion to security.
    5. Bureaucrat is the imposer of a tight grip of control, who crucifies and exiles new prophets and barbarians, assuring the loss of creativity and expansion.
    6. Aristocrat is the inheritor of wealth, alienated from those who do productive work, he is the cause of rebellion and disintegration.
    7. Synergist is the leader who maintains the balance, who continues the forward motion of a large and complex structure by unifying and appreciating the diverse contributions of the Prophet, Barbarian, Builder, Explorer andAdministrator".

12. (a) Hari C. Arora, Book Reviews of Lawrence M. Miller's Book. 'Barbarians to Bureaucrats" IJPA. July-Sept.-1990.

    (b) NF Iannone "Supervision of Police Personnel." p. 47.

11

Police Organization

The authors who studied public administration in detail and evolved various theories were mostly concerned with identification of tasks, grouping of departments and other factors responsible for effective functioning of the organization. Some of them like Henry Fayol dwelt with the functions of manager in detail.[1] Drawing heavily on his experiences as an industrialist, he initiated administrative principles for the guidence of administrators. Luther Gulick, further elaborated these principles and came out with 'Posdcorb' formula.[2] Further neo-classical theorists challenged the economic man's concept and concentrated on the three elements, i.e., individual, work groups and participation management. Later on Mason Haire, Simon and others viewed the organization in totality and laid emphasis on synthesis in the organizational phenomenon.[3] Nobert Wiener described the organization as a system consisting of in puts, process, out-puts, feed back and environment. Organization as an organism, is dependent for its well being on the smooth functioning of its various sub-systems.[4] Social systems (Police Organization) are contrived systems, they are made by men and hence are anchored in the needs perceptions, attitudes and motivation of human beings. Further, they form patterns of internal relationships for processing inputs (man and materials) into outputs (the handling of called for service).[5]

All open system possess nine characteristics, i.e., input, processing, output, cyclic character, arresting of disorganization, information, stable state, specialization, equifinality can reach the final state from differing initial conditions and by a variety of paths. In addition to above characteristics, every large and complex organization performs certain functions through sub-systems such as operations or technical care (they transform inputs into the primary outputs of the organization), supportive sub-system procument and development of supportive relationship such as research, advertising and public relations) maintenance of sub-systems (inputs of human skills-personnel functions of all types) adaptive sub-system (anticipation and response to changing environment) and managerial sub-system which are also called administrative structure which is responsible for co-ordination and direction of other systems.

"Organization systems, like social systems are considered to be cybernetic in their behaviour with regard to external environment. They develop mechanisms to collect, interpret and apply feedback in their decision making processes so as to acquire the capacity to adapt evaluate performance and to correct errors".[6] The recent researches in the field of public administration resulted into new contingency model for leadership (different from hard-nosed management techniques and human relations techniques). Fiedler conducted research and came to conclusion that hard-nosed worked best for 'highly structured tasks' and creative groups are best supervised by human relation type leaders. Fiedler proposed a seven-part model for leadership effectiveness. This approach based on contingency model shall have to take into consideration, the problems of politics, responsibility, distribution, equity, law, coercion respresentation and morality as they were the primary conditions which dictate the choice of strategy in a particular field.

Police organization is a complex unit and cannot be compared with companies or other corporate units with well defined tasks. Police organization is a social system which involves so many complexities at the input, output and feedback stages and cannot be and should not be controlled in hard-nose management fashion but requires a lot of human relations component. The strategies of administration selected for a particular situation may not hold good for similar situations two years hence, therefore, they remain in a state of perpetual flux and require constant examination of state of health of the organization by a specialist leader.

Good Leadership

"The executives (manager's, job consists mainly of creating by word and action, by decision and example, by orders and organization an atmosphere with which people are motivated to work willingly and effectively with continuous high effort; it is a job of leadership".[7]

As discussed earlier, the supervision in an organization like police is full of complexity and requires lot many functions and operations. The organizational leader who has to direct his men to give best results possible must have to perform certain roles. The role determinants decide the tasks that the police supervisor has to perform. In the beginning Police Supervisor's role was only to control his men who were supposed to obey orders with the passage of time and changes brought about in societal environment and quality of human raw material, the leader, in addition to traditional role of controller exercising authority over his subordinate, has to perform the role of leadership and trainer. The police supervisory leader's role amount to controlling, training and leading the man and material resources of the police organization.

The study of leadership traits has been taken up from various angles. Jack L. Kuykendal and Peter C. Unsinger have given following four theories of leadership:[8]

1. Great man approach.
2. Trait approach.
3. Situational approach.

4. System approach.

1. **Great man approach** in determining leadership qualities presumes that all greatmen were effective leaders and as such the qualities which were responsible for their excellence are the qualities which other leaders should also possess. Once these qualities have been identified an attempt can be made to select or develop leaders on that consideration.

This postulate marked the beginning of the serious study of leadership traits and at present has no following.

2. **Trait approach** : This theory aims at determining leadership traits on the basis of observation of effective leaders. This includes two sub-schools.

(a) Intuitive trait approach.

(b) Research trait approach.

Intuitive trait approach determines the traits in a general way such as sincerity, dependability and character etc. Research trait approach has identified intelligence (above the average) communication, skill (written and verbal), self-confidence, confidence in task performed, perception, sensitivity to individual and group feelings moderate boldness in social situation (somewhat extroverte) emotional maturity, high tolerance for frustration, breadth in interests and activities, strong motivation for achievement, and high concern for the needs and feelings of public and subordinates from other side.

3. **Situational approach** : The style, behaviour and response changes with the changing situations. Possible situations which can be dealt with include situations concerning individual, situations among individuals, situations concerning job, and the situations concerning relationships between jobs. Individual centred situation involves personalised response. A Constable has personal problems. A leader can solve the problem by placement. If the situation seeking response concerns a group of policemen then response involves study and quick decision. If situation is with respect to a particular job then the leadér has to organise task orientation, or guide all concerned to

acquire necessary expertise. If situation concerned various jobs then response will involve study of the system and a well thought of solution has to be given.

4. Systems approach to leadership proposes an absolute style for managerial effectiveness. Rensis Likert suggested four systems of management.[9]

(a) Exploitive autocratic (authoritarian).

(b) Benevolent autocratic (paternal).

(c) Consultative.

(d) Participative (democratic) management.

Internal Police Leadership

Organization sets certain goals of performance for itself but the individuals who join the organisation have their own goals when they join organization. If the goals of organization and goals of individuals manning the organization are integrated then maximum output and maximum satisfaction can be achieved when these goals are at variance then there is decline in production or decline in satisfaction standards or it may bring decline in both. Grid system has been developed around these two variables, i.e., concern for the people (individual goals) and concern for production (organizational goals)[10] from the degree of integration. Baker and Monton identified five managerial styles as follows :

I. 9/9 Style	High concern for production and people.
II. 5/5 Style	Moderate concern for production and people.
III. 9/1 Style	High concern for production and low concern for people.
IV. 1/9 Style	Low concern for production and high for people.
V. 1/1 Style	Low concern for production and low concern for people also.

9/9 style is the best style and, can be called as style of

optimum motivation and style of integrated goal. The grid system does not take into consideration the traits of the fellow workers and the stress situations. The internal leadership style should take into account the organizational maturity of the followers. The organizational maturity means willingness and ability to take responsibility. In this one can also add 'ethos' of the organization. When a subordinate has low organizational maturity then his work has to be closely monitored. The leader should maintain concern for the individual and his needs. The task has to be very well structured. As the follower matures the degree of supervision should be reduced and more and more participation be allowed ultimately resulting into self-controlled and self-motivated subordinate. If the supervisory leader does not vary the degree of control then it will lead to frustration and he will contribute to the creation of permanently dependent subordinate.

Stress situations need a particular response from the leader. In dangerous situations a task oriented leader is required and any attempt at participative or democratic style will bring disaster. In stress situations or in emergency prompt, strong and decisive action is necessary which leaves no room for participative style of functioning.

Jack L. Kuykendal and Peter C. Unsinger have suggested characteristics of an effective police manager: [11]

1. Shows confidence and trust in employees as they mature.
2. Acts in a supportive role to achieve goals.
3. Attempts to understand individual and organizational problems and never avoids dealing with them.
4. Provides the necessary training for the employees development.
5. Shares all important information about the organization.
6. Friendly and easily approached.
7. Generous in credit and recognition of successful performance.

8. Constructive action instead of criticism.
9. Respects others, ideas and criticism.
10. Will not 'walk over' others to achieve personal goals yet strives to 'get ahead'.
11. 'Plays square'and does not 'work angles' even for his own advantage.
12. Bases managerial efforts on a coherent plant.
13. Is objective and values facts and adequacy of information.
14. Has positive, as opposed to negative assumptions about people.

External Police Leadership. So far we have discussed characteristics of a leader which concern his followers or subordinates. But as a leader of the organization he has to work in society, therefore, his characteristics which come to the front while having inter-action with various societal groups are important for his image in society.

It is generally presumed that society appreciates a supervisor who can deliver goods. A leader who cannot control his men is of no worth to the society. The police manager who only reacts to a given situation is not appreciated by society. A police leader has to be pro-active and not reactive. One has to think ahead of time and constructive measures are to be taken. If in a given locality drug trafficking increases and public starts clamouring for action, then a reactive manager will only catch hold of some of the traffickers and ask for the additional staff for investigation. A proactive manager will think in advance and will suggest to voluntary organizations to take up preventive measures and will also encourage opening of treatment centres. Society wants proactive leaders and not the reactive pen pushers.[12] The credibility of an organizational leader in society plays an important role in controlling public disorders. Public co-operation which is so essential at the time of natural calamities shall not be forthcoming if he has very low credibility in society.

An organizational leader has to deal with other systems or sub-systems in order to achieve the departmental goals. If he lacks clarity of vision, professionalism and personal attributes of a balanced personality he will suffer isolation which will affect the organization as a whole bringing discredit to the leader.

The leader works as a link between government and the organization. The smoothness of the relationship is an indication of good leadership.

A good leader will increasingly affect the policy formulation at government level with respect to the subjects having bearing on police work.

The leadership in the context of an organization is an all encompassing term and includes all the roles and tasks of an effective manager. The leader has to lead the organization without any jerks and breakdown which means that he should maintain a happy blend of the concern for the goals of the organization as well as of its constituents and help them to self-actualization. Some of the personality traits are fundamental for a good leader while others can be acquired by training and experience as superstructure on the foundation of good personality, good manners and high moral character[13].

REFERENCES

1. Henry Fayol, 'General and Industrial Administration', London, 1949.
2. Luther Gulick, Duties of supervisory group or chief executive can be described by POSDCORB—which stands for:
   (a) Planning
   (b) Organising.
   (c) Staffing.
   (d) Directing.
   (e) Co-ordinating.
   (f) Reposting.
   (g) Budgeting.
3. (a) M. Haire 'Psychology in Management, New York, 1964.
   (b) A.H. Simon, D.W Smithburg Victor, A. Thomson, "Public Administration", New York, 1961.

4. "Every system is a system of some larger system and is itself made up of a hierarchy of sub-systems, sub-subsystems, sub-sub-subsystem etc. each of which is a system in its own right". Albert Shapero and Chales Bates Jr, "A Method for a performing Human Engineering Analysis of weapon Systems" quoted by Paul M. Whisen and in his "Police Supervision. Theory and Practice", 1976.
5. Paul M. Whisen and "Police Supervision. Theory and Practice", 1976.
6. Om Prie Srivastava, 'Quandary of Public Administration'. The Indian Journal of Public Administration, April-June, 1990.
7. S.K. Ghosh, 'Police leadership and man management',1977.
8. Jack K. Kuykendal and Peter C. Unsinger, "Community Police Administration", 1979.
9. Rensis Likert, "The human organization", 1967.
10. Robert Blake and Jane Monton, "The Managerial Grid", 1964.
11. N.F. Iannone while analysing leadership traits has suggested following twelve characteristics based on the works of Pratt, Bass, Ordway Tead, and Emory S. Bogardus.
    1. *Friendliness, sincerity, affection for others, und personal warmth.* A long face should be seldom, if ever, the face of the leader. Neither should he have a pessimistic or negative attitude. A sincere expression of pleasure when a greeting is indicated, especially to subordinate, has inestimable value. A person's birthday, a promotion, his wedding, or the birth of his child is one of the big events in his life. A warm, sincere handclap or a word of congratulation takes little time and is worth every moment it takes in these and similar cases.
    2. *Enthusiasm for the job and all it entails.* Sincerity and the ability to display it are vital traits of the leader. Zeal to do the right thing and to get the job done are extremely contagious and are quickly felt by others.
    3. *Ambition.* Within reason, ambition is desirable; however, it must be controlled or it can become a millstone around the supervisor's neck. It should never result in the taking of credit which belongs to another. Neither should selfishness and vanity be allowed to corrode the supervisor's career.
    4. *Physical and nervous energy and vitality.* Being a leader requires much physical and nervous stamina and a high frustration tolerance. Good leadership and hard work seem to go hand in hand. Diligence and industry are essential to effective leadership.

5. *Moral and physical integrity.* The real leader has moral as well as physical courage. He has a sense of direction and purpose with clear goals in mind. He has personal responsibility. He doesn't make promises he does not intend to keep because his word is his bond. It is more important that he be trusted than liked. Subordinates expect their leaders to be honourable, to know right from wrong, justice from injustice, and to be fair with all without prejudices. A leader is expected to pursue the truth at all times. He is expected to keep the personal and professional life above approach and, by his conduct, to be a credit to those in the organization, and his profession.
6. *Intelligence.* It has been shown that the successful leader almost invariably has more intelligence than those he leads. He has a sense of imagination and humour. He is capable of making objective observations. He has a questioning attitude which helps him in his search for truth in all matters. He has vision and insight, for without them he will fail as a leader. He has a highly developed ability to see all sides of a question and draw commonsensical conclusions from the evidence at hand.
7. *Technical skill.* The most successful leader has a technical mastery of his job including the teaching skill.
8. *Faith.* The leader has faith and confidence in himself and his subordinates.
9. *Verbal aptitude.* A large amount of experimental work supports the conclusion that the most successful leaders are verbally capable. They are persuasive and tactful. Few attributes are more important in dealing with others without generating friction.
10. *Courtesy.* Common courtesy demands that politeness is a civility which must be practised at all times. The superior cannot afford to be cut down in it by his subordinates.
11. *Modesty.* The real leader can afford to be modest and practice humility. His accomplishments will attest to his value without his constantly reminding others of his greatness.
12. In addition, those characteristics of self-control, dependability, empathy for others, short of sentimentalism, good judgement, originality, versatility, and adaptability are usually found in the most successful leaders.

12. According to Jack L. Kuykendal and Peter C. Unsinger the characteristics of proactive leadership are as follows :
    1. He identifies and speaks out on all police related community

problems.

2. He offers alternatives to these problems consistent with democratic principles.
3. He advocates rule of law.
4. He advocates active citizen participation in police policy formulation in areas that are not covered by legal rules.
5. He advocates fair and impartial policing.
6. He seeks support for progress and solution to problems consistent with democratic principles.

13. Paul M. Whisen, "Police Supervision Theory and Practice", p. 236 has given role tasks constituting leaderships as follows:
Integrity (Infrastructure)
Optimism (Infrastructure)
Social Perception (Infrastructure)
Communication (Super structure)
Co-ordination (Super structure)
Job enrichment (Super structure)
Conflict resolution (Super structure)
Change agentry (Super structure)

12

Criminal Conspiracy and Indian Penal Law

The word 'Conspiracy' means 'a secret plan to commit a crime or do harm, often for political ends; a plot' (The Concise Oxford Dictionary, 1990), but in English Common Law it had its roots in Civil Law which later on was applied to Criminal Law as well. Indian Penal Code has borrowed it from English Case Law (1901) though law relating to conspiracy first appeared on Statute book in first decade of the 14th century in England.

The Indian Penal Code deals with 'Abetment' in Chapter V and 'Offence against the State' in Chapter VI. While the Sections 120-A and 120-B dealing with conspiracy have been added in separate Chapter V-A not without reason. The offence of abetment has been covered in Chapter V and Sections 116 and 119 have been included to cover certain categories of criminal activity. Again in Chapter VI, the offences against State have been adequately provided for. Section 121-A I.P.C. was added by the Indian Penal Code (Amendment) Act of 1873 to make the law more comprehensive so as to include conspiracy to wage war against the government. Sir James Stephen, the then Law Member, was of the opinion that Indian Penal Law should not suffer the anomaly that existed in English

Law that waging war against the King was a treason while conspiracy to wage a war against the government was considered only a misdemeanour. The addition of Section 121-A (Chapter VI) was primarily aimed at removing this anomaly prevailing in English Law and Chapter V-A Sections 120-A and 120-B were added to fill in the gap in dealing with offences of abetment (specially when no act or illegal omission has taken place) or criminal conspiracies with respect to other offences on one hand and attempt or conspiracies to wage war against the Government on the other.

This Chapter V-A of the Indian Penal Code (Sections 120-A and 120-B) was enacted in the year 1913 by Indian Criminal Law Amendment Act (Act VIII of 1913). The Indian Penal Code was enacted in 1860, and the Indian Evidence Act was enacted in the year 1872 after the unsuccessful struggle for Independence. Though Britishers had overcome the struggle initially yet the fight for freedom was going on in one form or the other. The revolutionaries were incessantly exploring new methods to throw away the yoke of foreign rule. The Partition of Bengal also brought in its wake a wave of revolutionary activities. The political environment was surcharged with emotive issues and younger generations motivated by the events in Europe and America were waging war against the establishment both from within the country and also from England and America. To deal with this situation the Penal Law was updated from time to time. In the year 1873, Section 121-A (Chapter VI) was added while in 1913, Chapter V-A was added to the I.P.C. The Statement of Objects and Reasons for the enactment was published in the Gazette of India—1913 (Part V, p. 44) which mentions that, "Experience has shown that dangerous conspiracies are entered into in India which have for their object aims other than commission of the offences specified in Section 121-A of the Indian Penal Code and that the existing law is inadequate to deal with modern conditions. The present bill is designed to assimilate the provisions of the Indian Penal Code to those of the English Law with the additional safe-guard that in the case of conspiracy other than a conspiracy to commit an offence some overt act is necessary to bring the conspiracy within the purview of the criminal law.

The Criminal Conspiracy and its English Roots

The offence of criminal conspiracy entered Common Law as private injury simply as misdemeanour not indictable but later on it was considered indictable. It was only around 17th century that it was recognized as substantive law by the courts. In earlier stages, it was considered as an agreement of persons who joined to carry on illegal acts in a improper way but afterwards the criminal aspect of agreements of this nature evolved into a substantive offence. The criminal conspiracy first entered Statute book in A.D. 1305 when an Ordinance was passed to deal with persons who conspired to corrupt the Course of Justice. Afterwards, Statutes were passed to penalize criminal conspiracies to commit offences of murder (1861) to cause explosion (1883) regarding Unions and for formenting trade disputes.

The essence of this offence is the agreement which may be expressed or implied. The offence is complete as soon as the agreement is made and it continues till this agreement continues to exist which may, however, terminate by the execution of the act or abandonment by the parties to the agreement.

The offence of criminal conspiracy has been divided into following three categories by Fitzgerald, J. (in. *R.V. Parnell*—1881) : (a) Where the end to be attained is in itself a crime, (b) Where the object is lawful but the means are unlawful, and (c) Where the object is to do injury to other but were to be effected by single individual. In third category, it is not a conspiracy : "An agreement to constitute a conspiracy must be to do that which is contrary to or forbidden by law as for instance, to violate a legal right or to make use of fraud or violence, or to do what is criminal."[1]

The conspiracy to 'undermine the principles of commercial or moral conduct' or conspiracy to 'corrupt the public morals' was considered to be indictable as a criminal offence by the

Common Law Courts as the courts are supposed to be *custos morum* of the people and they have superintendency of offences *contra bonos mores*.

Definition and Ingredients of Criminal Conspiracy

The definition of criminal conspiracy in Section 120-A has been taken from Lord Brampton who defined conspiracy in a case in the year 1901. Lord Brampton in *Quinn V. Leatham* defined conspiracy by holding that, "if two or more persons agree together to do something contrary to law or wrongful or harmful towards another person or to use unlawful means in the carrying out of an object not otherwise unlawful, the persons who so agree commit the crime of conspiracy.[2]

The ingredients of the offence of criminal conspiracy as enumerated in Section 120-A may be listed as :

1. There must be two or more persons.
2. They must be in agreement.
3. They must agree to do (a) an illegal act or (b) an act by illegal means (which may not be illegal).

The explanation further clarified that it is immaterial whether illegal act is ultimate object of the conspirators or it is incidental to their objective of conspiracy.

The Criminal Conspiracy must have two or more Persons

Section 11 of I.P.C. defines that the word 'person' includes any company or association or body of persons. In this way the 'juridical' or artificial persons can also be included in this definition. It is well known principle that where it is physically impossible to commit an offence or where *mens rea* is essential ingredient of the offence, such juridical persons cannot be prosecuted. In such cases, at least two persons should be 'natural persons' capable of entering into an agreement. An agreement with one man company and its director (sole member of the company) is not sufficient for the purposes of this section. Similarly, a child in the womb, however sufficiently developed, cannot be prosecuted along with mother of the child, for conspiracy.

The Criminal Law (Amendment) Act, 1977 Section 5(8) provides that unless the conviction of one of the two conspirators become inconsistent on acquittal of other, even one of the two conspirators can be convicted. Prior to this Act of 1977 single person could not be convicted if all but one have been acquitted or were in exempted category (*Faguna Kanta Nath V. State of Assam*—1959). Following new Criminal Law Act of 1977, the court convicted single person where one of the two persons was acquitted for want of proper sanction u/s 197 Cr. P.C. being a public servant. It was held by the court in the case of *Pradumna V. State* (1981) Bombay that acquittal was on technical grounds and the ingredients of the offence of the criminal conspiracy as required u/s 120-A stood proved.

In a case of criminal conspiracy, as in other cases also, it is not necessary to prosecute all the persons at the same time. One of the conspirators who is in custody can be tried alone and while others are still evading arrest.

Essence of Conspiracy Agreement

The gist of the offence of conspiracy has in forming of the scheme or agreement between two or more parties. A conspiracy consists not merely in the intention of two or more but in the agreement of two or more to do an unlawful act or to do a lawful act by unlawful means. So long as design rests in intention only, it is not indictable.

A criminal conspiracy may persist as long as the persons in agreement continue to act in pursuance of the agreement. The conspiracy can be terminated other by abandonment, accomplishment or detection and resultant route by law enforcement. It is a continuing offence.

It is not essential for agreement that the members of conspiracy meet each other or know all the members or even majority of the members to the conspiracy. It is also not essential that all should know all the details of conspiracy. As a matter of fact, a criminal conspiracy has to be inferred from the circumstances as held in *Gutta Sriramulu Naidu V. State* (1963) wherein the court held that, "Conspiracy is a matter of inference deduced from certain criminal acts of the parties accused, done in pursuance of an apparent criminal purpose common between them."

An act in furtherance of conspiracy is not required in case of an agreement to commit an offence. In case of a criminal conspiracy, conspirators can be punished for conspiracy though individually they may not be prosecuted for substantive offence of theft or criminal breach of trust (*K.C. Kapoor V. State*—Alld.. 1959).

The offence of criminal conspiracy is different offence from the object of the conspiracy and as such it starts even before the beginning of actual offence which is the object of such conspiracy and it is complete even before the attempt or completion of the offence so agreed upon.[4]

Illegal Act

The provisions of Section 120-A (1) specifically mention 'an illegal act' in the context of agreement to do or cause to be done to make it indictable as criminal conspiracy. The definition of 'illegal act' has been given in Section 43 I.P.C. The word 'illegal' includes (a) offences, (b) which is prohibited by law, and (c) which furnishes ground for civil action. It also includes omission which a man is legally bound to do. The definition is very comprehensive in scope and makes the Sections 120-A and 120-B very wide in implication.

"Sections 120-A and 120-B have brought the Law of Conspiracy in India in line with the English Law by making the overt act unessential when the conspiracy is to commit any punishable offence. The most important ingredient of the offence of conspiracy is the agreement between two or more persons to do an illegal act. The illegal act may or may not be done in pursuance of agreement, but the very agreement is an offence and is punishable" (Shetty, J. *Kehar Singh V. State*—S. Court decided on 3-8-1988 AIR 1988, pp. 1886-1887).

When Object may not be Illegal

The end does not justify the means in Criminal Law. If, therefore, one conspires with another to employ illegal means to achieve a legal purpose, one may be convicted of conspiracy. It is not difficult to conceive of such cases, for instance, it is not illegal to under-sell a rival trader but it would be illegal for the latter to combine to ruin the seller of cheap goods by inducing to give credit to a bankrupt purchaser and thereby cause him loss.[5]

In Criminal Conspiracy as defined in Section 120-A I.P.C. four ingredients are required : (i)an agreement between persons, (ii)to do an illegal act, (iii)to do a legal act by illegal means and (iv)overt act done in pursuance of conspiracy. In English Law only first three ingredients are required while u/s 120-A I.P.C. overt act in furtherance of conspiracy is also required if the act to be done or cause to be done is not illegal (Proviso to Section 120-A I.P.C.). Held in *State V. Jai Govind Raj* (AIR 1951), "In Indian Law, a distinction is drawn between an agreement to commit an offence and an agreement of which either the object or the methods employed are illegal but do not constitute an offence. In the case of former, the criminal conspiracy is completed by the act of agreement, in the case of the latter, there must be some act done by one or more of the parties to the agreement to effect the object thereof that is there must be an overt act." In English Law, the agreement itself is treated as overt act and no separate overt act is necessary unless the rule is limited by Statute.

Section 120-B I.P.C. provides punishment for criminal conspiracy where no express provision is made in the Code (I.P.C.) for the punishment of such conspiracies. The offences of conspiracies which have been punished under other sections are not covered by Section 120-B I.P.C.

Conspiracy Punishable Under I.P.C.

1. Abetment by conspiracy (Section 107, Clause2)
2. Conspiracy to wage war against the Government (Section 121-A I.P.C.)

3. Thugee (Section 311 I.P.C.)
4. Being a member of thieves (Section 401 I.P.C.)
5. Being a member of an assembly of dacoits (Section 402 I.P.C.)

In addition to above offences, conspiracy u/s 120-A is also punishable.

Plurality of Objects

For the offence under Section 120-A it is not essential that the object should be one. The individual conspirators may have more than one objects. It is also not permissible in law to distinguish between primary and secondary objects of the conspiracy.

Sanction as Required for Prosecution u/s 120-B I.P.C.

The offence of criminal conspiracy has its roots in English Common Law as has been discussed above. In Common Law, the powers were wrested gradually by the Common Law Courts and this is a long history of evolution of this branch of Common Law. During the period of its growth, the cases came where it was held that individual should be protected against the oppression of the State.[7] The wide scope and vagueness of this crime further afford the opportunity for oppression by the Government against its own citizen, therefore, at the time of addition of this new chapter precautions were taken to prevent any misuse of these two sections.

Section 120-B provides for the punishment for the criminal conspiracy only in those cases which were not already covered by the existing sections of the Code as discussed earlier. Further, the section provides for different punishment for serious offences which are punishable with death, imprisonment for life or rigorous imprisonment for a term of two years or upwards. For the criminal conspiracy with respect to this category of offences, section provides punishment in the same manner as if he had abetted such offence. In this way the punishment has been graduated in accordance with gravity of the offences. In criminal conspiracies with respect to other offences (not provided for in the section above), the punishment is 6 months (maximum) or with fine or with both. Further, safeguard has been provided in Section 196 (IA) (2) Cr. P.C. subject to the provisions of which Section 195 Cr. P.C. requires previous consent of the State Government or the District Magistrate to prosecute in respect of criminal conspiracies to commit an offence punishable with less than two years' imprisonment.

The requirement of the previous consent under Section 196 Cr. P.C. is fully met if consent is obtained before filing charge-sheet in Court of Law. The authority competent to remove a public servant from the office is also competent to give sanction for prosecution under this section. An authority higher in rank to the appointing authority is also competent to give sanction for prosecution. An authority inferior to appointing authority is not competent to give such sanction (*K.M. Mathew V.P.K. Thungan*—1990 Cr. L.J., p. 247).

The absence of sanction does not prevent the court from proceeding with the trial under substantive sections, in a case where accused was standing trial for conspiracy u/s 120-B I.P.C. and also offences under Sections 409 and 477-A. I.P.C. The conspiracy to commit an offence is by itself an independent offence, therefore, the offence if actually committed would be the subject-matter of separate charge. If sanction is not obtained then accused persons can be tried and punished under substantive sections (*Madan Lal. V. State of Punjab*—1967). No sanction u/s 196 Cr. P.C. was considered necessary for the prosecution of offfences u/s 120-B and under Sections 161 and 162 I.P.C. as they were cognizable offences having punishment of three years (*State of Maharashtra V. Ram Chandra Vasudeo Desh Pande*—1974).

The Provisions of Section 10 of Indian Evidence Act

The provisions of Section 10 of Indian Evidence Act introduce the 'Doctrine of Agency' which means that if the conditions laid down in the section (there is reasonable ground to believe, that two or more persons have conspired together to commit an offence or an actionable wrong) are met then the acts done (anything said done or written, by any one of such persons in reference to their common intention was first entertained by any one of them) by one are admissible against other accused persons of the conspiracy case. Anything so said done or written is a relevant fact for the purpose of proving the existence of the conspiracy and the conspirators were members of the conspiracy (*Bhagwan Swaroop Lal Bishan Lal V. State of Maharashtra*—AIR 1965). It cannot be used in favour of the other party or for the purpose of showing that such a person was not a party to said conspiracy (*K. Kunhaman V. State of Kerala*—1974).

The offences of conspiracy can be proved, like any other offence by direct evidence or by circumstantial evidence. As discussed above this section introduces the Doctrine of Agency of Civil Law into Criminal Law. The provisions of Section 10 of Indian Evidence Act will not operate unless conspiracy is not proved. The mere intention is not indictable as such it does not prove conspiracy, therefore, in criminal conspiracy cases, one has to go a bit further and establish with the help of direct or circumstantial evidence, the 'agreement to act in consent'. When conditions laid down are met to the satisfaction of the court, then and then alone evidence should be adduced to prove the acts and declaration of one accused against other member of conspiracy. In such cases, the rule of prudence embodied in Section 30 of Indian Evidence Act has to be kept under consideration. The evidence to prove the case against the co-accused persons is also subject to provisions of Sections 14/15 of Indian Evidence Act, therefore, the evidence of similar acts can be given but it must be of same specific kind and it should also possess proximity in time.

The provisions made in Section 10 of Indian Evidence Act are by way of departure from the recognised principles of Criminal Law, because generally, a conspiracy is hatched in secrecy and it may be difficult to adduce direct evidence of the same.[8] The prosecution will often rely on evidence of act of various parties to infer that they were done in reference to their common intention. The prosecution will also more often rely upon circumstantial evidence. The conspiracy can be undoubtedly proved by such evidence direct or circumstantial. But the court must enquire whether the two persons are independently pursuing the same end or they have come together to the pursuit of the unlawful object. The former does not render them conspirators, but the latter does it is, however, essential that the offence of conspiracy requires some kind of physical manifestation of agreement. The express agreement, however, need not be proved. Nor actual meeting of two persons is necessary. Nor it is necessary to prove the actual words of communication. The evidence as to transmission of thoughts sharing the unlawful design may be sufficient. The relative acts or conduct of the parties must be conscientious and clear to mark their concurrence as to what should be done. The concurrence cannot be inferred by a group of irrelevant facts artfully arranged so as to give an appearance of coherence. The innocuous, innocent or inadvertent events and incidents should not enter the judicial verdict.[9]

Criminal Conspiracy and Common Intention u/s 34 I.P.C.

In case of criminal conspiracy, the mere engagement or meeting of minds to break the law as given in Section 120-A is essential but in all cases illegal act is not necessary and in case of Section 34 I.P.C. it is essential that some criminal act should have been done in furtherance of a common intention of all the accused persons which indicates 'unity of criminal behaviour'.

Section 71 I.P.C. and Criminal Conspiracy

The provisions of Section 71 I.P.C. does not come into play in cases of criminal conspiracy as defined u/s 120-B. Section 120-B I.P.C. provides punishment for conspiracy and it is unreasonable to say that persons can be punished under that section so long as they conspire but do not commit an offence and the sections become inoperative if they actually proceed to commit the offence agreed upon (*Bhagwan Das*

Keshwani V. State of Rajasthan—AIR 1974).

Criminal Conspiracy and *Mens Rea*

It is well-settled English Law that a person can be held guilty of conspiring to commit an offence without knowing a material fact which constitute the offence so that his mind remains innocent of criminal intent. The offence of conspiracy is the making of an agreement to do an unlawful act. It is the character and the content of the agreement that matters, and the accused's knowledge of what in fact has been done is relevant if it throws light on that, therefore, one can safely infer that *mens rea* is not a necessary ingredient of the charge of conspiracy to commit an offence.[10]

The Law of Conspiracy is very delicate. If it is not used with discretion then it can cause more harm to the people than it purports to prevent. Since privacy and secrecy are the essential elements of conspiracy, the direct evidence is not likely to be available to establish it in Court of Law and it is to be proved by circumstantial evidence, and the conduct of persons involved before and after the act. The Indian Evidence Act makes special provisions to govern relevancy of facts once court is satisfied about the commission of criminal conspiracy. The court has to be very careful in taking decision in such cases as explained by Shetty, J., "In the past, the judges and lawyers spoke of a 'golden rule' by which Statutes were to be interpreted according to grammatical and ordinary sense of the word. They took the grammatical or literal meaning unmindful of the consequences. Even if such a meaning gave rise to unjust results which Legislature never intended, the grammatical meaning alone was kept to prevail. They said that it would be for the Legislature to amend the Act and not for the court to intervene by its innovation. During the last several years, the 'golden rule' has been given a go-bye. We now look for the 'intention' of the Legislature on the 'purpose' of the Statue. First, we examine the words of the Statute. If the words are precise and cover the situation in hand, we do not go further. We expound those words in the natural and ordinary sense of the words. But, if the words are ambiguous, uncertain or any doubt arises as to the terms employed, we deem it as our paramount duty to put upon the language of the Legislature rational meaning. We then examine every word, every section and every provision. We examine the Act as a whole. We examine the necessity which gave rise to the Act. We look at the mischiefs which the Legislature intended to redress. We look at the whole situation and not just one-to-one relation. We will not consider any provision but of the framework of the Statute. We will not view the provisions as abstract principles separated from the motive force behind. We will consider the provisions in the circumstances to which they owe their origin. We will consider the provisions to ensure coherence and consistency within the law and as a whole and to avoid undesirable consequences. This adventure, no doubt, enlarges court's discretion as to interpretation. But it does not imply power to courts to substitute its own notions of legislative intention. It implies only a power of choice where differing constructions are possible and different meanings are available"(*Kehar Singh and Others V. State*—S.C. 1987 D/3-8-1988).

REFERENCES

1. Sir John Woodroffe and Saed Amir Ali; *Law of Evidence*, p. 579.
2. Dr. Hari Singh Gaur, Penal Law of India, p. 1062.
3. *Ibid.*, p. 1071.
4. *Kehar Singh and Others V. State*—1987 (Paras 272, 273)—AIR 1988, p. 1887.
5. Sir John Woodroffe and Syed Amir Ali, *Law of Evidence*, 1993, pp. 582-83.
6. Ratan Lal and Dhiraj Lal, *The Indian Penal Code*, 1992, p. 133.
7. "The Law of Conspiracy is a brand of Jurisprudence to be narrowly watched, to be jealously regarded and never to be pressed beyond its true limits" Fitzgerald, J. (Irish State Trials, 1867).
8. "Guilt must be wiped out by punishment but there is no reason why the victim should be one person rather than another." (Salmond on Jurisprudence, 12th Edition, p. 105).
9. *Kehar Singh and Others, appellants V. State*, 1987 (G.L. Oza, B.C. Ray, K. Jagannath Shetty, JJ.).
10. Dr. Hari Singh Gaur, *Penal Law of India*, pp. 1078-79.

13

Drug Dependence and Society

Drug abuse in all its varied form and with all its complexities and colossal cost both individual and social, continues to remain at the centre of all discussions at national and international level, aimed at improving the quality of life. This ever-increasing awareness of the problem and the dedicated research work into the causative factors leading to dependence on drugs, has not changed the scenario which continues to remain grim and gloomy despite all efforts, on the part of national governments and responses received at international level in many regional conferences held under the auspices of United Nations.

In the last few decades, man has made incredible strides in the fields of explorations both within and without, and has managed to unlock some of the basic riddles of human existence by delving deep into the fundamentals of the life on the universe. In his efforts he got immense help from the scientific knowledge he collected on his way from homo sapien errectus days to the present juncture of human history when he has already succeeded in walking on the surface of the moon. This vast load of scientific knowledge though aimed at ameliorating the conditions of life, has also given us some of the problems now crying for solution and drug addiction is one of them.

The cost of drug-abuse is immense particularly when we take into account its inevitable spin-off crime, corruption and social degradation. The drugs which symbolise the human effort put in decoding the secrets of life in our quest for disease-free life, also brought untold miseries to mankind and decay of the social institutions which in turn breeds tainted money responsible for moral degeneration besides blocking the path of progress and diverting the national resources for self-annihilation. Thus, the struggle against drug-abuse is essentially and intrinsically linked with welfare of the mankind and our failure in this area will lead to socio-economic problems of the magnitude that will threaten the very existence of human beings on *terra firma*.

The speed and precision in the fields of transport and communication have reduced the world to a global village when no corner can remain as an island, insulated against the ill-effects of evils of progress.

Since the abuse of drugs is a global phenomenon, it has aroused global reaction and from 19th century onwards efforts are being made to fight out this menace in cooperation with other nations. The political boundaries, emotions linkages with certain practices and national sovereignty concepts could not block the path of international cooperation in the field of research with respect to the causative factors, treatment and social relation besides the method of detection and investigation.

Most of the drugs that are misused have proper or legitimate use also and are being used as such for a long period of time. New discoveries, and successes achieved in the field of science have provided technical knowhow to isolate the psychoactive chemicals from the plants having medicinal value. In the above process, some new drugs have come into being and some adventurers developed the drugs from the chemicals to produce similar physical or psychological effect on human mind and body. In course of time, these substitutes also attained same notoriety and are placed in the category of psychotropic substances. These psychotropic substances are also a cause of concern and occupied central position in International Convention in 1971.

Any drug having legitimate use is likely to be misused. Misuse may be defined as the use of a drug to the point of being harmful to the health of the user as well as to the society. The consequences of drug use are dependent on the pharmacologic effects and properties of the drugs as well as on the social factors. Social factors which may be considered responsible for abuse of the drug in case of one individual may not have same effect with respect to other individuals. The factors responsible for drug-abuse may be grouped in following categories :

A—Individual factors.

B—Social factors.

C—Drug factors.

Individual Factors

Despite our best efforts and advances made in the study of various components of brains it has not been possible to predict with authority the social behavioural pattern of individuals solely on the basis of the study of certain inherent physiologies. It is difficult to quantify the dependence of individual behaviour on the basis psychopharmacological drives whose origin and functioning is still the subject-matter of conjecture. Our understanding of functioning of brain and its effect on individual response with respect to certain drugs also remains at best marginal. On the basis of data available some researchers contend that the psychosomatic make-up of some animals affects their susceptibility to addiction. From the study of the personality of some of the addicts, some authorities contend that dependence is brought about by the metabolic disorder or severe maladjustment of body's internal chemistry.

The brain receptors are thought to be sensitive to stimulation caused by various chemicals having addictive quantities. It has been suggested that either some individuals have more receptors or their receptors are more sensitive to particular chemicals.

The studies made into the behaviour of the addicts points out that many drug-users are immature. The immature person fails to cope with the demands of life with its problems, anxieties and frustrations. This feeling of inadequacy is taken care of by the drugs and they feel, under the influence of drugs, quite adequate, hence, the need for continuous intake of drug.

For some individuals the drugs provide escape or time-out from the miserable conditions of life. The tolerance limit of individuals with respect to tensions, anxieties and setbacks in life, is very low and draws them close to drugs which give them pleasurable experiences. Chronic stress conditions produce symptoms of neurosis in many people. When such people go to medical man he gives them drugs on which these persons become dependent and even without medical advice they continue to take drugs until the drugs take control of them.

In certain cases, the drug is taken to experience the "*euphoria*", the exaggerated sense of well-being artificially induced. The user after persistent use loses the interest to lead a normal life and he becomes dependent upon a drug which further increases his craving for the drug and thereafter for most of the time his activities are centred around the drug its procurement, use and experience of euphoria induced by it and this condition may be described as the state of addiction.

Social Factors

The social factors also have a bearing on the initial use of drugs by the individuals. These social or environmental factors are operative on a wide range of people living in particular social environment but all the people do not get involved with the drugs. Among these are : (a) the case with which dependence producing drugs may be obtained in a given locality; (b) social acceptance of the use of drugs to relieve discomfort or to modify mood or perception; and (c) the geographical mobility now possible for persons, ideas and objects. In addition, consideration must be given to the influence of the family, peers and subcultures, as well as proselytizing by conformed users. The sources and quality of the available and accepted information about drug-use are also of interest. Why drug-use becomes indiscriminate and heavy for some users, remains experimental or controlled for others and is totally rejected by still other persons, needs further examination.

Availability

Where certain drugs can be obtained only with great difficulty, the users of these drugs must be few. For example, fresh khat and coca leaves are widely available and used in certain limited regions of the world but are essentially lacking elsewhere. However, there are few, if any, regions where at least some forms of dependence-producing drugs are not available, even if they are limited to those produced locally. Nevertheless, despite the fairly ready availability of dependence-producing drugs, they are not used at all, or are not used in damaging amounts, by a great many persons.

Social accceptance

In areas where a number of dependence-producing drugs can be readily obtained, many persons are exposed to culture that facilitates attitudes towards drug-use. Here both young and old are exposed to cultural pressures to accept and value modification of mood and perception. These pressures may arise from mass media sensationalism concerning the non-medical use of drugs, particularly by widely known and popular figures. They may also stem from some types of advertising for an increasing variety of socially accepted drugs (e.g., alcoholic beverages, tobacoo, many medicaments). Underlying such advertising may be vested interests in governmental tax revenues as well as corporate or individual profits. All these influences may tend to foster the use of available mood modifiers, including those capable of producing dependence.

Mobility

The extent and rapidity of mass communication and transport now enable persons in one part of the world to learn quickly of the activities of others in distant places, to obtain drugs that do not deteriorate too rapidly, and to travel to many parts of the world. Such travel is now possible and acceptable for many younger, as well as older persons. Travel facilitaties, contacts with social groups and subcultures that are not accessible to those who must or do stay at home. Further, the effectiveness of external (as contrasted with internal) controls by parents, neighbours, acquaintances and other socio-cultural factors is diminished when persons are away from their immediate influence. This phenomenon is not limited to young people, but youth may be affected to a greater degree than older persons who have had a longer time in which to establish particular patterns of living. There also seems to be a ready supply of dependence-producing drugs in certain areas frequented by young travellers.

Peer Groups

The interests and expectation of peer groups have an important bearing on whether or not a person will try a dependence-producing drug. The majority of youthful non-medical users of such drugs obtain those that are socially deprecated from persons of their own age, not from adults. Boys tend to receive drugs from other boys of about the same age, but girls tend to get them from boy friends or men somewhat older than themselves. A friend or peer group is likely to be the source of information for drug-users about the availability of drugs and their alleged effects. Futhermore, a desire for acceptance and social interaction in a particular peer group may result in starting and maintaining the use of drugs if some influential members of that group happen to be intermittent or regular user. Joining a drug-oriented subculture is usually a sign to indicate that exploratory stages of drug-use, are over and that a commitment to beaviour or less discriminating use is being made.

Pushers

At times, a group of persons who are themselves addicted to drugs becomes dependent on drugs for their livelihood as well. This group is dangerous for the society as they try to win over their prospective clientele from well-to-do families, so that they get regular money to earn their livelihood. The vendors selling ice-cream laced with drugs at the school gates are the examples of such pushers who are prepared to earn their comfortable living at the cost of decay and death of others.

Information

Some people believe that relevant information about the nature and effect of drugs on human behaviour and health will go a long way to discourage the drug affliction of the society while others feel that these exposures should not be such which enkindles the curiosity for the use of drugs. The programmes of media should be so designed as to bring forth the adverse effects to the forefront and should not in any way encourage the youngsters to emulate the example.

Once a person starts using drugs, then it becomes very difficult to break away from the habit because of the following factors:

1. Dependence—Physical and Psychological.
2. Rejection by society.
3. Pull of subculture group.

Social Attitude and Responses

(a) Why people take drugs—same as in the case of V.D. and AIDS etc.,

(b) Immediate and delayed effect of using drugs,

(c) Aspects of society's broad value system—relative worth of material possessions spiritual, cultural and traditional belief and experience—meaning and value of life.

Drug Factors

Some drugs are very quick in forming habits while others are very slow. As soon as a particular drug is taken it is absorbed by the body through its membranes and ultimately finds its way to human brain. The psychoactive agents lodge themselves in fat, water etc. and affect the nervous system depending upon their soluble properties. The efficacy of the drug depends on the method of intake, i.e. through stomach and intestines (oral); through lungs (smoking or otherwise inhaling); directly mixing with the blood (muscular or intravenous) and then to brain. Once the active agent acts on the brain receptors, they become used to it and develop tolerance to the particular quantity of drug. This tolerance physical as well as psychological forces the man to increase the dose of the drug, so administered and also conditions the reaction in case of absence of the drug, i.e., the withdrawal symptoms. The acuteness of these withdrawal symptoms depends on the tolerance level of the person which is dependent on the potency of the drug quantity of dose, interval between administration, mode of administration and also general health condition of the subject. The excessive regular use of drugs leads to physical and psychological dependence.

Some drugs produce only psychological dependence while others induce physical dependence as well. The feeling of relaxation and *euphoria* is generally associated with the effects of the drug, the ultimate goal of the user. When psychological dependence develops the subject's thinking process is affected and he always thinks about the drug and drug alone. His thought process becomes drug-centred and he is treated as *hooked* on the drug when he develops continuous and uncontrollable craving for the drug.

As the widespread use of drugs is threatening our modern civilized society, causing disintegration of basic family unit and casting dark shadow on the future generations even those who are not even born at present, can we remain silent? No.

As a citizen we have to remain alert not to help the pushers (even inadvertently), and inform the authorities and parents in case of children. As parents and custodical guardians we have to communicate with susceptible or potential addicts and advise them to consult de-addiction centres working in the area without stigmatising the user. Remember, the user is a sick person who needs treatment and assistance so that he can reintegrate himself with society and does not remain a *drain* or *dead weight* for the community.

We should always remember that the problem of drug-abuse can be fought only with the help of society in general. Any governmental or voluntary agency cannot fight this menace alone. To fight this menace one has to create atmosphere which is not very conducive for drug-use or its continuance and for this participation of broader section of society is needed. Society's permissive attitudes has to be changed and it has to be prepared to bear extra cost for the controls and effects on discouraging use of drugs and also for providing attractive alternatives and correctional services.

14

Money Laundering and Enforcement Efforts with Special Reference to Drug Trafficking

The organized crime, specially one like drug trafficking generates substantial amount of cash as profit which is further pumped into underworld economy to finance the operations and purchase men and material for the upkeep and betterment of the organization. Such organizations collect a large amount of unaccounted money and enlist services of armed men, who have scant respect for law, become threat to social order and hold government to ransom and assume invincibility. Since drug trafficking is essentially a trans-national crime the sharing of profit is also done at international level. The poppy or coca-growers get little share in the tainted money while the manufacturers and the distributors reap the maximum benefit. The maximum profit one gets at the consumer's end which is mostly in the progressive countries, which necessarily makes them more vulnerable to the economic crime or money laundering.

The problem of underground money transactions may be more serious in rich countries when considered in absolute terms (in USA the estimates run in the region of $50-75 billion) but their economy is also capable of bearing such strains. The conditions in developing countries are different and such transactions destabilize the economy and deplete the resources required for the developmental efforts to improve the quality of life to their teaming millions. The economic balance is also so delicate that slightest stress on the economy can damage the economic fabric and threaten the integrity of the country which indicates pressing need for introducing effective legal and fiscal measures to check accumulation of unaccounted money or its conversion into white money by dodging the enforcement agencies.

In the past our Criminal Justice System was mostly concerned with arresting and prosecuting the criminals responsible for certain offences. The economic offences were not recognised as crime till very recently and those who collected money by illicit sources were considered successful entrepreneurs. Later on with the increase in the financial power of some of the syndicates even the governments felt threatened and then the need for introducing accountability for assets so collected was felt and most of the governments imposed certain restrictions on the commercial transactions. With the growth of the concept of Welfare State certain fiscal measures were introduced by body politic to raise financial resources to finance the Welfare Schemes. The international trade between the countries at different stages of development also attracted corrective measures in the form of customs duty to safeguard the national interest. Both at national and international levels the economic activities which hitherto enjoyed complete freedom, were brought under discipline in consonance with the political philosophy of the State. With the increased tax liability, the entrepreneur felt robbed of his assets and engaged best brains to outwit the government machinery by bypassing the legal provisions by using the loopholes provided in law to check such robbery. In this fight against the State to save one's assets the criminals also joined the race and introduced criminal tactics. The Narco-criminals are new entrants to the ring but with their organizational skill and criminal back-up they overwhelmed others in this field very quickly. The Narco-criminals added intimidation, extortion and elimination to corruption, deceit and subversion adopted by other syndicates engaged in laundering the 'dirty money'.

The drug trafficking or illicit trade in drugs is one of the fastest growing industries in the world and most profitable as well. The raw material for the most of the drugs is very cheap and the manufacturing cost is also very low but at the end of the tunnel the consumer has to pay very high price for the purchase of his daily dose. In India the price of opium at government rate can be found anywhere between Rs. 250-300 per kg. which can easily fetch about Rs. 5000-15000 (175-500 US dollars) in underground market. When this raw opium reaches Hong Kong it can fetch about Rs. 124800 (U.S. $ 4160). When this is the amount of profitability in raw form one can imagine the extent of profitability in the trade of heroin or cocaine manufacture and its illicit trade. The traders have to conceal this income from the enforcement agencies to save the tax, forfeiture (being connected with illegal activity) and criminal liability for interconnected infringements of law. Louis Kraar, the Investigative Reporter of *Fortune* estimated that international trade may run upto U.S.$ 500 billion a year which he calls more than double the value of all U.S. currency in circulation, let alone other countries which are quite low on the ladder of prosperity.

Process of Money Laundering

The concept of money laundering as the subject for serious study is a recent phenomenon and the direct result of the policy of certain governments to prove the dictum that 'Crime does not pay'. The dealer in the drug with good international link-up and backing of political and bureaucratic heavyweight in some of the countries and fired with the allurement of huge profits, enrolled services of best of the brains to ensure that the assets created from the profits of illegal activities escape the drag-net of enforcement agencies and remain with the criminals to be used for the expansion of the trade and protection of the criminals by corruption, intimidation and elimination, if needed. The process of money laundering aims at concealing the source of ill-gotten money and also the illegal application of the income and then disguises that income to make it appear from legitimate sources. It simply means that 'tainted money' is converted into 'white money', thus making the criminal to appear as successful entrepreneur. The means to convert this 'dirty money' into 'clean money' will differ with the sources of income and the legal and fiscal provisions of the country, the trader is operating in. Since there are numerous sources of generation of 'dirty money' so are the means to change its colour depending on the creative imagination and expertise of the criminal entrepreneur.

The illicit money is generated at every level that handles the drug and in every leg of journey to its final destination. The money laundering problems for a large syndicate engaged in the trafficking of drug is more important than the distribution of the drug while to the lone operators at the lower level distribution problems outweigh the laundering problems. The drug trafficking not only generates illegitimate capital in the hands of the criminals but it also showers liberally the part of the money on the corrupt system of enforcement and political leaders. In certain countries both of them have tried to buttress their positions in the cloak of special protections granted in law by way of special provisions of sanction before prosecution.

In the context of drug trafficking there is general awareness about the nefarious activities of the traders and its impact on economy of the nation which necessitated stringent provisions in law to arm police and other enforcement agencies to unearth such transaction but still many areas of the world have a legal and fiscal climate that is optimal for the growth and prosperity of money laundering industry. The places like Gayman Islands, the Bahamas, the Netherland Antilles, Panama and Switzerland have been regarded as safe haven for money laundering process. In most of the above countries the 'Bank Secrecy Laws' are quite strict and any wilful disclosure may expose the banks and their employees to criminal liability. Such closely guarded bank information system is most favourable for the launderer and most difficult for the Investigating Officer. Such countries obtain significant competitive advantage in attracting secret money but at the cost of others. This tendency has encouraged others also to impose similar restrictions on banks. Pakistan also introduced criminal friendly foreign exchange regime in 1991 which is a safe haven for the launderers. Sri Lanka has already assumed notoriety in this connection. A report of the US State department referred in *The Times of India*. April 30, 1993, indicated appearance of Sri Lanka and Pakistan as new safe havens for drug money. The chart given below will show how the drug-money is converted into white money or legal money ready to be reinvested.

How Drug-Money laundered and becomes legal

Transfer to A/C in tax havens → under-invoicing imports and over-invoicing exports → Payments through A/Cs in tax havens

↑

Deposit in a single A/C

↑

Buy money instruments

↑

Use hawala route to send money abroad → Procure local money

NARCO - DOLLARS | LEGAL MONEY

↓

Buy property, half payment in cash → Sell and payment by cheque.

Buy gold in black

↓

Documents to prove gold purchased by own cos

↓

Sell gold to dealers and banks

↓

Paymet to A/Cs in tax havens. → Shelf cos sells shares in forward to group Co. → Group Co. makes profit

The Times of India, April 11, 1993.

There are as many ways of conversion of tainted money

with white money, as there are people doing it but the main problem remains the same, i.e., taking out the money from the countries of generation and its receipt in the country of operation in the cloak of strictly legal transaction. As compared to global laundering domestic laundering is simple specially in the countries having complicated fiscal problems and pressure groups claiming protection by way of exemption in one form or other. In investigation firstly it is very important to identify the money flow and approaches to the real source of the flow. The money is visible in the form of assets including deposits in banks, shares in Companies and investment in real estate etc. but the source, in the present context drug trade, remains underground. Other problem, equally difficult is to prove it to the satisfaction of the court that the assets were generated by the conduct of illegal activities and third party interest are not affected in indiscreet way. The evidence to be collected to prove this in Court of Law may fall in different jurisdictions having different legal system. Further the implementation of the judgement regarding seizure and forefieture in foreign lands is another problem. The money launderers thrive on these weeknesses and devise means to overcome such difficulties in a very intelligent manner.

The money laundering may be conducted through domestic financial transactions. The lone low-level operator normally convert cash payments into capital goods such as jewellary, cars, air-condition, VCRs, video cameras and other gadgets. Those who are more enlightened and serious in the business create assets and purchase land and houses in urban areas. In former case the moveably property thus accumulated is totally concealed or it is undervalued on paper. In the second case real estate is created in fake names or as *Benami* transaction to conceal the source and to cover the track leading to the real owner. Since our Income-Tax laws have not touched agricultural sector, therefore, some of the dealers in narcotics have purchased agricultural land and show exorbitantly inflatal returns from it to cover income from dubious means.

In the wake of proliferation of economic activities, a new class of juristic persons have come into being as Corporations. Through shares, a large amount is collected which defies all investigations if papers are properly maintained with the help of experts. These fake corporations normally show huge profits to cover inflow of tainted money. Once this tainted money comes to mainstream it changes its colour. Since the shares are in the names of different shareholders, at the time of court proceedings, the interest of third party will come in the way of successful seizure or forfeiture.

The lotteries and other games like horse-race etc. are other instruments in the hands of manipulators to conceal the source of income. The winning tickets of lotteries are purchased by the small underworld traders and that much black money is converted into white money by simple operation. The actual winner may be a small-time farmer who has immense capacity of concealing dirty money hence his interest lies only in money. The launderer repurchases the ticket making payment from black money and gets white money in lieu thereof. The agents of such launderers develop intimacy with the staff of Directorate of Lotteries and on announcement of prize immediately contact the holder of the winning ticket. This racket is going on and corrupt people placed at high places having access to and influence upon the employees connected with Directorate of Lotteries, are getting prize money again and again through dubious means thus converting their ill-gotten money into white money to ward off any difficulty at the hands of enforcement agencies and Income-tax department.

During elections the political leaders collect election funds presumably from Electorates. In some cases it was reported that amount reported by the political parties was inflated and actually it was not given by the Electorates but by the underground dealers. Similarly, the birthday gifts collected by some of the political practitioners is their own money generated from illicit sources and after such public demonstrations it becomes white without any trace of its origin. Sometimes the black money is liberally spent on elections without any mention in the election expenditure statements escaping action under People's Representation Act. The means to launder money are many and exhibit novelty and originality depending on the resourcefulness of the launderer.

The money generated out of trafficking when involves a complicit with other countries then distribution of assets and further laundering problems assume entirely different dimensions. The countries like USA, UK and Japan have strong currencies and are likely to be accepted by the criminals as it is but in case of other currencies exchange of currency is involved besides custom laws of the countries concerned. As mentioned earlier largest share of the illicit money is generated in the consumer countries which are incidentally prosperous and their currencies are quite strong in the international fiscal market.

In India the profits of illicit drug trade are reportedly brought in cash in aeroplane without declaration and then deposited in a bank after exchanging it by making false statement at the point of exchange. Illegal courier service is also rampant in some part of the country. The money to be remitted to India is given to a courier service in foreign country then by telephone or telegram instruct their agents to make payment to the payee in India the equivalent amount in rupees. The hard currency is deposited in the country in original itself or in a country having Bank Secrecy Law. Since our country is facing foreign exchange crunch and every effort is made to boost export, therefore, the traders contact these exporters and send their money by over-invoicing and the equivalent amount can be collected in the country. Now with liberalisation and encouragement to NRIs it has become very easy to bring foreign money in the country in the shape of loans etc.

In countries like USA or United States the problem has entirely different dimensions. Bank Laws are quite strict and the government is pretty serious about the flow of the currency outside the country. In USA the money launderers commonly use following methods for transfer of cash outside the country :

1. In USA illegally obtained cash may be taken from the United States to a foregin country physically without filing any statement and then depositing in a bank in the country having Bank Secrecy Laws.
2. Cash is deposited in a Bank in USA and then transferred by wire or through cashiers cheque to a foreign bank located in countries having Bank Secrecy Laws.
3. Illicit money is deposited into a fake account (in the name of non-existing person) in USA and then transferred by wire or cashier cheque to a foreign bank.
4. The money is given to an Attorney or an Accountant as a cash transfer without filing any statement required in law and then deposited into the trust account of the Attorney or Accountant and then transferred by wire or male and taken physically.

Once the tainted money is taken out of the country, then it may be deposited into banks in fake individual or corporate accounts. Once Accounts in countries like Switzerland, Bahamas, Panama are open, then it can be taken back into the country after filing regular declaration in the shape of assets acquired in foreign countries as proceeds of a loan granted to a citizen of United States, as fee paid to a citizen of US services or by way of over-invoicing the goods exported from the country. The net result of this process is that cash generated in the country out of illicit trade in Narcotics will be hidden from Law Enforcement Agencies to avoid tax, seizure, forfeiture and the illicit trader will escape of criminal liability. The operations La-Mina will serve as an example on the subject:

Once cash is physically taken out of the country and deposited in one of these havens, then there is no problem in financing illegitimate activities such as terrorism and anti-establishment activities in the country. This phenomenon may be new but the companies like Lockeheed Aircraft Corpn. Gulf Oil Corporation, Mc. Donnell Douglas Corpn.. and many

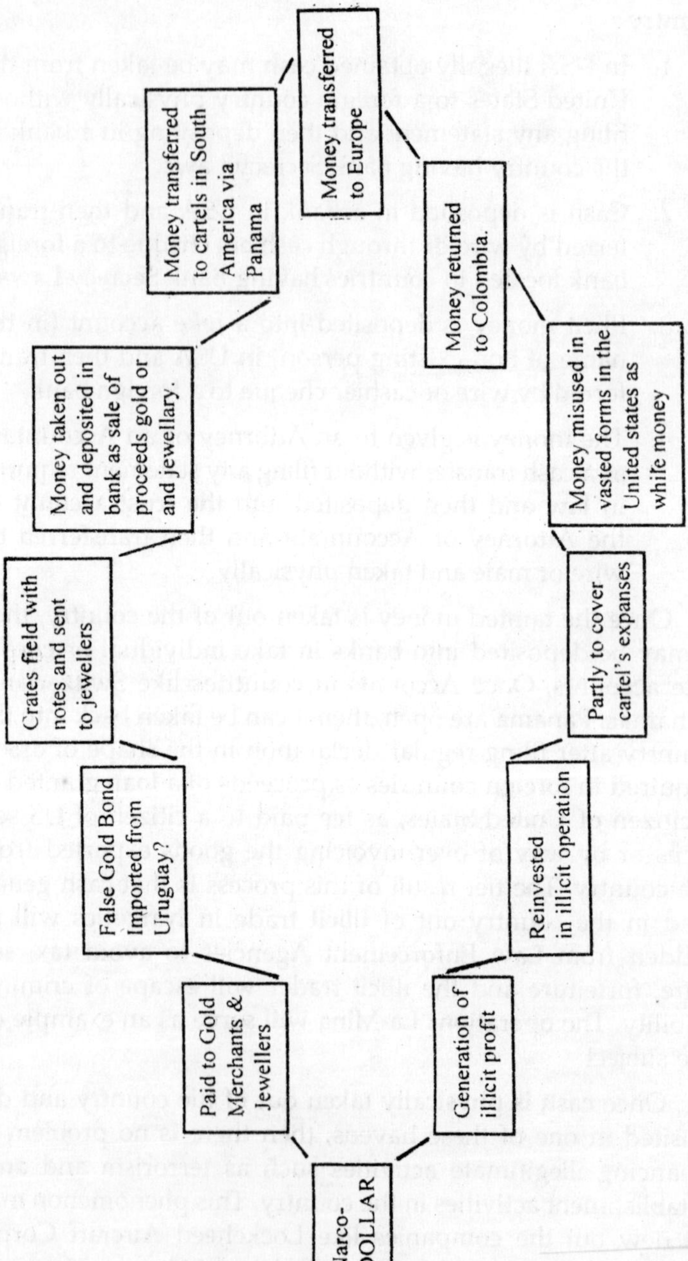
Narco-DOLLAR
Paid to Gold Merchants & Jewellers
False Gold Bond Imported from Uruguay?
Crates field with notes and sent to jewellers
Money taken out and deposited in bank as sale of proceeds gold or and jewellary.
Money transferred to cartels in South America via Panama
Money transferred to Europe
Money returned to Colombia.
Money misused in vasted forms in the United states as white money
Partly to cover cartel's expanses
Reinvested in illicit operation
Generation of illicit profit

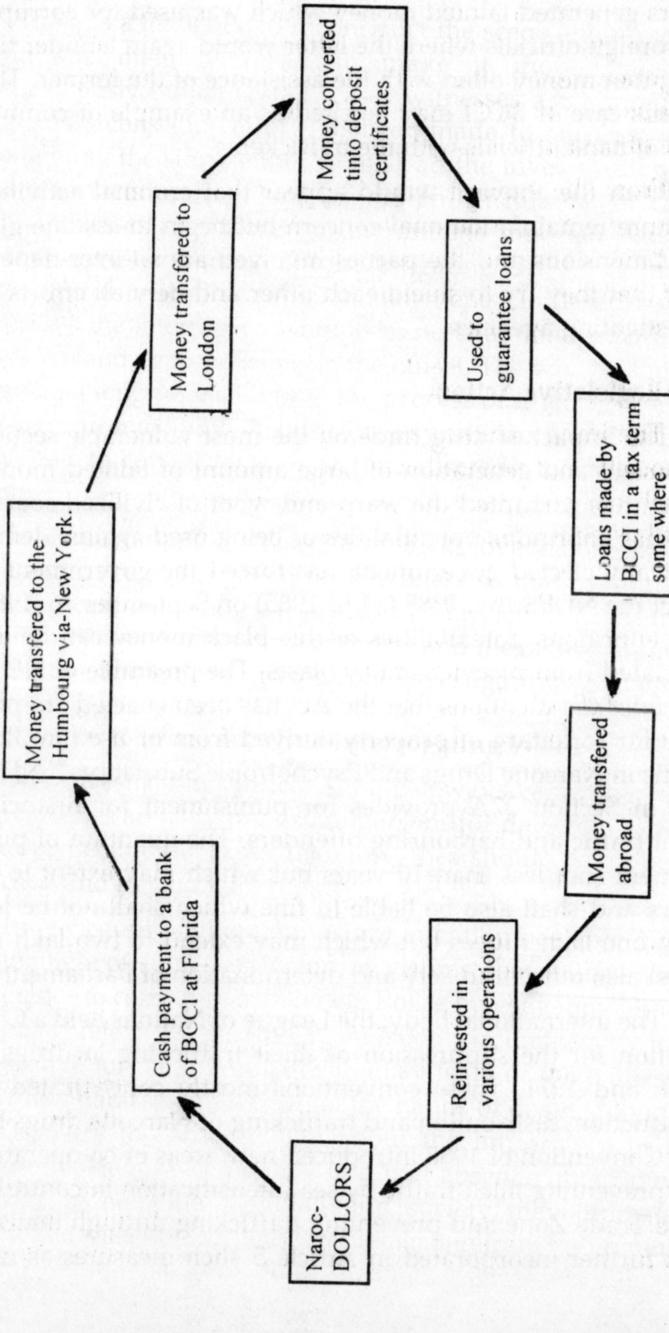
Naroc-
DOLLORS
Cash payment to a bank
of BCCI at Florida
Money transfered to the
Humbourg via-New York.
Money transfered to
London
Money converted
tinto deposit
certificates
Used to
guarantee loans
Loans made by
BCCI in a tax term
some where
Money transfered
abroad
Reinvested in
various operations

others generated tainted money which was used for corrupting foreign officials where the latter would again launder the ill- gotten money often with the assistance of the former. The famous case of BCCI may be cited as an example of connivance of bank officials with the traffickers :

From the above it would appear that criminal activities no more remain a national concern but begin to assume global dimensions and the parties involved are so inter-dependent that they try to shield each other and defy all efforts of investigating agencies.

The Legislative Action

The impact of drug trade on the most vulnerable section of society and generation of large amount of tainted money which has corrupted the warp and woof of civilized society and has enormous potentialities of being used against democratically elected government, has forced the government to enact the NDPS Act, 1985 (61 of 1985) on September 16, 1985. The enormous potentialities of this black money can be appreciated from recent Bombay blasts. The preamble of NDPS Act *inter alia* mentions that the Act has been enacted "to provide for forfeiture of property derived from or used in illicit traffic in Narcotic Drugs and Psychotropic Substances". NDPS Act in Section 27A provides for punishment for financing illicit traffic and harbouring offenders. The quantum of punishment (not less than 10 years but which may extent to 20 years and shall also be liable to fine which shall not be less than one lakh rupees but which may extend to two lakh rupees) also reflects anxiety and determination of Parliament.

The international body, the League of Nations held a Convention for the suppression of illicit trafficking in drugs in 1936 and 1971. These conventions mostly concentrated on production, distribution and trafficking of Narcotic drugs but the Convention of 1988 introduced new areas of co-operation for preventing illicit traffic by sea intensification in control of Free Trade Zone and preventing trafficking through mails. It has further incorporated in Article 5 such measures as may be necessary to enable confiscation of proceeds derived from offences established in accordance with Article 3 or property value of which corresponds to that of such proceeds. In the same Article the Convention enjoined upon the signatories to adopt such measures as may be necessary to enable its competent authorities to identify, trace and freeze or seize proceeds, property, instrumentalities, or any other things' for the purpose of eventual confiscation. The provisions in Convention against illicit traffic in Narcotic Drugs and Psychotropic Substances, 1988 are so broad-based that if implemented the traffickers cannot escape the drag-net of Law Enforcement Agencies. Government of India ratified this Convention in December 1988. Being the signatory to Convention of 1988 Government of India have appended Chapter V-A to NDPS Act, 1985 which provides for for forfeiture of property derived from and used in the illicit traffic. Again the provisions are broad-based and it includes not only the sale-proceeds but the assets created from them not only in the hands of criminals but also in the hands of associates, relatives and even in the hands of third parties. The peculiar feature of the legal provision in Chapter V-A is that it raises certain presumptions in favour of prosecution and the most important being that the burden of proving that the property specified in the notice served u/s 67 H is not illegally acquired property lies on the person who has received the notice. To avoid further delay in adjudications in Courts of Law the Act provides for the constitution of Appellate Tribunal u/s 68N of the NDPS Act. Government of India in exercise of powers conferred by NDPS Act notified the Appellate Tribunal for Forfeited Property (Procedure) Rules, 1989, on 22nd January, 1990.

From the above it would appear that Government of India in consonance with United Nations Conventions have made legal provisions to counteract the activities of money launderers. Now the enforcement agencies are fully equipped to deal with traffickers and their associates the money launderers.

In international field the difficulty lies in collection of evidence to provide the connection of the assets with the drug trafficking. The Bank Secrecy Law and the principle of the dual criminality come in the way. Since relations between the two States depend on the bilateral basis, United Nations in its Convention of 1988 have taken a very pragmatic stand and have provided that if two nations decide to take measures on the basis of bilateral treaty then the parties shall consider the Convention of 1988 as the necessary and sufficient treaty basis. Article 7 envisages that signatories to the Convention shall afford one another the widest major of mutual legal assistance in the course of prosecution in the judicial proceedings in relation to the criminal offences related to Narcotic drugs. The mutual legal assistance will include taking evidence or recording of statements of persons, service of judicial documents, execution of searches and seizures, examination of objects and sites providing information and evidentiary items, identifying or tracing proceeds, property and other things for evidentiary purposes. Not only this in Article 7 also it envisages that the parties shall facilitate or encourage to the extent possible in their domestic law the presence of availability of persons who assisted in investigation and shall not decline to render mutual legal assistance under Article 7 on the ground of Bank Secrecy.

The net result of these provisions of Convention of 1988 is that it will help in overcoming the considerations of dual criminality and absence of mutual treaty in case of member-nations who signed the Convention. The removal of difficulties will definitely arm investigating agencies with the additional instruments and will also foster a new era of co-operation between the signatories.

Role of Interpol

The growing concern about secret flow of tainted money from the place of origin to the desired place in the form of white money has moved Interpol also to take some effective and stringent measures. In the General Assembly of Interpol a Resolution was passed in 1989 for the indepth study of the problem specially with respect to money laundering, the confiscation of assets of illicit origin, financial investigation techniques and international co-operation in investigation. A specialized group FOPAC (Fonds Provenant d'Activities Criminelles—Funds derived from illicit activities) was set up for the above purpose in 1989 after Interpol Conference held in April 1989 in Paris.

The FOPAC study group has published an encyclopaedia—FAPE (Financial Assets Programme Encyclopaedia) in co-operation with CCC (Customs Co-operation Control). This encyclopaedia incorporates information regarding financial law in operation in various countries and methods of financial investigation etc. FOPAC group under the auspices of Interpol is also running training courses with a view to providing basic knowledge and to promote multi-disciplinary investigation team and to foster close co-operation with investigation agencies of different countries. With growing awareness about the harms caused by flow of the Capital and its likely use has led many countries to set up financial Action Task-Force to deal with such flow in a planned manner.

UN Convention on Narcotic Drugs

UN Conference for the adoption of a Convention against illicit traffic in Narcotic Drugs and Psychotropic Substances, held at Vienna on 25th November and 20th December 1988, "reaffirmed the guiding principles of existing treaties in the field of Narcotic Drugs and Psychotropic Substances and the system of control which they embody". This Convention in its preamble desired, "to conclude a comprehensive, effective and operative international Convention that is directed specifically against illicit traffic and that considers the various aspects of the problem as a whole, in particular those aspects not envisaged in the existing treaties in the field of Narcotic Drugs and Psychotropic Substances". The parties to the Convention agreed to recommend for adoption of measures as may be necessary to establish offences under its domestic law (committed intentionally) to control, cultivate, manufacture, sale and purchase, transport financing of any of the offences and also about the conversion or transfer of property in Article 3. In article 5 of the Convention, the measures to facilitate confiscation of property has been provided for. For mutual assistance, in the sphere of extradition and mutual legal assistance articles 6 and 7 have been enacted in a very comprehensive manner to take care of all conceivable situations. With growing consciousness about the harms likely to be caused by illicit money the enlightened countries have launched schemes in a determined way to combat illicit trafficking and laundering of illicit gains to save society from the corrupting influence of tainted money.

15

Protection for Victims of Crime : A Study in Victimology

Maintenance of order and safety is one of the most important functions of study without which modern civilization cannot sustain itself. Maintenance of order involves punishment to the offenders and protection to the victims of crime. The offenders were considered enemies of the society and very harsh punishment was meted out to them. Later on a view was taken that criminals are pushed into the alleys of crime because of certain social factors. Therefore, they should be treated as sick persons requiring treatment. From international forum also concern was voiced to ensure basic fundamental rights to under-trials as well as convicts. In our anxiety to ensure basic fundamental rights to the criminals or the offenders we ignored the sufferings of the victims of the crime. These persons were losers in the society, therefore, required more compassion.

Law has also taken note of problems of the victims in court and in-built mechanism has been provided in the legislation in certain countries for the information and participation of the victims in process of law.

"Order and Safety, although they are not themselves civilization, are things without which civilization would be impossible. They are as necessary to our civilization as the air breath is to us, and we have grown so used to them that we do not notice them any more than we notice the air.[1] When we say safety, we mean safety to all those who abide by law, safety to all those who conduct themselves in accordance with the norms set by society for the enlightened humanity, and safety to all those who adhere to the lofty principles of "सर्वे भवन्तु सुखिनः सर्वे सन्तु निरामयाः"[2] From times immemorial, the violators of law were classed as 'Offenders' or 'Criminals' and it was considered most important duty of King or the State, as the case may be, to dispense justice, protect the people and thus ensure order in society and safety to all, by punishing these offenders.[3]

With the passage of time and increasing interaction with islands of civilization the principles of justice also crystallized and certain rights were considered inalienable rights of Individuals which were condidered justiciable on petition of individuals while State took care of offences against State or society. The offenders were considered enemies of the society and very harsh punishments were prescribed. The punishment or the *danda* to the criminals was considered very essential for the well-being of the people (*praja*). Administration of justice with proper consideration of time, place and other relevant factors was one of the very important duties of Kings as explained by Manu,[4] the ancient law-giver of the country. The deterrence of punishment was considered important to control crime and recidivism thus basic to maintenance of order.[5] The punishment administered with proper care and caution endeared the ruler to his subject while absence of it was mutually destructive.[6]

Above situation continued in India and in other countries as well upto medieval period. The Industrial Revolution, the Renaissance and French Revolution brought about a sea-change in every walk of life and in every corner of the planet and social sciences never remained an exception to it. The attention of criminologists was also drawn towards the condition of prisoners, and other under-privileged in the society. The criminologists focused their attention towards the rights of the criminal offenders and advocated that they should not unduly deprive of their rights and as a result came very many doctrine ensuring fair play and justice to those who had earlier perpetrated injustice on other members of the society. The doctrine of "defense sociale" brought about the study of the person of the criminal from many angles such as social conditions, attitude of society towards crime and criminals. The attempts were made to free society from deviant behaviour by eliminating factors which were considered responsible for generating crime and with this came to light the futility of deterrent punishment as sole factor to deter criminals from committing crime.

Further analysis of the factors responsible for criminals conduct changed the attitude of sociologists towards offender who regarded him a sick person who needed treatment rather than punishment. In this context after Second World War, anxiety was shown from national and international forum for the treatment and restitution of the criminal offenders generating interest all over the planet which brought about reformatory measures in jails, establishment of after-care units, and legislation to restore dignity to the convicts. The anxiety was shown to the convicts but it was felt that the persons who suffered at the hands of the criminals were not given their due. The sufferers thus suffered the gross neglect by sociologists, criminologists and social voluntary organizations as well which led to disillusionment towards treatment theory. In the words of Erich Corves "The huge swing towards a view which focused attention almost exclusively on care for the criminal offender has inevitably resulted in a degree of widespread disillusionment after the euphoria of the two decades of treatment of offenders after the war. Consequently, this has given rise particularly in North America to a new approach, the so-called 'just desert' models (North American Neo-Classicism)."

The greater attention towards the victims is the imperative need of the society as they are the persons who can be termed as losers. It is also true at the same time that the competitive society that stresses on achievement never sides with the loser, hence, this neglect of victims, so far. The recent developments in socio-political fields have forced social organizations to raise voice against this criminal neglect of victims or victimization of a particular section of society and in this context movements regarding protection to the victims of rape (specially custodial rape) and dowry can be cited as glaring examples. "More recent developments have manifested themselves in a growing number of research studies dealing with the situation and problems of the victims, as well as in agendas of national and international conferences in which the victim has found himself increasingly at the centre of interest in such discussions."[8]

Victimology—Its Growth and Approach

Victimology is the science which makes victims the centre of study and aims at intensive understanding of the victim-offender relationship, investigates the victims' share in crime causation, examines the ways and means to protect the victims before commission of the crime during investigation and trial of the offender and also analyses restitution and reparation of the damages caused to him by perpetration of crime.

Mendelsohn coined the world 'Victimology' for the scientific study of all victims of crime as well as that of accidents.[9] He also planned to have an International Institute of victimology under the auspices of UNO besides holding international congress to discuss all aspects of Victimology. After Second World War there was growing concern for the plights of the victims of every type and it was in this climate that B. Mendelsohn developed this branch of criminology. Kurt Weis and Sandra S. Borges in their paper "Victimology and Rape : The Case of the Legitimate Victim,"commented, "Mendelsohn had far-reaching gobal plans and predictions for the continued historical development of the field of Victimology. He envisioned a central institute of Victimology in every country, an international research institute of UNO at UNESCO, professorships, an international terminology and congress of Victimology — the first to be held in Jerusalem."[10] The first International Conference was held in Jerusalem in the year 1973 (September 2-6). The term 'Victimology' has also been adopted in international nomenclature. The Conference in Jerusalem was followed by another Conference at Boston in 1976. International Association for Victimology was found in Munich in 1977. After the hesitant beginning the subject was discussed at length in 6th UN Congress in Caracas in 1980 followed by inclusion of the subject 'Victims of crime' on the agenda of 7th UN Congress in 1985 in Milan. The intervening period between 6th Congress in 1980 and 7th Congress in 1985 there were number of Congresses, Seminars and Studies at international, regional and national levels highlighting the "problems of victims", "the legal position of the injured party in criminal proceedings", "Research on Victimization."[11] Unlike West, Asia was not so eventful as far as study of Victimology was concerned. In India besides research work on certain victim communities and agitations demanding legislative changes to ensure justice in cases of female victimization (dowry deaths and cases of rape specially custodial rape) nothing worth mentioning was done on national or international level.

In the initial stages Victimology concentrated on the victim as an individual unit of study in understanding the causative factors responsible for commission of crime. Kurt Weis and Sandra S. Borges has aptly pointed out that, "The offender is the centre of the attention and other agents involved in his criminality are primarily seen as they affected his behaviour and thus reduce his personal guilts. Criminology deals with the offender; sociology of deviance emphasized the role of social control in generating and maintaining the offender's deviance; and Victimology stresses the victims' responsibility for the offender's act."[12] In view of above the study of victims' problems in a scientific manner suffered and it became only the study of crime causation through the victim ignoring the positive orientation towards the victims. This approach leads to assigning guilt to victims to a large measure and rationalizing the deviant behaviour by the denial of responsibility, denial of injury and denial of victimization. (as victim himself was the wrongdoer), the condemnation of the condemners and finally by appealing to higher loyalties as a justification for the deviant behaviour.[13] In short, it only supports the concept of victim-precipitation which may not be considered as the legitimate area of study for Victimology. The discipline of Victimology aims at ameliorating the circumstances of the victims of different categories. In this connection, Van Dijk, in Criminological Research Conference of the Council of Europe in Strassburg, identified following approaches for the benefit of the victims:–

(a) Care approach,

(b) Rehabilitation approach,

(c) Retribution approach,

(d) Abolition or anti-criminal justice approach.

All the ideologies or the approaches mentioned above do not apply to all the victims in all the situations. In this context analysis of personal situations, victims' personality including subjective sensitivity to a particular type of crime; categories of crime, intensity of the injury (physical and mental), social outlook of the victim and hordes of other factors are to be taken into account.

Victim Identification

Who is victim in the context of the study under the discipline of Victimology? If we take various types of victims who suffer because of human acts (criminal, negligent or otherwise), living conditions in society, natural disasters or by their own acts done under mistaken belief etc., then perhaps we may not be able to focus our attention on the problems of victims in proper perspective and will defeat the very objective as envisioned by B. Mendelsohn.

The preparatory meeting held in Ottawa in July 1984 worked out a draft for declaration on 'justice and assistance for victims' in the 7th UN Congress in Milan in 1985. This conference considerably widened the scope of the study and declared that "Victims means persons who individually or collectively, have suffered harm including physical or mental injury, emotional suffering; economic loss or substantial impairment of their fundamental rights, through acts or omissions that are in violation of criminal laws operative within a country, including those laws prescribing criminal abuse of power."

Above definition appears to be quite exhaustive and can include various types of victims such as who are having weak position in society due to social discrimination, physical and mental handicaps or handicapped due to age and sex, victims of abuse of political and economic power or socio-economic marginality. The victims of traffic and industrial accidents are also covered by the above definition. The liberal interpretation of the definition will lead to the inclusion of victims of pollution, victims of economic abuse like corruption, tax evasio, nvictims of social discrimination, apartheid and political persecution and scores of other victims. B. Mendelsohn has grouped these victims on the basis of evaluation of their responsibility for the commission of crime such as innocent victims, victims having minor contributory guilts, voluntary victims (cases of suicide), victims who are more guilty than the offenders (who incite others to commit crime such as drug-pedlars) and finally the victims who commit crime against other and get killed in the process.

Victims of Conventional Crime

The violent crime like homicide, bodily injury causing permanent impairment, rape and disfigurement are some of the crimes which leave behind a very traumatic effect on the victim. Besides physical injury it leaves behind scars of agonizing hurt psychology which takes a very long time for reparation. The victim of violent crime against person is often stigmatized and the society does not want to be associated with the losers and this is specially true of the victims of rape who are partly held responsible for causation of crime as states Hans Von Hentig. "In a sense victim shapes and moulds the criminal." The insignificant role assigned to the victims in trial proceedings, the attitude of law enforcing agents and freedom of lengthy and brutalizing cross-examination in court of law makes the victim attack the criminal justice system. The Women Associations all over the world have taken up this issue with success and forced governments to change law and its procedure. The victims of violent crimes against body need medical care, greater role in criminal proceedings, facilities of victim-offender mediation and reconciliation, legal aid, restitution and compensation. Such victims in certain cases need moral and psychological support to overcome initial trauma characterized by acute distress including disbelief, dismay, emotional breakdown before they attempt pseudo-adjustment to overcome in the anxiety for the protection of self and others.

The victims of traffic accidents, need immediate medical care, restitution and compensation besides speedy justice. Such victims also suffer from concern for crime and need reassuring hand of law enforcement agents and insurance agencies. The fear of crime affects quality of life and can be harmful to a group if multiple victims were involved.

The victims of property crime (without violence) do not suffer mental agony comparable to violent crime but on the other hand need financial help and compensation to save them from uncertain future besides speedy trial and professional advice to avoid the trap in future.

In case of victims of violent conventional crime, the situational aspect is very important while determining help and assistance to the victim. The offender-victim relationship has been considered quite important in determining the guilt as also the quantum of punishment. In certain cases even the exception has been made in criminal law (Ss. 88 and 89 IPC).

The relationship can also be a determinant in respect of psychological shock suffered by the victim and to a large extent determines the course of action for future adjustment.

The effect of violent crime such as physical injury to a child or an old person can be of immense consequences and will certainly need different treatment. Similarly, the psychological background of a victim also decides to a large extent the quantum of mental injury caused to him in terms of abstinence from perfectly normal behaviour and also his interaction with society which affects quality of life. This draws attention of the students of Victimology.

Victims of Non-Conventional Crime

With the advancement of Science and Technology, larger groups are exposed to unforeseen risks and slightest negligence can affect lives of millions and in this connection Bhopal gas-leak tragedy, can be cited as an example. In certain cases people living in other countries, can also be involved as was the case with the leakage in USSR nuclear plant and again leakage of poisonous gas in Kazhakistan. The victims of tragedies on such a higher scale cannot escape attention of victimologist. The tragedies affecting multiple victims such as victims of environmental pollution as a result of dumping of nuclear wastes in oceans, and discharge of untreated affluents in the rivers and lakes also need help in terms of health care, economic support, compensation, education, training and job facilities for victims' children. The victims of consumer fraud, graft and corruption in society, should be given speedy judicial redress.

Victims of Political and Social Excesses

The victims of atrocities committed on political opponents in countries having dictatorial forms of government apartheid, discrimination exercised on ethnic minorities, all come under these categories. Political and administrative excesses directed against any particular group of people result into exodus such as one during partition of India, and again in 1970-71 from Bangladesh. The recent influx of Tamils from Sri Lanka also makes them victims of circumstances which have roots in politics.

The victims of inhuman treatment by law enforcement agencies (Bhagalpur-like incidents), deprivation of fundamental human rights resulting into child labour force and inhuman working conditions in certain factories also attract victimologists.

Whatever may be the source of injury, "Severe encroachments on the persons physical integrity of financial situation demand immediate aid in the form of intervention to solve the crisis and sustained support measures for rehabilitation. Psychological impairments, in particular, with regard to the victims' role in criminal proceedings and in the event of personal settlement between offender and victim should not be left out of consideration. They will have a significant bearing on the different needs for reconciliation with the offender particularly in cases involving offences committed within the family or neighbourhood. For this reason the utmost sensitivity is demanded in this field in order to avoid provoking undesirable reactions."[15]

Grievances of the Victims

The formal protection of victims is a recent phenomenon but as part of criminal jurisprudence it was recognized in many countries in varying degrees. If victims feel that criminal justice system does not take into account their difficulties then they lose faith in judicial system and do not have moral courage to face criminals in self-defence. This concern was voiced by many criminologists in Western countries specially in USA in recent years.[16]

The grievances of victims are many and they take number of forms. Sometimes it is felt that in our effort to ensure fair play and justice we are ignoring the victim of the crime. When Acharya Vinoba Bhave initiated surrender of dacoits in Chambal Valley followed by Jai Prakash Narain and other political leaders, it was raised by many that soft option has been accepted and all facilities were given to dacoits and their family members but the victims and their family members were grossly ignored. When criminals responsible for ghastly crimes are released on bail cheaply then it becomes difficult to prevent hostility of the complainants, leave alone the witnesses. In certain cases even the police witnesses find it difficult to stand on their feet because of fear of reprisal at the hands of desperadoes having political links.

The grievances of the victims start right from the beginning and they feel handicapped in lodging the complaints with the Police or in Court of Law. There may be number of factors responsible for this but the most important one is the police attitude at reporting Police Station.

The victims' grievances with respect to judicial procedure have been summed up by B.J. George Jr.[17] as follows :

1. Lack of a voice in decisions whether to prosecute of settle criminal cases.
2. The general failure on the part of police and prosecution to keep the victims informed about the progress of the case.
3. Inconvenience of going to court again and again, and incurring expenses on transport, child care, loss of income minimally offset by the allowance given by the court. This also remains unpaid for long.
4. Physical surroundings are not congenial. Friends and relatives of the offenders frequently visit and intimidate the victims and witnesses.
5. When witnesses including victims take witness stand they are not treated with dignity and they feel humiliated.

To the above list a few can be added being the outcome of peculiar local conditions. In our country delay in disposal of cases erodes the interest of victims as well as the witness in the case. The apprehension of reprisals is still another point which unnerves the victims specially a victims of rape or grievous hurt.

The grievances mentioned above relate to only procedure

of judicial system but more important are the grievances with respect to concepts of law relating to particular offences. In this connection law relating to rape can be examined at length. The analysis of law relating to rape hinges around corroboration, consent and character. Justice V.R. Krishna Iyre in *Krishna Lal V.* State of Haryana (AIR 1980 S.C. 1252) has very aptly said, that "to forsake these vital considerations and go by obsolescent demands of substantial corroboration is to sacrifice commonsense in favour of an artificial, concoction called 'Judicial probability'."

Another essential ingredient to be proved in court of law for successful prosecution is non-consent[18] of the victim which is to be inferred from the struggle or resistance she has put up in thwarting the attempt of the offender. The third important ingredient is character. In court of law, prosecution in its anxiety to prove the case to the hilt forces the victim to relive those moments of agony and trauma while the opponents try to discredit her by casting aspersions on her character and also to disbelieve the circumstances only to add to her misery.

Existing provisions in law and social structure for the prevention of victimization and protection of victims.

As pointed out victims have a number of problems which cry for help and grievances which demand immediate redressal. We can group these problems as follows in order to find out existing provisions in law and social structure :

1. Problems related to communication between victims and governmental agencies.
2. Problems related to reparation, restitution and compensation.
3. Problems of resocializing the victim.

1. The problems related to communication start even before victimisation actually begins, therefore, it is related to preventive action of law enforcement agencies and social endeavours by way of voluntary organisations or private

enterprise. In this connection, the persons who are likely to fall prey to any of the special situations which is in the knowledge of governmental agencies have every right to have the information such as advance warning with respect to oncoming storm in coastal areas or floods in river valleys. Similarly, presence of a particular type of risk in a particular area such as firing range of the army, or seismic unrest in particular region have to be notified to the people inhabiting the risk area. In most of the countries these provisions do exist but the educational aspect regarding measures to be taken for securing property etc. have been neglected except in some of the countries who have adopted the Scandinavian system of Advisory Boards on crime prevention.

The victims are mostly very sensitive regarding lack of communication from investigating and prosecuting agency both at investigation level as well as prosecution level. In most of the legal systems the provisions do exist to keep the victim informed about the acts governing criminal trial but the apathy of governmental agencies involved are much to be blamed as they mostly prefer to remain *incommunicado*.

Though system provides that criminal proceedings can be sent rolling on the complaint of the victim but participation in criminal proceedings has been kept bare minimum. May be in certain cases State takes full responsibility to avoid confrontation between victim and the prepetrator of the crime. In private complaint cases the victims have full participation which is wanting in police cases. Similarly, the decision regarding filing appeal against the acquittal does not rest with the complainant. This right, if granted to the victims, will create problems in cases having victims more than one.

2. The provisions regarding redressal of health damage can be considered conjointly with the general public health provisions and insurance schemes. In most countries free medical assistance is available, therefore, no need was felt for separate arrangement for health care of the crime victims. Since scope of help to victims is not confined to immediate medical attendance but includes future treatment, 'occupa-

tional therapy assistance in professional rehabilitation such as retraining and similar schemes, disablement pensions, pensions for surviving dependents and assistance in particular predicaments'. It has been provided for in Federal Republic of Germany and some of the States in USA while in other countries it has been left to the direction of the court by making discretionary provision in criminal law.

The provisions of compensation to the victims is recent concept in modern criminal jurisprudence but in our country even *Manusmriti* made provisions for compensations to the victims of bodily injury to the extent required for the treatment.[19] Similarly, for the loss of property the compensation was provided for in *Manusmriti*.[20] In Cr. P.C. also provisions have been made for the compensation to the victims u/ss 357, 358 and 359 Cr. P.C. Section 5 of Probation of Offenders' Act, 1958 provides for the payment of the compensation to the victims. The compensation to the workmen and to the victims of road accidents has been provided in the respective acts. The payment of compensation has raised certain policy issues as identified by B.J. George Jr. in American Jurisdictions :

- Generally only crimes which cause death or bodily injury support a claim.
- The power to adjudicate claims has been vested in special administrative board.
- *Delimitation of eligibility to apply*—In this connection seven categories have been identified :
  - (a) Victims of violent crime.
  - (b) Surviving spouse or dependent child of a deceased victim of violent crime.
  - (c) Any other legal dependent of the deceased victim.
  - (d) A 'good Samaritan' injured or killed while trying to prevent a violent crime.
  - (e) A surviving spouse or dependent child of a 'good Samaritan' killed to prevent a violent crime.

(f) A person legally dependent for support on a slain good Samaritan.

(g) A person injured or killed while aiding a law enforcement officer in performance of official duty.

In the field of eligibility there are notable exceptions such as offenders, accomplices and family members of either of the two :

- Most State legislation requires that the victim claiming compensation should be resident of the State.
- Compensation legislation requires prompt reports and swift commencement of the compensation proceedings.
- Nature of the injuries for which compensation is claimed.
- Comprehensive Crime Control Act of 1984 envisages creation of victims' fund which finance victims'compensation plans. This fund gets money from fines imposed during trial, from the special forfeiture of collateral profits of a crime of physical violence, in the form of proceeds from a contract for sale or literary entertainment rights to the depiction of crime and third source of the money is forfeiture of appearance bonds, bail bonds and fines paid by the convicts.

3. As discussed earlier the victims can be termed as losers in criminal encounters. Once a man has been seriously injured, a woman has been raped and a child has been abused, it becomes very difficult to win the same social esteem and this is specially more significant for the women who have been raped or molested. In most countries voluntary organisations have taken up this task of rendering help to victims in resocializing.

Recommendations

So far we have been clamouring for the reforms in jail administration, protection to under-trials, scrutiny of the legal system to ensure fundamental rights to the under-trials and convicts, transfer of prisoners from one country to another and scores of other measures to improve the quality of life of the offenders or suspects but in the process we almost ignored the plight of victims and their dependents. Now time has come for the riddance of the sufferings of the losers of the society, i.e., a raped woman, maimed child, permanently handicapped youth, the multiple victims of industrial accidents and future generations of deprived human beings who are condemned to drink contaminated water and breathe polluted air. Following adoption of victims protection in UN Congress and other international conferences, certain regional conferences have worked out recommendations which are quite useful in designing programme for victim protection.[21] The sufferings of the victims can be reduced to a large extent if proper system is introduced and adhered to for registration of complaints which may involve compensation. In this connection education of the masses is very essential to enlighten them about their rights and procedure to seek redress.

The information regarding risks involved in any particular area is to be disseminated promptly and failure of it should entail punishment. Similarly, Crime Advisory Boards may be set up for general advice of the risk-prone public and also to collect feedback with respect to police preventive measures.

The victims should be taken into confidence at every stage of investigation. At this stage his legal interests should be carefully watched and strict privacy be maintained.

At prosecution stage more interest be cultivated in the victim about the success of the case. In the beginning, copy of FIR has to be given u/s 154 (i) to the informant and again communication has to be given to the victim regarding action taken by Investigating Officer as enjoined by Sec. 173 (2) (ii) Cr. P.C. Despite these provisions action is not taken promptly which adds to the annoyance of the victim. The grievances of victims regarding lengthy trials, cross-examination, loss of wages can be overcome if there is change in the attitude of prosecutors as well as that of presiding officers of the court. If witnesses and victims are given proper respect in court they will feel more involved in the outcome of the trial. Some funds should be provided to help the victims who are found in great financial difficulties.

The change in the concept has brought about increasingly the provisions of health-damage reparation, restitution and compensation in the legislative amendments to the existing law. The payment of compensation to crime victims should be institutionalized and it should be ensured that claims of compensation are disposed of speedily.

Public awareness should also be promoted regarding rights and obligations of the victims, the procedures for filing claims for compensation and other benefits available to the victims. Even the literature regarding LIC schemes be kept at the police station to be given to the victims of crime. Police officers and officers of the court should also be given training in various programmes designed for the protection of victims.

Further government should sponsor and fund research in the field of Victimology for refining procedure of law affecting victims and promoting public awareness about the plight of victims and their rights and obligations.

REFERENCES

1. Joad, C.E.M., *Our Own Civilization.*
2. सर्वे भवन्तु सुखिनः सर्वे सन्तु निरामयाः
   सर्वे भद्राणि पश्चन्तु मा कश्चित् दुःख भाग्गवेत।
3. *Manusmriti*-Chapter 7: दुष्येयुः सर्ववर्णाश्च भिद्ये रन्सर्वसेतवः
   सर्वलोकप्रकोपश्च भवेद्‌दण्डस्य विमात् (24)
   x x x
   यत्र श्यामो लोहिताक्षो दण्डश्चरति पापहा,
   प्रजास्तत्र न मुङ्चन्ति नेता चेत्साधु पश्चति (25)
4. *Manusmiriti*-Chapter 7: तं देशकालौ शक्ति च विद्यां चावेक्ष्य तत्वतः
   यथार्हतः संप्रणयेन्नरेष्वन्यायवर्तिषु। (16)
5. *Manusmiriti*-Chapter 7: तस्यार्थे स सर्वभूतानां गोप्तारं धर्ममात्मजम्।
   ब्रह्मतोजोमयं दण्डमतृजत्पूर्वमीश्वरः (14)
   x x x

स राजा पुरुषो दंडः स नेता शासिता चसः
चतुणामाश्रमाणां च धर्मस्य प्रतिभूः स्मृतः (7)

6. *Manusmiriti*-Chapter 7: समीक्ष्य सः घृतः सम्यक्सर्वा रज्जयति प्रजाः
असमीक्ष्य प्रणीतस्तु विनाशचति संर्वतः। (19)
7. Dr. Erich Corves, Ministerialrigent (Federal Ministry of Justice, F.R. Germany), "Policy Planning for the Protection of Victims".
8. Dr. Erich Corves, *Ibid*.
9. B. Mendelsohn, Revue International de Criminologie et de Police Technique—Vol. 10-Sereva, Switzerland 1956.
10. Kurt Weis and Sandra S. Borges, "Victimology and Rape: The Case of the Legitimate Victim." Published in issues in Criminology, Vol. 8, No. 2, 1973 Issue.
11. 1. European Regional Preparatory Meeting, June 1983.
    2. Seminar "Towards a Victim Policy in Europe—Helsinki Institute for Crime Prevention and Control", November 1983.
    3. UNO Preparatory Meeting in Ottawa, July 1984.
    4. Law Congress in Hamburg in 1984.
    5. 16th Criminological Research Conference of the Council of Europe in Strassburg in November 1984.
12. Kurt Weis and Sandra S. Borges, "Victimology and Rape: The Case of the Legitimate Victim" in "Rape Victimology", ed. by Leroy G. Schultz.
13. G.M. Sykes and David Matza, "Techniques of Neutralization. A Theory of Delinquency", American Sociological Review, Vol. XXII (1957).
14. Hans Von Hentig, "The Criminal and His Victims, Studies in the Sociology of Crime", 1948.
15. Erich Corves, "Policy Planning for the Protection of Victims.", Paper presented in UNAFEI, Tokyo.
16. Special mention may be made about authors like Turpen (The Criminal Injustice System: An Overview of the Oklahoma Victim's Bill of Rights, 1981). Anderson Woodare (Victim and Witness Assistance, 1985). Kelly (Victims of Perception of Criminal Injustice). Herrington (Victims of Crime : What Government can do?—1984). Diane K. Shah (Women Attack Rape Justice, 1971).
17. R.J. George Jr. Prof. of Law, New York School, U.S.A in his paper "New Developments in Victim and Witness Protection in the United States."
18. H.A. Snelling—"What is Non-consent?" Australian Journal of Forensic Sciences, Sydney, Australia.
19. *Manusmriti*-Chapter 8.

20. *Ibid.*
21 Recommendations made in the Report of Asia and the Pacific Region International Experts Meeting on the Protection of the Human Rights in Criminal Justice (February 17, 1987).

16

The Art and Science of Interrogation

The administration of justice is one of the most important functions of the State and its effectiveness reflects the vigour of State organism. From the dawn of human civilization, the dispensation of justice was inalienable attribute of sovereignty of the State. The dispensation of justice extends to protection of people from men who indulge in deviant behaviour or who infringe the right granted to people by society and State. The king, who was considered fountain-head of justice, was enjoined upon to punish the guilty man but at the same time he was supposed to ensure that innocent persons are not punished.[1] A criminal was to be punished only after proper investigation of the facts and circumstances which brings in existence the agency now known as police.[2]

Police have multifarious duties to perform these days but most important of them is the prevention and detection of crime. The detection of crime involves the facts and circumstances leading to commission of crime, the ascertainment of criminals, collection of available evidence (physical as well as testimonial evidence) and also the opinion of police investigating officer about the case. The facts and material evidence so collected, are put up before the court in cogent manner with a view to helping the court in dispensing justice. All these steps are taken within the limitations set by law. In view of above, the investigator has to establish commission of crime, to identify and apprehend the suspect, to establish in Court of Law the guilt beyond a certain degree of exactitude but he has to do all this and more within a prescribed period and within the established legal framework without infringing the rights of the accused and without usurping the powers of the court. The achievement of the objectives enumerated above requires attainment of a certain degree of expertise in the fields of skills and techniques generally called upon during the course of investigation including interrogation.

The evidence required for the prosecution of the case may be physical, documentary or testimonial. The physical evidence mostly connects the criminal with the crime and needs expert opinion on the subject. It includes biological evidence and tell-tale, marks left on the scene. The documentary evidence is also supportive evidence which can be of immense value in proving or disproving alibi etc. in criminal cases. The best and most direct evidence is testimonial evidence, i.e. statements of the persons who have seen the perpetration of crime, who heard of the commission of crime and also those who either committed crime or were victims of crime. All such statements throw light on the facts and circumstances relating to commission of crime hence very important for police and prosecution and serves as the anchor-sheet for the adjudication of the case in Court of Law.

Testimonial Evidence

A person's testimony 'is a formal statement' about something which is to be proved or disproved in a court or before anybody which is enquiring in its truthfulness. The information regarding facts and circumstances of the criminal case can be obtained by talking to the persons in possession of such information. Such conversion is essentially motivated by the desire to collect as much information as possible which reflects on the commission of crime and involvement or otherwise of the persons so suspected. In an interview, it is presumed that the information shall be voluntarily given. In case of interrogation, it is implied that certain amount of resistance shall be offered by the person interrogated. It includes an element of testing the information collected from other source. "The interrogation of subjects is an extension of the art of interviewing Complainants, Victims and Witnesses".[3]

The collection of information from witnesses and victims is normally voluntary and least resistance is to be met in the course of conversation therefore we tend to term them interviews while the term 'interrogation' is generally used with respect to 'suspects' or his associates. At times, witnesses and even the victims 'conceal' or twist the information with a view to giving a different colour to the incident. At times, even the victim of crime may turn out to be the real accused person. The distinction between interview and interrogation as maintained by Anglo-American author has not been maintained strictly, as I consider it to be of academic interest only. Similarly, the word 'examination' is also in vogue and has been used extensively in Cr. P.C. and Indian Evidence Act. In the present article the word 'examination' has been used in the context of testing trustworthiness of pieces of evidence both material as well as testimonial.

Objectives of Interrogation

The interview or interrogation can be conducted properly only when the investigator knows the objective of this exercise. The aim of interview or interrogation and collection of testimonial evidence from various sources is to probe and gather data to ascertain facts and circumstances of the case by legal means and in accordance with the procedure established by the Law of the Land with a view to solving crime. Therefore, the objectives of an interrogation *inter alia* includes the following:

1. Hearing the truth about the commission of crime including mode of operation;

2. Ascertaining the perpetrators of crime—both the principles and accessories (before and after the crime);
3. Ascertaining the part played by individuals;
4. Recovering property connected with commission of crime;
5. Collecting physical evidence and examining their trustworthiness with the help of information given by the persons interrogated;
6. Identifying the real culprits and eliminating the suspects;
7. Getting information throwing light on the criminal antecedents of the suspects;
8. Obtaining the suspect's version of the crime; and
9. Developing information which may be useful in prevention and detection of other crime.

Examination of Witnesses

The Code of Criminal Procedure, 1973 empowers any Police Officer making an investigation to examine orally any person supposed to be acquainted with the facts and circumstances of the case [Section 161 (1)]. The Code gives powers to Police Officer to examine any person which includes witnesses, victims and suspects. Such persons are bound to answer such questions truly. The Constitutional safeguard reflected in Section 161(2), however, protects the person to be examined with respect to such questions, "the answers to which would have a tendency to expose him to a criminal charge or to a penalty or forfeiture".

The Code of Criminal Procedure in Section 163(2) lays down clearly that "no Police Officer or other person shall prevent, by any caution or otherwise . . . any statement which he may be disposed to make of his own free will". This provision will not affect the provisions of Section 164(4) Cr. P.C.

The law laid down in relevant Sections of the Code of Criminal Procedure sets the parameter for the police officer as far as interrogation of witnesses is concerned. The objectives of interrogation as discussed earlier, is only to ascertain truth so that it can be put up before Court of Law to facilitate court to arrive at appropriate conclusion in the process of dispensing justice. The Investigating Officer must formulate his plan meticulously so as to include important things (physical evidence, weapons, distances, visibility, sounds, etc.) places (places of entry and exist, construction, doors, windows, etc.), persons (number, names, dress, conversation, etc.) and other relevant factors, relating to the witness such as physical peculiarities (stammering, impaired hearing, colour-blindness), emotional peculiarities, dialect, and intelligence quotient. Before the start of interrogation, the emotional stability, relationship (hate, love, closeness, enemity, etc.) and interest in the case should also be ascertained.

Witnesses

Eyewitnesses or the witnesses of 1st degree will include witnesses who have either seen, heard, tasted, smelled, felt or perceived the commission of crime themselves or have come to know about commission of crime by seeing, hearing or smelling a thing or event which was intimately connected with the crime. Such witnesses are very important to police for detection as well as for prosecution in Court of Law.

There are a number of factors which can affect the perception of the witnesses. During an interview or interrogation one tries to find out the facts as perceived by the witnesses, therefore, the factors responsible for influencing the perception are of immense value to the Investigating Officer during the course of investigation and to the prosecution in the court-room, further, these factors enhance or mitigate the competence and credibility of the witnesses.

The factors affecting competence of the witness include his age, state of mind, level of understanding and presence of certain handicaps. Indian Evidence Act specifically provides for determining the competence of the witness. The personal relationship including privileged relationship affects the competence of the witness in ways more than one.

The credibility of the witnesses is determined by the physical possibility, presence, consciousness and attentiveness at the crucial or critical time. The questionnaire must be prepared in the light of above factors. The distance, condition of light, line of sight, etc. must be clearly established. Similarly, the facts such as drunkenness or impairment of senses temporarily (by sudden injury or shock) should also be thoroughly established.

The witnesses must be tested thoroughly on the grounds on which his trustworthiness can be assailed in Court of Law. His special relationship with the accused (hate, love or jealousy), his own involvement, and also his previous history are relevant facts which will affect his credibility in court-room, hence, deserves utmost attention even at the time of preliminary investigation.

The statements given by the witnesses during the course of investigation are to be thoroughly examined, checked and rechecked before accepting them. The witness may be reliable, honest and conscientious still the statement may not be correct and faithful narration of facts because of the complex nature of the perception process of human mind. The perception is a decision-making process influenced by numerous factors such as intelligence, attitudes, association, self-esteem, social perception besides the opportunities to make observation.[4] The statement given by a witness is the result of memory recall and perfect recall is exceptional and imperfection of various degrees is a rule. This imperfection in recall can be the result of expectancy and filling the gap tendency of human beings and one should remember that, "The eye, the ear and other sense organs are, therefore, social organs as well as physical ones."[5]

Each individual has his individual peculiarities and needs different treatment at the time of interaction. If a man does not get proper treatment at the hands of the interviewer then one can easily anticipate the reaction of the witness. In order to get maximum information from the witness one should know the individual traits and the process of interview can be tailored accordingly. The operative variables are too numerous and individualized to be categorised in specific classification systems, nevertheless, an attempt has been made to classify witnesses on the grounds of discernible traits conditioned by the factors like motivation, attitude, perception, expectancy and social status by the authors on the subject of criminal investigation.[6] The witnesses to be examined could be either straightforward type or deceitful. In both the cases the interrogator has to prepare his questionnaire very carefully. The witness to be examined may be honest and straightforward. Such witness will try to give facts correctly but his testimony will also be exposed to the factors which influence all witnesses, namely, age, emotional factors, physical impairment, and also the tendency to fill up void left in the story. So, his statement will also suffer from expectancy which includes 'biases or prejudices' and considerations of social norms. Such witnesses should be interrogated if possible on the spot itself but in any case no time-lag be provided otherwise in valuable evidence is likely to be affected by the adjustments made by the person to fit in the new emerging picture after preliminary investigation and interrogation of the witnesses. In such cases in his anxiety to be very useful he may fabricate parts of his recall of memory in order (to make imperfect but natural, memory) to appear more plausible to the investigator.

The deceitful witness can to spotted out initially without any difficulty. The investigator must find out the motive behind such deceitful behaviour. If sufficient motive is discovered then his replies to the questions should be properly weighed and cross-checked with the help of other evidence on the point. The inconsistencies should be properly recorded and then the witness may be confronted with them, which may be quite helpful in breaking the shield of deception.

Occasionally, one comes across a witness who may be a 'pathological liar'. The tendency to fabricate memory is known as 'pseudologia phantastica'. In this case a witness can relate without any remorse or regret a totally false picture by adding false and incorrect facts to his recollection. Such witnesses are dangerous and should be identified at first instance and consistencies be pointed out to discredit them after giving him a very long rope.

In serious cases involving gangsters most of the eye-witnesses show disinterestedness and more often than not exhibit reluctance to come near the police investigator. Even after persistent questioning it becomes difficult to exact information from them. In such cases one has to find out motive behind such behaviour and then to proceed to remove the mental block. The reluctance in such cases may be due to a strong apprehension that the suspects of the case are likely to seek revenge or also that the Investigating Officer is not likely to act on their disclosure then why should they unnecessarily involve themselves. Such apprehensions and suspicions are to be removed and then alone the witnesses can provide useful clues. Such mental blocks must be removed at the outset otherwise such a reluctant witness can turn hostile in Court of Law later on.

During the course of investigation at times one comes across witness who are unreliable due to mental deficiency, immaturity of age, or persons having bouts of vivid imagination. Such witnesses should be allowed to talk freely then gently the discrepancies be pointed out and efforts be made to correct the inconsistencies. In such cases the credibility of the witness has to be determined properly after ascertaining the factors such as opportunity to observe, his capacity to observe, veracity, personal attitude, and his relationship with suspect or the victim.

The biased or interested witness can be identified by the investigator by his mannerism, his interest in the case and character and extent of discrepancies in the information given by other persons. Such a biased person may be under the influence of either of the parties to the case. In such cases patient hearing be given and if possible the conversations can be recorded on tape then discrepancies and inconsistencies are analysed properly and brought to the notice of the witness rather forcefully. The vested interest of the witness should also be found out.

There is a tendency to reconstruct the scene and improve upon the memory recall to make it more plausible unconsciously but in certain cases witnesses are tutored. In such cases conscious effort has been made to fabricate very intelligently the story, either to mislead the investigator or to twist the facts under cover up design. In number of cases such witnesses are tutored to incriminate innocent persons by the interested parties. The Investigating Officer has to be very careful in evaluating such statements. In case of such witnesses the interrogator should in no situation disclose his suspicion and apprehensions in the outset. The witness should be given a long rope so that in the process of interrogation he can be confronted with inconsistencies and inaccuracies which may lead to correct facts or to total discredit to the tutored witness.

In some cases the investigator in its overjealousness to rope in real culprits tries to tutor witness so that in Court of Law the case is found flawless and a conviction is ensured. Such practices besides being immoral and illegal are counter-productive and in turn discredit the investigating agency.

Precautions to be taken while Interrogating Witness

The Investigating Officer should always remember that the witnesses are very important persons for detection as well as for prosecution of cases, therefore, they should be properly handled and treated with dignity.

In our country where only scant attention has been given to the plight of witnesses, including victims, they always show reluctance to come forward to help Police Investigating Officer on one pretext or the other. In such circumstances it is imperative for the investigator to allay fears of the witnesses regarding harassment in court at the hands of defence counsel and also try to convince him about the importance of his testimony. He may be politely told that absence of testimony is likely to help the criminals and society may ultimately suffer. The witnesses normally fear retaliation from the criminals or their friends, therefore, witnesses should be assured of secrecy as much as possible in our legal system. The witnesses should always be given proper protection of law. It is noteworthy that witnesses should not be given false assurance or promises which could not be kept.

In case of children and women, every care should be taken not to hurt their feelings. Their statements should be recorded separately and if possible by the woman officer.

'On the Scene' Interrogation

In certain cases where scene of crime is very difficult to describe and due to differences of dialect the true meaning of the words is likely to be misinterpreted it is always advisable to interrogate the witnesses on the scene of crime. In such cases the witness gets an opportunity to reconstruct the crime in his mind fully and relative distances and sequence of events are correctly depicted by him. The defects in the perception are also avoided. This visit to scene of crime also equips investigator to cross-examine the information given by the witness. The scene of crime in such cases should not be disturbed before the interrogation, if disturbed it has to be reconstructed.

Group Interrogation

In cases where gangs of criminals are involved, people are afraid to say anything separately but in a group they feel emboldened. In such cases outline of the crime can be ascertained and later on witnesses can be interrogated separately in the context of group discussion.

Informal Interrogation

In such interrogations, the investigator does not ask any specific questions but interrogation proceeds like conversation and the witness is given a long rope. There is every possibility that some seemingly irrelevant facts are narrated by the witness with useful facts thrown in-between. It is the duty of the investigator to pick up these threads and then combine them to correct facts of the case.

Follow-up Interrogation

In case of interrogation of suspects or accused there is prescribed procedure but in case of witnesses there are no such constraints and a witness can be confronted with facts that come to light during the course of investigation after the statement of witness is recorded for the first time. The witness should be taken into confidence during the investigation which gives him a sense of participation and pride so essential to keep him interested in the case and prepares him to withstand grilling by the defence counsel. Such confrontations with facts as disclosed by defence witnesses will also revive his memory and additional light can be thrown on the case which may help the prosecution in countering defence arguments.

The follow-up interrogation is also necessary because certain discrepancies in the story of other prosecution witnesses need to be cleared by subsequent interview. Such discrepancies may be the result of physical or mental impairment, lack of observation, special skills etc. Such special skills or handicaps can be discussed during follow-up interrogation.

Interrogation of Witnesses—Police Powers

The Police Investigating Officer has powers to order attendance before himself, of any person who appears to be acquainted with facts and circumstances of the case (Section 160 Cr. P.C.). In such cases provision for the payment of reasonable expenses may be made by the State Government. The Investigating Officer has to record statement of children below 15 years and women only at the place of their residence and they should never be called to police station for their statement as witnesses.

The persons called by the Police Investigating Officer are bound to answer truly all questions relating to such case. The witness, however, cannot be compelled to answer questions which would have a tendency to expose him to a criminal charge penalty or forfeiture of property.

In connection with examination of witnesses the provisions of Section 24 of the Indian Evidence Act, 1872 have to be kept in mind. No person in authority should offer any inducement, threat or promise to obtain statement of the witness but at the same time no Police Officer or other person shall prevent by any caution or otherwise, any person from making in the course of any investigation any statement which may be disposed to make of his own free will. The provisions of Section 163(2) are not to affect provisions of Section 164(4) of Cr. P.C. which deals with recording of confessions of the suspects.

Interrogation of Suspects/and Men in Police Custody—Objectives

The main purpose of an investigation is collection of evidence but it must be conducted by a Police Officer or any other person so authorised.[7] It *inter alia* includes arrest, medical and other examinations, recovery of physical evidence, recovery of property and all other steps that help in true detection and prosecution of the case. In view of the above objectives of investigation, the interrogator should proceed with interrogation only with a view to finding out truth and collection of evidence to prove it in Court of Law as per procedure laid down by the Law of the Land. Though admissions and confessions are of immense probative value yet they are only incidental to interrogation. The information exacted from the suspect or the men in custody in most of the cases, is of immense detective value and can certainly lead to taking preventive action to prevent recurrence of such occurrences.[8]

The aims or goals include such objectives as :

1. Learning the truth;
2. Obtaining an admission of guilt;
3. Ascertaining the identity of participants, principals and accessories;
4. Recovering evidence and property;
5. Discovering crimes in which the suspect has been

involved;

6. Eliminating the suspects from the real core of criminals;
7. Obtaining all the facts, method of operation and circumstances of the crime in question;
8. Gathering, information enabling the investigator to arrive at logical conclusions (to corroborate or disprove some facts);
9. Recording, reporting and furnishing the results of interviews to the prosecutors for prosecutive opinion or court action; and
10. Developing intelligence information that might uncover unlawful activities and identify persons and criminal groups.

John J. Horgan says that "The interrogation of subjects is an extension of the art of interviewing complainants, victims and witnesses. It is a process of proving and gathering available data in crime solving."[9]

Preparation for Interrogation

Interrogation of the suspect needs thorough preparation before embarking on the job because the results are proportionate to the efforts of interviewer spent on planning and preparation. Each case must be viewed separately in the context of circumstances attending to the case and preparations should be made in accordance with the requirements of the case.

In police investigation at times the exigencies force the investigator to interrogate the person immediately without having recourse to records of the case and help from other supporting agencies. To meet such situations the interrogator should remember basics of interrogation and after preparation attempt recording interrogation. In case of on-the-spot arrest the interrogator has to question him about his associates, their whereabouts, property if it was subject-matter of crime and so many other points requiring immediate attention. In such cases the interrogator has to rely on the information readily available and also the basic guidelines. In case of planned interrogation, more attention can be paid to selection of place of interrogation, persons helping in interrogation and other facilities.

Basic Guidelines

1. Suspect must be treated as human being and his rights must be respected.
2. Never lose patience and confidence.
3. Language should be adjusted to the level of the subject of interrogation. The questions should be short, forthright, and intelligible considering the social, economic and intelligence level of the suspect.
4. Suspect be allowed to speak and too much interruption be avoided.
5. Interrogator should not lose temper. Arrogance and belligerent attitude is always counter-productive.
6. Try to establish rapport with the suspect. If need be, interrogator can be changed so that a person who can establish rapport be given chance of interrogation.
7. The suspect being under the shock, a little sympathy is likely to be more than repaid in terms of correct information.
8. The suspect must be sized up early and technique be selected accordingly.
9. The objective of interrogation should always be kept in mind. The interrogator should always try only to find out truth and should always remember that "No case is ever important enough to justify falsification."
10. The question on important points should be asked in a normal way so that suspect does not attach any extra significance to it. At times, a single piece of information can be elicited in two or three questions.
11. The suspect should not be given the impression that he is disbelieved by the interrogator. However, he

may be confronted with facts just to elicit true facts.

12. Leading questions should not be aked as a rule when one's aim is to find out the truth.
13. The interrogation is conducted to gather the information and not to educate the suspect.
14. The investigation should not be unduly aggressive otherwise it is likely to build up defence mechanism.
15. The interrogation should be conducted in such a way that the suspect is not unduly embarrassed. He should also be assured of confidentiality as much as possible within the four corners of law.
16. The questions should be so planned that important points are covered.
17. The behaviour pattern during interrogation should be seriously studied for the suspect might be giving body signals while answering questions. Before starting interrogation the interrogator must prepare himself for the job. He must have full knowledge of facts of the case. In this connection, copy of FIR and the report regarding scene of crime should not only be studied carefully but its copy should be readily available to the investigator. The examination reports regarding physical evidence should also be studied before hand. The interrogator must study the crime pattern of his area having some resemblance with the crime in question.

Criminal history of the suspect should also be known to the Investigating Officer. Personal details of the suspect, his family members, relations and associates in crime should also be known to the investigator.

The Time and Place

The time, place and duration of interrogation depends upon the exigencies of the case. Normally, interrogation room should be plain, and having only the necessary furniture required for two or three persons. No objects of distraction should ever be kept in the room unless for psychological reasons it is considered necessary.

Time should be so fixed that the suspect should not feel that particularly odd time has been selected to interrogate him. Normally, time should be normal working hours but to avoid disturbance odd time can be fixed in certain situations.

Proper arrangement for light should be there so that the interrogator can comfortably watch physical and mental response to the questions.

Further, the interrogator can also read the body language in proper light.

The distraction like telephones and other appliances can be avoided if not required for psychological impact. Dummy telephones can be fixed in the room fitted with microphone connected with record in devices. Two-way mirror may also be useful in the room so that subject is watched by other persons at other place who can draw inferences of their own.

Basic Amenities

At the time of interrogations it is essential that interrogator must deal the subject in a very humane way. Cruelty, torture or neglect on the part of interrogator is likely to develop defence mechanism in the subject and he will not come out with any fact and the very purpose of interrogation can be defeated. The provision of food, drink, smoke, etc. can be taken care of and similarly provision of toilet, etc. should not be neglected. These petty things are likely to change the mental response of the subject. As a rule all the facilities which an ordinary man is entitled should be given to the subject, if he is in police custody. If he is not in police custody then his freedom of movement should be restricted to the extent permissible under law and required for the purposes of interrogation. Imposition of restrictions in the movement beside inviting complaints are also detrimental to the interrogation processes as it hardens the attitude and infuses aggressiveness in the subject.

Interrogation of Juveniles

The juvenile offenders are a class by themselves and legal

protection has been provided to them. This fact should always be kept in mind while making preparations for interrogation of juveniles. It is also essential that thorough preparations be made keeping in view the protections given by law. Further, it is presumed that juveniles are immature in understanding, therefore, a leading question, excitement, inducement, threat, etc. will have immediate effect on their minds, therefore, every care should be taken to avoid such deviations to creep in. The interrogator should adopt a friendly gesture and it should start with friendly tone. Every care should be taken that important questions are put to the subject only after establishing a friendly rapport. The conversation may start from the subjects of common interest and the subject should be encouraged to do most of the talking and interrogator should have more patience to listen even the irrelevant and superfluous story. At any point of time the interrogator should not give an impression that he is not giving the importance to the witness he deserves.

During the course of interrogation with the juvenile it is always necessary to encourage him in telling facts but in case of any inaccurate fact, the discrepancies should be politely pointed out, so that he has a chance to save face. No attempt should be made to embarrass the juvenile subjects. Use of vulgar language should always be avoided while dealing with juveniles. Similarly, nothing should be said to him to suggest that interrogator has any ill will against the family members of the juvenile, otherwise he will start considering interrogator as his enemy. The juveniles may be asked to put their version if they can write it coherently. In case of juveniles body language should be read carefully. The non-verbal communication in case of juveniles shall be of utmost importance.

Interrogation of Women

Certain provisions have been in law regarding custody of women. Similarly, female suspects should also be shown all considerations to avoid any embarrassment and hardening of attitude. Restraint should be exercised with respect to language by the interrogator. The questions regarding sex and infidelity should not be asked normally. If it is absolutely necessary then female interrogator should be taken help of.

Interrogation Approaches

There are as many interrogation approaches as the criminals. The emphasis on a particular aspect of interrogation to exact true facts from the suspect can be treated as approach. The interrogation approaches have been divided into following categories :–

1. The logical approach, and
2. The emotional approach.

The logical approach is based on "Common-sense and sound reasoning". It assumes that person interviewed is reasonable and rational and there is considerable evidence available.[10] As discussed earlier, before proceeding with interrogation it is always desirable that interrogator must assess the suspect's personality and character traits and take decision regarding approach to be followed in his case. Normally speaking, educated persons and those who have committed crime for the first time are more amenable to logical approach. The interrogator must collect data with respect to crime as well as with respect to suspect before starting interrogation. The interrogator must allow the suspect to speak without any undue interruption. When suspect completes his story then discrepancies based on available data and statements of other witnesses may be brought to his notice and correction if any made in the story by the suspect, should be incorporated. In some cases the suspect might leave some parts of the story uncovered knowingly. In such cases direct questions should only be put up as a last alternative. It is advisable to ask clarification about the lapses indirectly. In logical approach greater emphasis is laid on physical evidence including corresponding reference in records maintained in normal course of business. The presence of fingerprint, footprint and pieces of clothes, papers connecting criminal with the crime can also be very useful.

The circumstantial evidence fixing the presence of the

suspect at the crucial time before and after commission of crime can be brought to his notice to compel him to divulge correct facts.

The discrepancies and evidence of other witnesses will force the suspect to come to truth. However, uneducated and ignorant suspects may have to be enlightened about the circumstances again and again rendering his story unacceptable. In this type of interrogation one has to prepare thoroughly before the start of interrogation and utmost patience has to be observed as the story is amended again and again by the suspect. It will be very useful to read body language specially while answering questions having bearing on incriminating circumstances because even hardened criminals are unable to control inadvertent signals transmitted by them.

The Emotional Approach

In emotional approach the interrogator appeals to suspect's sense of conscience, decency, morality and his family pride, etc. This approach is advisable for first-time offenders and also those who have committed offence in sudden rage. Such people have burden on their conscience and are always ready to give expression to their feelings as soon as appreciative recipient is found out. In some of the cases such suspects admit their guilt without any remorse. The interrogator should encourage them without taking sides. The suspect and human treatment meted out to the suspect establishes proper chain of communication so conducive to interrogation. The suspect can be reminded of his good character, good family background, honourable life led by the suspect till the commission of crime and then asking the questions related to commission of crime and also giving him a hint to the suspect to offer his defence or justification for the particular act.

In some of the cases the intimate relationship with the victim of crime can also emotionally compel the suspect to come out with the true facts. The objects connected with the victim such as his clothes, photographs, his voice recorded on a tape and other incidents can also have sound emotional effect on the suspect. In cases of murders of family members the suspect will not be able to see the face of victim. In case they proceeded to see the face of victim they generally break and divulge correct facts. In cases of molestation the mere sight of the victim will send the suspect in rage.

Cooperation from Friends and Relatives

In cases of interrogation of immature persons, the presence of understanding and emotionally attached persons, friends and relatives can further heighten their sensibility. Before introducing friends and relatives it is imperative to find out degree of intimacy with such friends or relatives. The embarrassing questions involving sex and other immoral acts in presence of relatives and friends may be avoided.

Truth Serum

The use of truth serums are also prevalent in some of the countries for detecting lies. The administration of these serums removes the inhibitions and thus encourage the suspect to make the true statement. The serums used in aid of interrogation include Sodium pnetothal, Sodium amytal, Pheno barbital solution or Hyoscine. The truth serum test should be given only in presence of a doctor and after observing legal precautions.

Use of Polygraph

The Polygraph is based on assumption that when a person conceals or tampers some information in response to certain questions certain physiological changes occur which are beyond the control of person put on Lie-detector or Polygraph. These physiological changes include pulse rate, blood-pressure, skin resistance and sweating. The data obtained from the Polygraph is analysed by the scientist and properly interpreted on the basis of certain recognised principles. Before the suspect is put on Lie-detector he is thoroughly examined. The expert explains the procedure and the nature of the test. The subject is also warned that the evidence obtained with the help of instrument can be used against the suspect. This pretest interview is very important and at times suspects divulge the truth even before applying the test. The instrument is attached to the suspect and then questions are put to the victim for correct answers. The instrument starts recording changes in breathing, blood-pressure, sweat activity, skin resistance, etc.

Psychological Stress Evaluator

In this instrument the voice of suspect is taped in response to questions put by the interrogator and immediately the connected computer starts analysing modulations of the voice and expert gives his finding on that.

When a man speaks then his voice is transmitted in two types of modulations : 1. Audible, and 2. Inaudible. The inaudible modulation is not received by human ear, while audible one's are received by human ear. The Psychological Stress Evaluator (PSE) can decipher inaudible modulations as well. The inaudible modulations reflect internal stress which are detected and measured by PSE. With the help of this instrument the guilt suggesting quality can be detected. In PSE simple questions are prepared which are designed to suit the specific subject, and answers to them will reveal patterns which are truthful and also those which are indicative of deeption. The subject would be asked to respond to a series of questions both truthful and deceptive. The results are then compared with previously recorded voice patterns which will indicate truthfulness or deception. The PSE has following advantages : 1) this instrument is very simple to operate and there are not many appliances, therefore, easy to operate, 2) PSE may also examine tape recordings of telephone conversations.

Mark-2 Voice Analyser

Mark-2 Analyser invented by John Reid & Fred Invau. This instrument does not require any attachment. Like PSE this instrument also records submodulations. It is capable of processing a recorded voice—one heard on telephone or spoken words. The instrument analyses certain quality of voice which is loaded with stress. This instrument of stress is indicative of deception. This instrument is very speedy and very simple to operate, therefore, it is in advantageous position as compared to Polygraph or ordinary Lie-detector.

Body Language

Within last few decades a very valuable Science has been uncovered which deals with non-verbal communication and is referred as Kinesics or body language which includes theory as well as scientific study on field survey. The subject of non-verbal communication is discussed in ancient books (Kautilya's *Arthashastra-Samyacharikam*, Stanza-5, *Prakaran*-93, Chapter-5) as well as by the social scientists in their books in middle ages. *The Expression of the Emotions in Man and Animals* (1872, Charles Darwin) and books of Freud influenced the scientific study of non-verbal communication. In normal communication there is no contradiction between verbal and non-verbal communication but when a person wants to conceal some facts such contradictions also appear and can be exploited by the interrogator while questioning the suspects.

Some of the body languages signals or non-verbal signals are inborn and genetically transferred while others are acquired later on. Much of our non-verbal behaviour is culturally determined though some of the signals may have universal acceptance. In the sphere of crime detection the interrogator has to be a very keen observer to read this body language and should also have local knowledge to interpret non-verbal communication signals. Some of the physiological changes can be measured with the help of instruments like Polygraph, Voice Analyser or PSE while signals take broadening of pupils, placing of arms, biting of nails, closing the palms of hands and arms gesture are still subject of interpretation and may differ from one cultural zone to another. Similarly, positioning of the seat of the subject, vis-a-vis the interrogator can affect the degree of compatibility achieved during interrogation should have basic knowledge of non-verbal communication and should be well-versed in local interpretation of such non-verbal signals of communication.

Policing is one of the most important functions of any Sovereign State. Policing *inter alia* includes prevention and detection of crime, apprehension of criminals, recovery of property prosecution of the offenders and to achieve this objective police has to carry out intensive investigation. The interrogation is one of the most important tools in the hands of police. The interrogation in its wider sense is pivotal to all investigation. The success of interrogation is directly proportionate to the intelligent efforts made to exact information. The investigator has to acquire expertise in the art of interrogation, solid grounding in scientific investigation and interpretation of facts discovered during the course of investigation. He has to be objective and straightforward. The investigator should remember that every case is important and unique in its investigation and justifies all efforts to work it out but at the same time, 'No case is ever important enough to justify falsification'.

REFERENCES

1. यानि मिथ्याभिशस्तानां पतन्त्यश्रूणि राघव।
   तानि पुत्र पशून घ्यन्ति प्रीत्यर्थमनुशासतः।। 59/100

   —*वाल्मीकीय रामायण*
2. गृहीतश्चैव पृष्ड्श्च काले दृष्टः सकारणः।
   कच्चिन मुच्यते चोरो धनलोभन्नरषंभ।। 57/100

   —*वाल्मीकीय रामायण*
3. John J. Horgan, *Criminal Investigation*, p. 78.
4. "Research and Court room Experience provide ample evidence that an eye-witness to a crime is being asked to be something and do something that a normal human being was not created to be or do"—Robert Buckhout, "Eye-witness Testimony", p. 25.
5. *Ibid.*, p. 24.
6. Types of Witnesses, (A) Criminal Investigation, Charles R. Swanson *et al.*
   (B) Criminal Work, John J.Horgan.
7. *State of U.P. V. Sant Prakash*—1967 Cr. L.J. -274/283 Allahabad.
8. John J. Horgan—Criminal Investigation, p. 78.
9. *Ibid.*
10. *Ibid.*, p. 837.

17

System of Punishment in Ancient India

स राजा पुरुषो दण्डा स नेता शासिता च सः।
चतुर्णामाश्रमाणां च धर्मस्य प्रतिभूः स्मृतः।।
दण्डाः शास्ति प्रजाः सर्वा दण्ड एवाभिरक्षति।
दण्डः सुप्तेषु जागति दण्ड धर्म विदुबुधाः।।
समीक्ष्य स धतः सम्यक्सर्वा रन्जयति प्रजाः।
असमीक्ष्य प्रणीतस्तु विनाशयति सर्वतः।।

Manusmriti—VII/17—19[1]

The administration of justice was considered as one of the most important functions of the State in pre-Vedic and post-Vedic period alike. Manu declares that God created King only to protect all living beings against the atrocities of the stronger people.[2] King being the incarnation of Dharma or Yama was also responsible for administering *Danda*. If kings fail in their duty to administer *Danda*, then stronger people will annihilate weaker people and anarchy will prevail all over.[3] *Danda* stands for the performance of Dharma in all the Ashramas and absence of it will result into chaos and as such Manu says that *Danda* stands surety for observance of Dharma in all the fourt Ashramas.

Sources of Ancient Indian Law

When Aryans came to India, they brought with them their culture, language, religion, rites, rituals, philosophy of life and their experiences in the form of Statecraft. All the knowledge was conveyed to disciples from Guru, orally and therefore, had enough scope for updated interpretation of their instructions. These instructions given by accomplished scholars and interpreted in the light of prevailing socio-economic conditions were the basis of innumerable Srauta/*Sutras* which came into being after proto-historic or Vedic period (C. 1500-500 B.C.) Vedas, Brahmans and some of the Upanishads became obscure and needed elucidation in the form of Sutras,[4] or 'the thread' which leads to proper understanding of the scriptures. After Srauta/*Sutras* came *Grah Sutras* and *Dharma Sutras*. *Grah Sutras* elucidate scriptures on domestic matters while *Dharma Sutras* form basis of ancient Hindu law.[5] Some of the better known *Sutras* include *Sutras* of Gautam, Baudhayan, Vasistha, Apastamba and Vishnu *Sutra*. The period of composition of these *Sutras* ranges between 600 B.C. to 100 B.C.[6] The geographical references given in these *Sutras* indicate that all the *Sutras* were composed in the territory north of Ganges except that of Apastamba, who probably composed his *Dharma Sustra* in Northern Deccan plateau. The rivers that are referred in these *Sutras* again indicate that the territory watered by rivers like Sindhu, Saraswati, Yamuna and Ganga was the centre of Vedic learning in that period. The rapid expansion of Aryans in this period towards south-west included Avanti, Asmata and Mulaka (in upper Godavari Valley) and towards the east reached upto Bengal and Orissa (Pundra, Subma, Vanga and Kalinga).[7] Newly Aryanized territories were thinly populated and cultural assimilation was also incomplete, with the result, some of the *Dharma-Sutras* prescribed atonement for the visit to these areas.

Later on, with the march of civilization these *Dharma-Sutras*-prose rendering of instructions regarding Aryan conduct gave way to Dharmasastras. These Dharmasastras were verse rendering of Sutras in an expanded form. These Dharmasastras were composed between 200 B.C. to a 600 A.D. i.e. roughly from the period of decline of Mauryan Empire to the period of Harshavardhan of Kanyakubja.[8]

Sutras and *Sastras* are known as *Smritis* i.e. recollections by Rishis. The Vedic literature including Samhitas, Brahmanas, Aranyakas, Upanishads and other Vedangas are known as Srutis i.e. 'one which is Heard' which gives them more sanctity and authenticity. Puranas and Epics also enjoyed almost same sanctity as enjoyed by Smritis. The passages found in Mahabharat are also found in Manu Smriti. In this connection special mention may be made of Shantiparva and Anushashan Parva wherein we find elucidation of principles of State craft and in-depth analysis of Nyaya and Dharma. Similarly Agnipuran and Matsya Puranas also contain treatment of subjects which find place in Dharmashashtra.

In addition to *Sruti, Smriti, Puranas* and *Mahakavyas* some of the commentories and treatises also contain references which reflect on contemporary Danda *Vyavastha*. Most important of these works include Panini's *Asthadhyayi* which was probably written in the 4th century B.C., followed by a commentary by Patanjali known as Mahabhasya. The commentaries on Sutras specially on *Manu Smriti* and *Yajnavalkya Smriti* have also contributed towards the growth of criminal law. These commentaries were composed between 800 A.D. to 1500 A.D.[9] Manu says that the Vedas (Sruti), the sacred traditions, the customs of virtuous men and one's own pleasure, are the sources of sacred law. He further defines that the custom handed down in regular succession (since time immemorial) among the four chief castes (Varna) and the mixed (races) of that country, is called the conduct of virtuous men."[10] Kautilya *Arthasastra* also gives sources of law and also indicates importance of King or the State.[11]

Some Basic Concepts

Discussion on the source of law above, does indicate that there was ample room for discretion on the part of the judge, in the case of ancient India, the king or his representative. The gravity of the offence was not the only consideration in inflicting punishment but other factors: such as caste, age, sex and status in the field of Sadhana were also taken into account while taking decision regarding punishment, as has been unequivocally mentioned in *Gautam Sutra*, *Vasistha Sutra* and in the *Dharmasutra* of *Apastamba*.

The purpose of inflicting punishment or Danda was to save the society from chaos and also to enable every creature to perform his duties or Dharma. Without Danda nobody can observe his Dharma properly.[12] Even Nirukta supports this view in "दण्डोददते धरियतिकर्मण:" which means that, it is because of Danda that everybody can perform his duty. One of the most important functions of Danda (punishment) was to maintain order. This order could be maintained by keeping the evil doers under check. The evil doers must be suppressed by Danda, if they cannot suppress their criminal instincts themselves. The word Danda takes its origin from Verb 'Damyati' and means 'one which suppresses'.[13] From the above, it is amply evident that purpose behind administering justice and inflicting punishment was the preservation of social fabric or ensuring social security so that all creatures get opportunity to observe their Dharma (Dharma taken in its broadest connotation).

According to the tenets of modern jurisprudence the punishment could be Deterrent, Preventive, Retributive or Reformative. While scanning through vast field of ancient literature, one could find elements of all the four theories behind punishment. In the early compositions emphasis was on deterrence and it was postulated that it was Danda which keeps all the creatures in their proper place because it is difficult to find virtuous men.[14] The punishment of exile and imprisonment is essentially preventive in nature. Angachhedan (multilation by way of serving limbs) may be both preventive as well as deterrent in nature. Sastrakar Brihaspati also says in so many words that, in cases of Sahasa fines equal to the value of the property stolen be imposed. In cases of more gravity, fine to the tune of double the value of the property stolen be imposed. He further prescribes that in order to prevent recurrence of such offence, even death sentence may be given.[15] Manu also says that to discourage recidivism in case of defiling a willing maiden, a fine of 200 panas be imposed.[16] While elucidating the functions of king Smritikar mentions that king should "restrain the wicked by three methods—by imprisonment, by putting them in fetters and by various (kinds of) corporal punishments. For by punishing the wicked by favouring the virtuous, kings are constantly sanctified, just as twice-horn men by sacrifices."[17] Though there are examples of punishments inflicted by way of retaliation specially when the accused was low caste member and the victim a high caste member of the society. Yet Hindu Law prohibited individual initiative generally speaking and it was enjoined as duty on the king to administer justice.[18] It is generally believed that modern reformative attitude towards the criminals is the gift of western jurisprudence. In oriental thinking and also in Hindu Law, the doctrine of reformation is deeply enshrined and purpose of inflicting Danda is always to correct the wrong doers.[18a] In this respect Gautam compares Danda with Guru, as both of them aim at bringing the subject to the right path. *Arthasastra* of Kautilya also enunciates the same principle.

Concept of *Prayschit* and *Punarjanma* (Penances and Rebirth)

The system of Danda envisaged that by committing crime, one violated the code of conduct prescribed for virtuous men and as such he has incurred wrath of Gods for doing sinful act, besides infringing the law of the land punishable by king. Danda as administered by king in proper way, will wash off the crime part of it from the person of the wrong doer, but the sin part of his act, has to be cleared, either by way of Prayschit or expiation or one has to suffer the punishment in the life after death. The concept of crime as violative of law of the land as well as of tenets of religion, is peculiar to Hindu Law because Hindu religion unlike any other religion of the world, was not only a way of life, but also the mode of life beyond this life. This unison of religious code of conduct, social morality and legal code, was the most important factor in giving enormous force to social sanctions which preserved Hindu society and even the kings had to surrender to the will of the people as expressed by the wisemen of the contemporary society by way of *Sastras*.

Expiation was possible by proclaiming one's offence, repentence, penance, and study of Veda. Manu says, "Sages prescribe a penance for a sin unintentionally committed, some declare on the evidence of the revealed texts (that it may be performed) even for unintentional (offence).

A sin unintentionally committed, is expiated by the recitation of Vedic texts, but that which (men) in their folly commit intentionally by various (special) penances."[19]

Those who could not wash off their sins in this life they will have to suffer in the next life.[20] In this context Hindu Law gives of ancient time invoked co-operation of God almighty. This concept was basic to Hindu mind and it still retains some of its efficacy among religious people.

Modes of Punishment

According to Manusmrti[21] the punishment which was meted out to criminals for various offences can be grouped into following four categories :–

1. Mild admonition
2. Harsh reprimand or reproof
3. Fine
4. Corporal chastisement

Manu further hastens to remark in the following *Shloka* that when king "Cannot restrain such (offenders) even by corporal punishment, then let him apply to them even all the four (modes conjointly)".[22] Other Sastrakars such as Yagyavalkya (1-367) and Vrddhaharita (VII-195) also broadly agreed with above modes of punishment. Yagyavalkya changes only the sequence of punishment in accordance with gravity of offence as he puts harsh reprimand (धिग्दण्ड) before mild admonition (बाग्दण्ड). Later Smritika namely Narad, Katyayan and Brihaspati mention only fine (अर्थदण्ड) and corporal punishment (बधदण्ड) which should be administered by the king and king alone.

As has been discussed earlier, in Hindu Law there was conscious effort to preserve the social morality and prevent recurrence of offence, therefore, at the time of pronouncing judgement, the judges used to keep in mind so many seemingly extraneous factors. In modern jurisprudence as well certain factors, such as mensrea, age of the culprit, his mental condition etc. has to be taken into account and in cases requiring compensation, the factors such as cost of reparation and status of the victim has to be given proper consideration. Gautam (XII-51-52) recommends that, "The award of the punishment (must be regulated) by a consideration (of the status) of the criminal of his (bodily) strength of (the nature of) the crime, and whether the offence has been repeated. Or a pardon (may be given) in accordance with the opinion of an assemblage of persons learned in the Vedas". In Danda Viveka, Vardhamana, also recounts certain factors which should be considered in the trial of the accused person. These factors include the caste of offender as well as the victim, subject matter of the offence, extent of the loss, gravity of the injury, determination of value of the loss or injury, real sufferer, age of the offender, his learning and capacity (physical and mental) his merit, fault including class of the offence and also the consideration whether it is the first offence.[23] From the above, one can very well infer that punishment was prescribed in accordance with causative factors responsible for commission of crime and also the capacity of the culprit and efficacy of punishment.

Admonition and Harsh Reprimand

Punishment by way of admonition and harsh reprimand was reserved for those who had some status in society, which means that even this type of punishment was quite adequate to prevent recurrence of such offence. The punishment of this type was also recommended for persons of tender age which aimed at reforming them and not forcing them to take to life of crime which has been of late adopted in juvenile and first offender legislation of 20th century. In certain categories of crime, the first offender was also leniently treated in the eyes of the law, as such admonition and harsh reproof was considered adequate enough to deter him to commit the crime again. This type of punishment was never considered for hardened criminals or those who belonged to the group of habitual offenders.

Fines (*Arthadands*)

Fines by way of punishment was prevalent in ancient India and almost all the *Sutrakars* from Gautam to Vishnu, *Sastrakars* from Manu to Parashari and poets of epics age have mentioned fines as mode of punishment. Even Kautilya's *Arthasastra* and *Mahabharat* discuss punishment by way of fine.

The fine imposed on the culprits could be either fixed or dependent on the status of the culprits and the property involved. In the former case, it was quantified in the gold, silver and copper coins in use during that period. In later case it was divided in three categories namely Pratham Sahas, Madhyam Sahas and Uttam Sahas.[24] In the beginning, fine in the form of cattle was also imposed. In *Dharasutra* of *Apastamba*, it has been mentioned that coins should be given by way of punishment for man-slaughter.

The fines imposed on the culprits were quite harsh in some cases but the judges had their guidelines alright. Just like present Civil Procedure Code, there were provisions that, when total property was to be confiscated, at least 1/4th of the property must be left for subsistence and also that the musical instruments of the musicians, weapons of the soldiers, ornaments of the prostitutes and the implements of artisans should not to be taken by the king by way of fine. It was contemplated that by taking such movable property, the economy of the state be harmed, which will affect the finances of the State, besides affecting means of livelihood of the subjects.

The property obtained by way of fine was part of king's treasury and the victim had no right to it save in exceptional cases. Ancient law givers never encouraged private enterprise in this connection. In Vedas, however, one finds mention of

Vairdaya, but in later scriptures, it is not mentioned. In some books methods of recovery of debt has been mentioned, which permit coercive methods.

1. Corporal Punishment

Vardhaman in his *Dandavivek* categorises corporal punishment in the following groups:

(i) *Peera* (Torture)—which could be *Kashaghat* (whipping), (ii) *Avrodhan* (incarceration), Bandhan (hand-cuffing etc.) and (iii) Vidamban (shaving of hair, making one ride a donkey, marking on the forehead etc.).[25] These punishments included whipping, slapping, roping in, nailing the nails, nailing elbows and knees, tying upside down and other such ingenuous methods.

Kautilya elaborates various types of tortures which were used in ancient times[26] some of which were quite unusual which made Spellman say that "some of these methods of torture seem rather extraordinary and one would have thought that physical limitations alone would have been an obstacle to their successful performance. However, we see no reason for believing that these methods were not used sometime."[27] These tortures were prevalent not only in Hindu India, but it even continued during Buddhist period of Indian history. Some of the technical terms used in Angattar, Nikay gives an indication of cruel nature of these torturous punishments.[28]

Marking on the forehead was also very common specially in certain serious offences. As Brahmins were exempted from all serious corporal punishments, the *Chinhankan* (marking) was the ingenuous method, to make the punishment deterrent despite exemption. Those markings differed with the nature and gravity of the crime. In a case where a person was found guilty of having affair with the wife of his teacher, punishment prescribed was to emboss the figure of female organ on his forehead. Similarly punishment for stealing was to mark figure of dog and for murder headless human body, was not be marked on the forehead. More often than not, such marking was followed by exile. If the criminals were not exiled they were treated as outcaste.

2. ***Angachhedan** (Mutilation)*

Manu prescribes ten places (parts) where punishment should be inflicted.[29] While Brihaspati gives fourteen places. These punishments were not applicable to Brahmins. Normally the part of the body which was involved in commission of crime was severed, for instance in case of assault by hand, hand should be severed and in case of using slanderous language, tongue should be severed. In case of adulterous intercourse, male organ should be severed. Similarly in other offences also mutilation was recommended by the Sutrakars either separately or conjointly with other punishments.

3. ***Pramanan** (Death Sentence)*

The sentence of death was known as *Vadha Danda*. However, some authors mention that *Vadha Danda* should be interpreted as corporal punishment because there was provision of inflicting other forms of punishment alongwith *Vadha Danda*.

Manu recommended the sentence of death to those who were guilty of murdering women, children and Brahmins; those who were guilty of debasing public morals, those who administered deceitful means and also those who served the enemies.[30] Other *Sutrakarrs* and *Sastrakars* like Yagnyavalkya, Katyayan, Brihaspati and Kautilya have also recommended sentence of death in public interest.[31]

In *Manusmriti* as well as those who followed Manu, Brahman was always treated as Avadhya, i.e., who could not be killed. Corporal punishment was never recommended for him. If Brahman committed an offence which fell in the category of Mahapataks, even then, he was not to be sentenced to death. He was exiled after confiscation of his property. There is mention of markings (*Chinhankan*) on his forehead, which resulted into excommunication by his social circle.

Not only that, Brahman was not to be slain, but also that, those who killed Brahman, had to suffer more stringent punishment than recommended for killing members of other

Varnas. Apastamba mentions that one who kills Brahman, had to pay more fine than one who killed Sudra or for that matter even other twice born (Dvij), such as Kshatriyas or Vaisyas. Though penances have been prescribed for various other offences, but the penances prescribed for killing a Brahmin are definitely more rigorous. To harbour or give shelter to one who killed a Brahman, was also considered as an offence and the offender was liable for punishment. From the above, it is more than clear that Brahmans were given a preferential treatment in the eyes of law; however, there are instances, where punishments imposed on Brahmans were more stringent than inflicted upon Kshatriyas, Vaisyas and even Sudras. For theft a Sudra will pay 8 times the value of property while Vaisya will pay 16 times, Kshatriya will pay 32 times, and a Brahman will have to pay 64 times or 128 times of the value of the property.[31a] Therefore, the system of punishment did not always favour Brahmans, but it was graduated punishment according to Class or Varna.

It is quite perplexing to note that ancient Indians, or Aryans, who were so liberal that the domestic servants and even animals were given a very respectable place, why they were so rigid about *Varnasharam*? At the time of Shradha in *Shikhodak Mantra*, Hindus remembered even the family animals who died.[31b]

The sentence of death could be administered by hanging, beheading by sword, drowning, burning, killing by elephants and in so many other ways. The mutilation could also be done before killing the criminals. At times some people were killed in public. Vardhaman in his *Dandavivek* elucidates the mode of inflicting the sentence of death on the criminals.

Imprisonment

The punishment by way of *Avrodhan* and *Bandhan* has been mentioned in *Dandavivek* but it does not appear to be very popular with the early writers, however, Manu mentions in dealing with punishment to Vaishya, who commits adultery with protected Brahmin.[32] In some of the *smritis* and in *Arthasastra* even Karawas finds mention. Some of the writers lament even the condition of persons imprisoned.

Exile

The punishment by exile was quite common. Some of the criminals who were found guilty of grave offences were exiled, while others suffered exile conjointly with punishment of mutilation and confiscation of property.

In Ancient India, like countries of other old civilizations, punishment was inflicted to preserve the society against the selfish acts of certain persons. The offences against human body and king were viewed very severely. The king was the fountainhead of law though there were other sources of law including religion,[33] and as such modes of punishment also differed in view of gravity of the offence, caste of the accused as well as that of victim, age of the accused besides other considerations reflecting morality of the contemporary society which immensely valued the welfare of the masses even under monarchy.[34] In ancient India the welfare of the individual or collection of the riches of the world, was not the goal of this worldly strife, but they distinguished and quite early in human history, between eternal and perishable. They also realised that knowledge of soul is most efficacious of securing supreme bliss.[35] The study of Vedas leads to an increase of happiness and cause continuation of mundane human existence, i.e., *Pravritta* and at the same time it ensures supreme bliss and cause *Nivritta* and he, who sacrifices to the self alone equally recognizing the self in all created beings and all created beings in self becomes self luminous.[36] In the field of administration of justice, this Vedic concept remained central to all law givers and they aimed at virtuous conduct which leads to 'Param Padam.'[37]

REFERENCES

1. Danda is king. Danda is Purusha. Danda is Neta (leader) and Danda rules every one. Danda as narrated by learned Rishis, stands surety to observance of Dharma in all the four Ashramas. Danda governs all the creatures. Danda alone protects every one, and Danda keeps awake when all others sleep. Scholars interpret Danda as Dharma.

Danda administered in accordance with scriptures and after proper thought pleases Praja, but it destroys everything if administered without proper considerations.

2. अराजके हि लोकेअस्मिन्सवंतो विद्रते भयात। रक्षाममस्य सर्वस्य राजानमसृजत्प्रभुः।।
इन्द्रानिलयमाकांणाभग्नेश्च बरुणस्य च। चन्द्र वित्तेशयोश्चेव मात्रा निहृंत्य शाश्वतोः।।
यस्भादेषां सुरेन्द्राणां मात्राभ्यो निर्मितो नृपः। तस्मादभिभवत्येष सर्वभूतानि तेजसा।।
तपत्यादित्यवच्चेष यक्षूंषि च मनांसि च। न चेनं भूवि शबनोति कश्चिदप्यभिवीक्षितुम।।
साअग्निर्भवति वायुश्च सोअर्ककः शोभः स धर्मराद्। स कुबेरः स वरुणः स महेन्द्र प्रभावतः।।

Manusmriti—VII/3-7

3. यदि न प्रणयेद्राजा दण्डं उण्डभेष्वतन्द्रितः।
शूले मत्स्यानिवापक्ष्यन्दुर्बलान्बलवत्तराः।।
अषात्काकः पुरोडाशं श्वा च लिह्याद्ध विस्तथा।
स्वाभ्यं च न स्यात्कस्मिश्चित्प्रवतंताधरोत्तरम्।।

Manusmriti—VII/20-21

3 (b) *Manusmriti*—VII/17.

4. "The term Sutra literally means 'thread' but was used with the secondary meaning of a manual of instructions in the form of brief aphorisms: the whole title may be translated 'Manuals Explaining the Scriptures". A.L. Basham, *The wonder that was India*, p.112.

5. (a) "Though the text of Dharma—Sutras has not always been preserved with perfect purity, they have evidently retained their original character. They do not pretend to be anything more than the compositions of ordinary mortals, based on the teachings of the Vedas, on the decisions of those who are acquainted with the law, and on the customs of virtuous Aryas". F. Max Muller, Editor—'The Sacred Books of the East' Vol. 25. The laws of Manu, p.XI.

5. (b) "Nobody can doubt for a moment that these manuals are written by the teachers of the Vedic schools for the guidance of their pupils, that at first they were held to be authoritative in restricted circles and that they were later only acknowledged as source of the sacred law applicable to all Aryas." —F. Max Muller—Editor—*the Sacred Books of the* East, Vol. 25. The laws of Manu by G. Buhler, p. XI-XII.

6. Period of composition of Sutras—according to Prof. Kane-*Dharma Shastra Ka Itihasa*—stands as follows :–
Gautam Dharmasutra—600-400 B.C.
Apartama Dharmasutra—600-300 B.C.

Bandhayan Dharmasutra—500-200 B.C.
Vasistha Dharmasutra—300-100 B.C.
Vishnu Dharmasutra—300-100 B.C.

7. T. Burrow. 'The early Aryans, in *'The Cultural History of India'* ed. by A.L. Basham, p. 28.
8. Period of composition of *Dharmasastras*—
Manusmiriti—c 200 B.C. to 100 A.D.
Yajnavalkya Smriti—100 A.D. to 300 A.D.
Vishnu Dharmasastra—c 100 A.D. to 300 A.D.
Narad Smriti—c 100 A.D. to 400 A.D.
Brihaspati Smriti—c 300 A.D. to 400 A.D.
Katyayan Smriti—c 400 A.D. to 600 A.D.
Other Smritis such as *Palashari, Sankla* and *Deval Smriti*—c 600—900 A.D. Based on Kane's *Dharmasastra Ka Itihasa'*, Part-I.
9. 1. Commentary on *Manusmriti* by Vishwaroop. C-800—850 A.D.
   2. Commentary on *Yajna valkya Smriti* by Vighyaneshwar. C-1080-1100 A.D.
   3. Commentary on *Manusmriti* Medhatithi. C-825-900 A.D.
   4. Commentary on *Manusmriti* by Govind Raj. C-1080-1100 A.D.
   5. Commentary on *Yajna valkya* by Aprark. C-1100-1130 A.D.
   6. Commentary on *Manusmriti* by Kallook. C-1150-1300 A.D.
10. वेदोडखिलो धर्ममूलं स्मृतिशीले च तद्विदाम्।
आचारश्चैव साधूनामात्य न स्मन स्तुष्टिरेव च।।
Manusmriti—II/6
11. धर्मश्च व्यवहारश्च चरित्रं राजशसनम्।
विवादार्थश्चतुष्याद: पश्चिम: पूर्व वाधक:।।
Arthasastra—3/1/51
12. तस्यार्थे सर्वभूतानां गोप्तार धर्ममात्यजग्।
ब्रह्म तेजोमय दण्डम सृजत्पूर्वमाश्वर:।।
तस्य सर्वाणि भूतानि स्थविराणि चराणि च।
भयाभूदोगाय कल्पन्ते स्वधर्मान्न चलन्ति।।
Manusmriti—VII/14-15
13. "दण्ज्ञो रमनादित्या हुस्तेनां दान्तान्दभयते"
Gautam Smriti.
14. "The whole world is kept in order by punishment, for a guiltless man is hard to find, through fear of punishment the whole world yields the enjoyment (which it owes)."
Manusmriti-VII/22—translated by G. Buhler—the laws of Manu.
15. *Brihaspati Samhita*—22, 27-28.
16. A man (of equal caste) who defiles a willing maiden shall not

suffer the amputation of his fingers, but shall pay a fine of 200 (panas) in order to deter him from repetition (of the offence).

17. अधार्मिक त्रिभिन्यायैनिगृहणी यात्प्रयसतः।
निरोधनेन बन्धेन विविधेन व धेन च।
निग्रहेण हि पापानां साधूनां संग्रहेसा च।
द्विजालय इवेज्यागिः पयन्ते सततं नृपाः।।

Manusmriti—VIII/310-311

18. King shall appoint men for protection of people. They must protect the town from thieves in every direction to the distance of one Yojan. They must be made to repay what is stolen within these boundaries—*Apastamba—Prashna* II, *Patal* 10 *Khand* 26.

18a. "The Hindu Law repeatedly insist that the purpose of the king should be to put the wrong doer back in the right path". . . . S. Vardacharian—quoted in Dr. Sadhana Shukla *Prachin Bharat Mein Apradh Aur Danda* 1987, p. 94.

19. *Manusmriti*—XI/45-46 translated by G. Buhler.

20. "Thus in consequence of a remnant of (the guilt of former) crimes, are born idiots, dumb, blind, deaf and deformed men who are (all diseased) by the virtuous.

.Penances, therefore, must always be performed for the sake of purification, because those whose sins have not been expiated are born again, with disgraceful marks."

Manusmriti—XI/53-54 translated by G. Buhler.

21. वाग्दण्डं प्रथमं कुर्यादिग्दण्डं तदन्तरम।
तृतीय धनदण्ड तू बधदण्डमतः परम।।

Manusmriti—VIII/129।

22. *Manusmriti*—Ch.VIII.Sh. 130 translated by G. Buhler.

23. (a) जाति द्रव्यं परिमाणो विनियोगः परिग्रहः।
वयः शक्तिर्गणो देशः कालो दोष चहेतयः।।
वर्धमान–दण्ड विवेक–पृष्ठ—36 quoted in
Prachin Bharat Mein Apradh and
Danda—Dr. Sadhna Shukla.

(b) S.C. Bannerjee, Crime and Sex in Ancient India, p. 10

24. पणानां द्वेशते सार्धे प्रथमः साहसः स्मृतः। मध्यमः पंन्च विज्ञेयः सहसं त्वेव चोत्तमः।।

Manusmriti—VIII/138

25. यातु कन्यां प्रकुर्यात्स्त्री सासद्यौ मौण्डयमर्हति। अगुल्योरेव वा छेदं खरेरमो द्वहन तथा।।

Manusmriti—VIII/370

26. Kautilya *Arthashastra*—4/83/8.

27. Spellman—*Political theory of Ancient India* p. 115 quoted in *Prachin Bharat Mein Apradh and Danda* by Dr. Sadhna Shukla.

28. Angattar Nikay (11/1/1) included terms like *Shankha Mundika*

(Shaving of head like a conch), *Rahumukh* (mouth extended upto ears) *Jyotramlika* (setting fire after wrapping with oil soaked cloth) *Hashtaprajyalika* (setting fire after wrapping hands with oil soaked cloth) *Kharapatachhika* (applying salt after causing wounds) etc.

29. उपस्थ मुदरं जिह्वावा हत्तौ जादौ च पंचमम्।
चक्षुर्न सा च कर्णे च धनं देहस्तथैव च।।

Manusmriti—VIII/125

30. कूट शासनर्तृश्च प्रकृतीनां च दूषकान।
स्त्री बालब्राह्मण ध्नांश्च हन्याद् द्विटसे विनस्तथा।।

Manusmriti—IX/232

31. Brihaspati—*Pratirnak*/26.

31.(a) अष्टापद्य तु शैद्रस्य स्तेये भवति किल्विषम्।
षोडशैव तु वैश्यस्य द्वात्रिशत्क्ष त्रियस्य च।।
ब्राह्मणस्य चतुः षष्टिः पूर्ण वापि शतं भवेत्।
द्रिगुणा वा चतुः षष्टिस्तद् दोषगुणविद्वि सः।।

31.(b) ये त्वाग्नि दग्धा जीवा येप्यदग्धाः कुले मम।
भूमौ दत्तेन पिण्डेन तृप्ता यान्तु परां गतिम्।।

Manusmriti—VIII/337-338

32. वैश्यः सर्वस्व दण्डः सस्यात्संवत्सर निरोधतः।
सहस्रं क्षत्रियो दण्ड्यो मौण्ड्यं मूत्रेण चार्हति।।

Manusmriti—VIII/375

33. धर्मश्च व्यवहारश्च चरित्रं राजशासनम्।
विवादार्धश्चतुष्यादः पश्चिमः पूर्ववाधकः।

तन सत्ये स्थितो धर्मो व्यूवहारस्तु साक्षिषु।
चरित्रं संग्रहे पुसा राज्ञामाज्ञा तु शासनम्।।

Arthasastra—3/1/51-52

34. राज्य बृक्षस्य नृपतिर्मूलं स्वन्धाश्च मंत्रिणाः।।
शाखा सेनाधिपाः सेना पल्लवा कुसुमानि च।
प्रजाः फलानि भूमागा कीजं भूमिः प्रकल्पिता।।

Shukraniti—4/1257-58

35. सर्वोषामजि चैतेदात्मज्ञानं परं स्मृतम्।
तद्व्यग्रयं सर्वविद्यानां प्राप्यते ह्यमृतं ततः।।

Manusmriti—XII/85

36. सर्वभूतेषु चात्मानं सर्वभूतानि चात्मनि।
समं पश्चन्नात्मयाजी स्वराज्यमधिगच्छति।।

Manusmriti—XII/91

37. एवं यः सर्व भूतेषु पश्चत्मा त्मानमात्मना।
स सर्व समतामेत्य ब्रह्मभ्येति परं पदम्।। *Manusmriti*—XII/125

18

Ordeals as Prescribed in Ancient Indian Law Books

सत्यमर्थ च संपश्येदात्मानमथ साक्षिणः । अध्याय 8/45
देशं रूपं च कालं च व्यवहारविधौ स्थितः । मनुस्मृति
सद्भिराचरितं यत्स्याद्धार्मिकैश्च द्विजातिभिः । अध्याय 8/46
तद्देशकुलज्ञातीनामविरुद्धं प्रकल्पयेत् । मनुस्मृति

The King sitting in his court and engaged in judicial proceedings, must pay full attention to the truth, object, himself (Atman), witnesses, place, time and aspect, i.e., the nature of the case or the looks of the parties. The King shall establish law as has been practised by the virtuous men if it is not contrary to the çustoms of the regions (*Desh*) families and castes. To find out truth and to dispense justice is the most important duty of the King. While sitting at a court, therefore, 'As a hunter traces the lair of a (wounded) deer by the drops of the blood, even so the King shall discover on which side the right lies, by inferences (from the fact).[1] In deciding a case one has to ascertain truth and then to administer punishment if the conduct of the person complained against is contrary to law.

The first stage, i.e., the investigation to ascertain truth becomes very simple if the accused person confesses his guilt otherwise one has to prove or disprove the contention on the basis of witnesses.[2]

Narad, however, declares that documents and witnesses are the two methods of clearing up doubtful matters.[3] In cases of dispute with respect to property the proof depends on documents, witnesses and possession.[4] In ancient times as well witnesses used to pay very important role in proving a case in court of law.

The earliest reference to a *Sakshi* or a witness is found in *Swetaswataro Upnishad* and it is used as an attribute to God Almighty who sees the whole universe.[5] Panini also makes a reference to *Sakshi* but he refers him as an eye-witness but later on those who possessed even hearsay evidence were also referred as Sakshi.[6] Elaborate rule have been provided for witnesses, their examination and punishment for giving false evidence. The credit-worthiness of the witnesses has also been discussed in detail in Hindu law books. In certain cases where there is no evidence or there is contradiction in the statements of witnesses then cases would be decided on the basis of oaths (*Shapath*) and ordeals (*Divya*).

The earliest reference to ordeals are found in Vedas. In one case there is a reference in Atharva Veda, when Vatsa jumps into fire to prove his case that he is Brahman.[7] Apastamba also makes a pointed reference to *Divya Sakshya* or ordeal in connection with doubtful cases.[8] Others *Sutrakars* and *Shastrakars* mention ordeals in their books with elaborate details.

The provision regarding Ordeals and Oaths or Swearing aims at providing divine basis for administration of justice in cases when there is no evidence or where there could not be any evidence, oral, documentary or circumstantial. In minor cases of claims and counter-claims, the case could be decided on the basis of oath only. Narad declared that 'Justice is based on truth and litigation on witnesses. When a case admits on divine test, human evidence (the testimony of witnesses) or documents must not be resorted to'.[9] In cases where due to negligence of the creditor both documentary and oral evidence is not available and the opponent desires the obligation that three methods were prescribed: the timely reminder, argument and lastly on oath (as a form of ordeal).[10] There is mention in the Puranas, that Vasistha when he was suspected by Visvamitra had to take oath to clear the allegation.[11]

Types of Ordeals

The ordeals could be of various types. Some were very simple such as ordinary oaths and sacred libation while others were of intricate type. Narad classified these ordeals in following categories[12] :—

1. Ordeal by balance (*Tula*).
2. Ordeal by fire (*Agni*).
3. Ordeal by water (*Jal*).
4. Ordeal by poison (*Visha*).
5. Ordeal by sacred libation (*Kosh Divya*).
6. Rice Ordeal (*Tandul*).
7. Ordeal by hot piece of gold.

Brihaspati[13] and Pitamah add two ordeals to the above list namely the plough-share ordeal and ordeal by Dharma or Adharma. In addition to above ordeals oath or *Shapath* was also administered to extract truth from the person who has been alleged against. In *Manusmriti* provision has been made for *Shapaths* of various types. Manu ordains that *Shapath* like any other punishment should also be graduated i.e. it should be in accordance with caste or Varnas. Brahman should swear by truth or veracity, Kshatriya by his weapons and chariot (*Vahan*), Vaishya by his kine, grain and gold and Sudra by imprecating on his own head.[14] In addition to above methods of *Shapath* a practice of touching head of wife and son was also recognized by *Manusmriti*.[15] Some of these practices are still in vogue in rural India and minor cases are decided on the basis of *Shapath* with local variations.

Ordeal by Balance

The apparatus for ordeal by balance *(Tula* or *Dhata)* consists of a beam suspended on two wooden posts. The elaborate details of the measurements have been given by Narad and Vishnu.[16] The beam should be made of Khadira or Tinduka wood, with three *Sthanas* for hooks. This could also be made of Simsapa or Sal wood, if wood of Khadira is not available. The scales should be suspended at the extrem of the beams by iron hooks. The scales should move in Toranas which facilitate the measurement of the movement of the *Tula (Scales)*.

When scales ready then the person undergoing ordeal weighed. He weighed in the scale on the northern side while the weights or stones kept on the southern side of the scale. In weighing and inspection of weighing apparatus, help of experts like goldsmiths, merchants and others experienced in the art of weighing taken. After first weighing the man asked to ascend the scales again but after the judge or Brahman should recite the following.[17]

"Thou art called Dhata (a balances) which appellation is synonymous with Dharma (Justice).

Thou knowest the bad and good actions of all being. This man being arraigned in a cause is weighed upon thee.

Thou art superior to gods, demons and mortals in point of veracity. (*Thou balance, hast been created*) *by the gods in time out of mind, as a receptacle of truth.*

Design, to speak truth therefore O propitious being and deliver me from this perplexity. If I am an offender take me down. If you knowest me to be innocent, take me upwards. Therefore mayst thou deliver him lawfully from the perplexity in which he is involved".

If on second weigh he i.e. he weighs less than the first weighing then he considered innocent. If his weight remain the same or increased he acquitted. Should the balance break or the beam or the hooks split or the string burst or the transverse beam split he declared innocent.[18] In the above circumstances Vishnu declares that he should be weighed again while Brihaspati holds him guilty. Katyayan and Vyasa also support Vishnu in this respect. Further Vishnu provides imprecation of the balance to be done in third person by the judge while in Narad the italics portion is in first person implying therefrom that the man undergoing ordeal also imprecates the balance.

The balance should be erected in a public place near the gates of the royal palace, in sight of a temple, (in a cross-road etc.) dug firmly in the ground after performing purificatory and auspicious ceremonies and after invoking the guardians of the world in public view. Such ordeals be administered in forenoon (Narad) and the person (to be tested) having fasted for a day and a night taken a bath and wearing his wet dress.[19] Any of the ordeals should not be administered unless the person declares himself ready for the ordeal. In cases of high treason, however, he could be forced to undergo the ordeal.

This particular ordeal is based on the common belief that when a Patak is committed by a person then this sin will stick to him which will increase his weight, i.e., the burden of the guilt. When Dharma is imprecated then due to divine intervention the weight should be reduced in second weighing if the person is innocent.

Ordeal by Fire

In this ordeal the person to be tested (Shodhya) had, to walk a distance of about 256 angulas with burning hot iron ball in his hands. If he succeed in walking that distance without having any marks of burning on his hands then he declared innocent.

The procedure has been described in detail in *Narad Smriti* (I/285-303).[20] Eight circles[21] have to be drawn on the ground and interval between the two circle was to be thirty two angulas, therefore, measuring 256 angulas in all. The hot piece of iron should be heated up by blacksmith. The iron ball should be fifty *palas* which is to be given in the hands of the person to be tested. The Shodhya should have seven leaves of holy tree (Ashwath) and these leaves be tied properly with seven threads.

Vishnu mentions only Mantras to be pronounced by the Judge which is in third person while Narad in addition mentions Mantra to be pronounced by the person so tested.[22] The man starts from first circle (facing east) putting one part in each circle and throws the ball after covering eighth circle. If his hands did not show any sign of burning or scarring then he is acquitted.

Ordeal by Water

In this ordeal a man has to ramain in the water for sufficient period of time. If the suspect successfully remains under water then he declared innocent otherwise he is held guilty.

This ordeal should be performed in the water of streams (which do not have swift current), oceans, lakes, ponds and pools.[23] The water should be free from mud, aquatic plants, vicious animals, large rapacious animals, fish, leeches and other animals.[24] This ordeal should not be performed in winter and dewy season.[25] Women, children, sick or feeble men should not be subjected to this ordeal. Similarly cowards or those tormented by pain have also been exempted from this trial.[26]

In this ordeal judge near the water and another man stands in the water navel deep. The suspect also stands in the water. The judge shots an arrow and sends another person to the place where the arrow lands. At this point of time the crime was written and placed on the head of the suspect who recites Mantra as in other ordeals.[27] The judge gives a signal when suspect dives and another young man runs to fetch the arrow. If suspect is not seen above the water during this period he is declared innocent. If his limbs are seen (even one limb) then he is declared guilty.

Ordeal by Poison

In this ordeal a particular quantity of specified poison is administered to the suspect and he is kept under watch upto sun set. If he does not show any violent symptoms of poison or does not become unconscious then he is acquitted otherwise held guilty.

In the ordeal by poison, the poisons like Kalkuta and Alabu are not to be administered. Only the poison derived from Sringa plant grown in Himalaya, should be administered that too of excellent quality having required colour, odour and tests.[28] The quantity of the poison has also been prescribed according to season.[29] The poison is administered in butter and the suspect is kept in shade and watched. Poison should not be given in the afternoon, twilight or at noon. The ordeal by poison should be avoided likewise in autumn, summer, spring and rainy seasons.[30]

The poison should not be administered to Brahman while Kshatriyas, Vaisya and Sudra could be subjected to it.[31] The poison should not be given to infants, ascetics, disabled persons or who have committed a very light offence.

Ordeal by Sacred Libation

In this ordeal consecrated water (three mouthsful) is given to the suspect for drinking. If misfortune falls on him within a fortnight then he is declared guilty otherwise he is announced innocent.[32]

The ordeal has been described in detail in Smritis of Yagyavalkya, Narad, Vishnu, Brihaspati and also by Pitamah. The water used for bathing the deities like Durga and Aditya is given to the suspect for drinking (three handsful) and one has to wait for a period of a week or a fortnight while in other ordeals the results are almost instantaneous. The weapons of the deities are bathed in water for instance Shula in case of Durga and other weapons in case of other gods. The consecrated water is given to the suspect early in the morning by a virtuous man. The ordeal by libation should not be administered to hardened criminals, irreligious men, eunuchs, low rascals, unbelievers, Vratyas and slaves.[33]

The Rice Ordeal

The rice ordeal involves chewing of rice by the suspect. If the suspect is guilty then blood should come from his teeth or gums or there may be other symptoms indicating hurt to the suspect or the defendant.

In this ordeal rice is cleansed properly and then put in earthen pot which is kept in the sun. The water is poured on the rice and then dried up. This dried up rice is then given to the suspect for chewing thrice. Later on the suspect is made to spit on the leaves of Peepal or Bhury trees. When rice is offered to the suspect or Shodya then he must face east. He is further asked to proclaim the charge. The rice ordeal has limited use as it is to be administered in the case of theft or larceny.[35]

The ordeal of the hot piece of gold

This ordeal is performed by the suspect by taking out gold or gold coin from the boiling hot clarified butter (ghee) kept into the vessel.

This ordeal involves taking out of hot piece of gold (Taptamasha) or mudrika from a vessel. This vessel could be of gold, silver, iron or earth. It should be filled by liquid which may be clarified butter (*Ghrit*). The judge recites the following Mantras :—

"Thou art the best instrument of purification O Clarified butter and comparable to Ambrosia at a sacrifice. Burn this man at once if he is criminal and be as cold as ice to him if he is innocent".[36] If the fingers are unhurt the man is considered innocent otherwise guilty.[37]

The ordeal by Ploughshare

This ordeal is neither found in *Vishnu Samhita* nor in *Narad Samhita* but it finds mention in *Brihaspati Samhita*. Dr. Kane mentions that this particular Divya is also found in *Smriti Chandrika* and *Vyavahar Prakash*.

In the ordeal a ploughshare is made of iron twelve Palas in weight. This ploughshare should be eight anguls in length. The thief is asked to lick the ploughshare after making it red hot. If he is not burnt he obtains acquittal, otherwise he loses his cause. This ordeal also finds mention in *Viramitrodaya* in Jibananda Vidyasagar's edition.

The ordeal by Dharma

In this method two idols are made one of Dharma and other of Adharma. Both these idols are kept in a jar then the suspect takes out one. If he gets Dharma pratima he is acquitted otherwise he stands convicted. In certain cases where it is not possible to have idols made of metal then the judge can make sketch depicting Dharma and Adharma on the leaf of Bhurj tree and then the suspect is asked to pick up one out of the two after reciting the usual Mantra. If he picks up Dharma he is acquitted and should be honoured.[39]

The administration of justice by way of ordeals was subject to certain general principles which have been given in Narad and Vishnu Samhitas.

The ordeals should be administered when no witnesses are forthcoming from both the parties. Further ordeals shall not be administered to anyone without consent. In a cause both the parties should be agreeable to the performance of ordeals.

The ordeals were to be administered only in serious crimes and in ordinary or trifling crimes only oath or Shapath be resorted to.[40] In case of criminal action against King or of violence the ordeals were to be administered indiscriminately, i.e., in cases of minor nature also.

During the rains the ordeal by fire was to be administered but it should never be administered in hot seasons. The ordeal by balance be undergone during the autumn season but never in stormy weather. The ordeal by water was to be applied in summer but never in cold weather. The ordeal by poison was to be applied in winter season but not in rainy season.

The ordeal by water was not to be applied to distressed, persons, asthmatic person, nor for those who earn their livelihood from water like fishermen etc. and the poison was not to be given to lepers, bilious persons, or Brahmans. The ordeal by fire was not to be given to lepers, infirm persons or blackmiths. The ordeal by sacred libation should not be given to atheists. Nobody was to be administered any of these ordeals when country is afflicted with disease or pestilence.[41]

In cases of breach of trust, larceny and robbery (Sahas) the ordeals were to be administered in accordance with value and Varna of the defendant. The value of the property was to be estimated in gold. If the value of the property in dispute was less than one Krishnala, a Sudra must be made to swear by a blade of grass, if the amount is less than two Krishnalas he has to swear by Tila if the value is more than two but less than three Krishnalas the Sudra has to swear by a blade of silver. If the amount is more than five Krishnlas but less than half a Suvarna then a Sudra has to undergo one of the ordeals prescribed. The Vaisya was also supposed to undergo same ordeals but in each case the amount in dispute was to be twice as high as prescribed for Sudra. Similarly for Kshatriyas the amount should have been thrice as high while in case of Brahman it was four times as high.[42] For instance the members of all the four Varnas will swear with Durva grass in hand if the amount involved in case of Brahmans was less than four Krishnalas, in case of Kshatriyas less than three Krishnalas, in case of Vaisya less than two Krishnalas and in case of Sudra less than one Krishnala.

In cases of previous convictions, an exception was made to the general rule and a person having previous convictions was required to undergo ordeals even for a trifling and as against this a man who was known to be honest among the virtuous men was not to be administered the ordeals even in matters of important contests.[43]

The anthropological studies have revealed that from the first day of the appearance of life on earth the cycle of change has become operational in all diverse fields. With the arrival of homo sapien errectus, on the world scene this change has been more perceptible. The early growth and dispersal might have been from one region but for considerable period of human history the islands of enlightenment and progress were separated by oceans of darkness and ignorance. These islands of progress later organized themselves as nations and developed their own civilization and culture. As Maitland has said that races and nations do not always travel by the same roads and at the same rate but there is striking similarity in the evolution of social institutions in these islands of progress separated by darkness and barbarism. In the evolution of jurisprudence also this fact is amply proved. In India in the early stages, various provisions were incorporated in Hindu law books and the same provisions were found in use in other countries having different political and legal systems. Some of the provisions of Manu's law were found mentioned in Chinese books. Similarly the provisions of ordeals were also in use in England. The ordeal by hot piece of iron and boiling water was prevalent in England. Ordeal by water was also practised there and it was considered to be honourable way of committing suicide.[44] In England such practices were banned by law in 1215 A.D.

The ordeals discussed in foregoing paragraphs have been in use in India for a very long time. There is evidence to point out that these ordeals were practised in India even upto 18th century. In India, the basic concept of social structure were enshrined in Vedic literature but it took a concrete shape in period of Sutras (Griha Sutra, Dharma Sutras and Kalpa Sutras). All the later writers writing *Samhitas* and *Nibandhas* were not giving new law but always professed that the law interpreted by them was laid down by Prajapati Manu and they were only interpreters of the same. All the changes in law necessitated by social evolution were accommodated by way of updated interpretation. This tendency continued till 10th-11th century A.D. which marks the beginning of Muslim influence. Muslim rulers did not interfere with Hindu law. They on the contrary encouraged compilation of Hindu law and results in the form of Narsimha Prasad (by Dalpati in 16th century) and Vyavahar-Saukhya (by Todarmal—Akbar's minister) were quite rewarding. In the last phase of the Hindu law the judicial system merged into English system gradually. The personal laws of Hindus were left untouched by Britishers. During early period the Hindu Pandits were consulted by the British Judiciary. The growth of the legal system stopped in India after 10th-11th century AD and mainly compilation work was taken up during Muslim and British periods. From the above it would appear that "the current of Hindu Judicial system and administration is an unbroken one even since the Vedic times, extending over many thousands of years and surviving inspite of many vicissitudes of fortune in the history of the country",[45] and it applies to the ordeals prescribed in Hindu law though they may appear quite absurd in the present context. In this connection it is desirable to evaluate Hindu legal system in historical perspective and appreciate the genius of those who evolved the system which is still alive and which held the society together for roughly 5000 years.

REFERENCES

1. G. Buhlr, *The Laws of Manu*, p. 261.

   यथा नयत्सृक्यातमृर्गस्य मृगयुः पदम्।
   नयेत्तथानुमानेन धर्मस्य नृपतिः पद्म।। मनुस्मृति-अध्याय 8/44

2. 'In disputed cases the truth shall be established by means of witnesses'. Gautam-XIII/I from the sacred books of the Aryas Pt. I by G.Buhler, p. 246.
3. "Documents and (the testimony of) witnesses are declared to be the two methods for clearing up doubtful matters, where two parties are quarrelling with one another." Narad-1/3 from the Minor Law Books, J. Jolly, p.5.
4. *Vasishtha*—XVI/10.
5. "एको देवः सर्वभूतेषु गूठः–साक्षी चेता केवलो निर्गणश्च।–श्वेताश्वतरोपनिषद्-6/11
   As quoted in '*Dharma Shastra Ka Itihasa*' by Dr. P.V. Kane translated by AC Kashyap Pt. II, p. 735.
6. Dr. V.S. Agarwal, '*India as known to Panini*'. p. 417.
7. (a) Quoted by Dr. P.V. Kane, '*Dharma Shastra Ka Itihasa*'—Pt. II, p. 747.

(a) आ दधामि ते पदं समिदे जातवेदसि।
अग्निः शरीरं वेवेष्ट्वसुं वागपि गच्छत।। अथर्ववेद-2/1218

(b) वत्सस्य ह्यमिशस्तस्य पुरा भ्राता यवीयता।
नाग्निर्ददाह रोमापि सत्येन जगतः स्पृशः।। मनुस्मृति अध्याय 8/116

8. 'In doubtful cases (they shall give their decision) after having ascertained (the truth) by inference, ordeals and the like (means). Apastamba II/II/29/6— The sacred laws of the Aryas—Pt. I by G. Buhler.

9. (a) "Where a heavy (grave) crime has been committed—the ruler shall administer one of the ordeals. In light cases, on the other hand, a virtuous king shall swear a man with (various) oaths.—Narad—I/249/100
10. Narad—I/18/235-236—Translated by J. Jolly. 'The Minor Law Books',pp. 96-97.
11. The story is mentioned in Puranas that sage Vishwamitra accused Vasistha in the court of King Sudas that the former had eaten his hundred sons in the form of a Rakshasa. Vasistha thereupon took oath and said, 'I will fall dead on the spot if I am a Rakshasa'. Saptarishis also accused one another of the theft of lotus fibres. The doubts were cleared by taking oath. Indra also had to undergo an ordeal when he was suspected with Ahilya.
12. Vishnu gives following types of ordeals (Vishnu X-XIV).
    1. Ordeal by balance.
    2. Ordeal by fire.
    3. Ordeal by water.
    4. Ordeal by poison.
    5. Sacred libation.
13. Brihaspati—X/5 translated by J. Jolly in 'The Minor Law Books' p. 315.
14. सत्येन शापयेद्विप्रं क्षत्रियं वाहनायुधैः।
    गोबोजकान्चनेवैश्यं शूद्रं सर्वेस्तु पातकैः।। मनुस्मृति अध्याय 8/113
15. (a) अग्निं वाहारयेदेनमप्से चैनं निमज्जयेत्।
    पुत्रदारस्य वाप्येन शिरसि स्पर्शयेत्पृथक।। मनुस्मृति अध्याय 8/113
    (b) "Truth, a vehicle, weapons, cows, seeds and gold, venerable gods, or Brahmans, the heads of sons or wives ; by these have oaths been ordained which are easy to perform and proper for trifling occasions".
    Brihaspati—X/6/7—in the 'Minor Law Books' by J. Jolly—p. 315.
16. (a) Narad I/261—266.
    (b) Vishnu X/2—6.
17. Narad—I/277—284 in the 'Minor Law Books' by J. Jolly, pp.107-108.
18. (a) 'In case of the strings bursting or of the splitting of the transverse beam the man should be placed in the scale once more. Thus the facts will be ascertained positively and a just sentence be the result'.
    Vishnu—XI/13 in the 'Minor Law Books' by J. Jolly, p. 57.
    (b) "Should the scale break, or the balance or beam or iron hooks split or the strings burst or the transverse beam split, he would have to be declared guilty", Brihaspati—X/20 in the 'Minor

Law Books' by J. Jolly, p.317.
19. Narad—I/268-269.
20. (a) Yagyavalkya—II/107.
(b) Katyayan—441.
(c) Narad—I/285/303.
(d) Vishnu—XI/1-12.
(e) Dr. P.V. Kane in *Dharma Shastra Ka Itihasa*, p. 752.
21. (a) "He must make seven circles, sixteen angulas in breadth each, the intervals being of same breadth".
Vishnu—XI/2 in the 'Minor Law Book', by J. Jolly, p. 57.
(b) Dr. Kane in his *Dharma Shastra Ka Itihasa* Vol. II (page 752) mentions about nine circles in the form of agni, Varun, Vaya, Yama, Indra, Kuber, Som, Savita and Vishwadeva, instead of eight of Narad, and seven of Vishnu.
22. (a) 'Thou O fire, dwellest in the interior of all creatures, like a witness. O Fire thou knowest what mortals do not comprehend. 'This man being arraigned in a cause desires to be cleared from guilt. Therefore mayest thou deliver him lawfully from this perplexity"—Vishnu—XI/11-12.
(b) Narad Smriti gives slightly different Mantras but there are also in third person but in commentaries Narad has been quoted differently and Mantra is addressed to fire is in first person : 'Thou O fire, dwellest in the interior of all deities as a flame. Thou conveyest burnt—oblation to the gods and givest peace of mind.
"Thou, O God, knowest the secret offends and merits of men. Thou, O deity knowest whatever mortals do not comprehend. "Arrainged in a cause, I am about to be tested by fire. Therefore deign to deliver me lawfully from the perplexity in which I am involved".
Narad—V/41-43—The 'Minor Law Book', by J. Jolly, p. 255.
23. Narad I/305.
24. Vishnu—XII/2.
25. Narad—I/304.
26. Narad—I/313-314.
27. 'Thou, O water, dwellest in the interior of all creatures, like a witness. O water thou knowest what mortals do not comprehend. 'This man being arraigned in a cause, desirer to be cleared from guilt. Therefore mayest thou deliver him lawfully from this perplexity".—Vishnu—XII/7-8.
28. (a) Narad I/321/322.
(b) Dr. P.V. Kane also mentions Vatsanasil (derived from Vatsa plant) in his *Dharma Shastra Ka Itihasa*, p. 753.

29. 'Six Yavas should be given in the rainy season, five yavas in the hot season, seven or eight in the winter season, in the autumn season this ordeal must not take place'.
    Narad I/324 in the 'Minor Law Books' by J. Jolly, p. 61.
30. Narad I/320.
31. Narad I/ 322.
32. "To whatsoever deity the accused happens to be devoted let (the judge) bathe the weapon of that deity in water, and give him to drink three handsful of it.
    "He to whom no calamity happens, within a week or a fortnight (either to himself or) to his son, wife or property, is innocent beyond doubt".
    Brihaspati—X/23-24—in the 'Minor Law Books' by J. Jolly, p. 318.
33. Narad—I/328/332.
34. This ordeal finds mention in Narad (I/337/342) and Brihaspati (X-25) but does not find any mention in Vishnu Samhita.
35. Narad—I/337.
36. Narad—I/346/347.
37. Brihaspati—X/26-27.
38. Brihaspati—X/28-29.
39. Brihaspati—X/33.
40. Narad—I/247-259.
41. Vishnu—IX/20/32.
42. Vishnu—IX/1-14.
43. Vishnu—IX/18-19.
44. Stephens in '*History of Criminal Law of England*' Vol. I, p. 73 as referred in '*Dharma Shastra Ka Itihasa*' by Dr. P.V. Kane, Vol. II, p. 755.
45. P.B. Mukerjee in 'The Hindu Judicial System p. 442 in the 'Cultural Heritage of India' edited by Dr. S. Radhakrishnan and others.

19

Environmental Crime and Legislative Response

"We are earth, the people, plants and animals, rains and oceans, breath of forest and the flow of the sea. We honour earth as the home of all the living things. We cherish earth's beauty and diversity of life. We welcome earth's ability to renew as being the basis of all life. We accept a shared responsibility to protect and restore earth and to allow a wise and equitable use of resources so as to achieve an ecological balance and new social economic and spiritual value."[1]

The environment is whole physical and biological envelope, in which all organism live and interact with each other. The quality of life depends upon the equitable and wise use of resources and disciplined interaction with other forms of life for mutual benefit. The man being capable of transforming the 'terrafirma' by way of utilization of physical resources and also taming the forces of nature has to act responsibly so that ecological balance is not disturbed. In nature nothing is irrelevant and without sufficient cause. In our keenness to improve our quality of life, if we negligently or intentionally disturb this balance in ecological terms, the nature is bound to react which may at times prove to be catastrophic in consequence not only to human beings but to all living beings and also to those who are likely to come to live hereafter.

The rapid population growth has increased urbanisation and the consumerism that follows which has led to depletion of resources. Rapid industrialisation besides using natural resources indiscriminately can also affect the elements of weather and at times change global climate, resulting into wide-spread changes and consequential readjustment of various elements of nature. Non-renewable resources of energy if depleted are likely to affect long-term viability of industrial development and resultant halt of economic growth. Rapid urbanisation and house building activity will cover the areas of arable land and the pressure of agricultural persuits can reduce floral cover which may affect climate and also the composition of atmosphere. If the present trend continues then in twenty first century will be more crowded, polluted with less natural resources facing crisis of energy, shortage of fresh water and breathing more polluted air besides damaging the protective ozone layer of stratosphere.

The industrialised countries are mostly confronted with the problems as a result of wanton use of natural resources for luxurious living while the poor countries suffer depletion of soil cover, pressure on forest land in their anxiety to feed teaming millions increasing despite best efforts.

Evolution of Environmental Legislation in India

The Indian Society from the very beginning believed in cosmic unity and treated not only other forms of life but also the objects of nature with dignity. The ritual prescribed in Vedic hymns also support this shared responsibility. The utilization of natural resources was also governed by the principles of utmost conservation. Kings were also ordained to issue orders not to kill animals capable of procreating.[2]

The high standard of hygiene maintained at public places can be guessed from Kautilya's *Arthashastra* wherein the deterrent punishment is prescribed for violation of normal conduct meant for responsible and respectable citizens.[3]

Mauryan edicts under the influence of Buddhist compassion preached total non-violence and tolerance. The ill-treatment of animals was strictly viewed by the State. Various *samhitas* also prescribed penances for common people for the lapses in violation of moral code. Specially the trees of primary leaves like peepal were worshipped.[4]

Cow and other useful animals were also given a special place.[5]

The rivers and the mountains were also worshipped in human form. The fruits of tree and water from rivers and ponds were considered gifts of God and were taken as *Prasada*.

So long as the religious hold remained paramount this code of conduct coupled with social sanction was observed strictly but with the dawn of industrialization in the west and intrusion and invasion from all directions of the country demolished the old values. The invaders who could not rule the country for the long period did not have any impact on socio-cultural life of the country and regulatory force of *samhitas* and *smirtis* remained uninterrupted. But with the arrival of Arabs and Moghals, the Hindu law lost its effectiveness. Precisely this was the time when Europeans came to India and later on Britishers established their empire. The Britishers consolidated Indian law. Most of the enactments dealing with various aspects of socio-political life came into being during this period.

Environmental Law in Pre-Independence India

Indian Penal Code was drafted in 4th decade of nineteenth century by Lord Macaulay but it could become law only in 1860. Before 1860 English Criminal Law was followed in Presidency Towns of Bombay, Calcutta and Madras but in other parts of British India the courts were administering justice on the basis of Mohammedan and Hindu Criminal Law. Chapter - 14 of the Indian Penal Code deals with offences affecting the public health, safety, convenience, decency and morals. Sections 268 to 291 of Cr. P.C. deal with subject affecting environment while other four sections deal with public morals. Broadly speaking the provisions of chapter - 14 deals with diverse subjects like public nuisance, infectious diseases, adulteration of foods and drinks making atmosphere noxious to health and dangerous negligent conduct. As far as environment is concerned the provisions contained in sections 277 and 278 are quite important.

Police Act of 1861 contains some regulatory provisions for convenience of general public. The Criminal Procedure Code of 1861 (Act XXV of 1861) which was replaced by Act X of 72 and again amended by Act X, 1882 also provides for removal of nuisance. The Criminal Procedure Code was amended and altered many a time before and after independence but it retains the original provision with respect to public nuisance. Other important Acts enacted during pre-independence India dealing with subjects of environmental protection include the Shore Nuisance Act of 1853, Indian Forest Act, 1865, North Canal and Drainage Act, 1873, Indian Fisheries Act, 1897 and others.[6]

Legislative Response in Post-Independence Period

With the dawn of independence the country became Democratic Republic under a progressive looking Constitution. The enactments that came into being after independence reflect the spirit of the Constitution as summarised in the Preamble of the Constitution. Immediately after independence the country embarked on the path of progress both in the field of agriculture and industry. Large-scale financial assistance from other countries was received with a view to accelerating exploitation of natural resources to ameliorate the living conditions of the masses. The land development no doubt accelerated economic growth and technological development but at the same time measures to improve the working conditions of labour force were also taken up and Acts like the Industries (Development and Regulation) Act, 1951, Insecticide Act, 1968, Atomic Energy Act, 1969, Radiation Protection Rule, 1971 were enacted.

The Stockholm Conference of 1972

The historic Stockholm Conference (1972) represented the

first major effort to tackle the problems relating to environment on an international plank. Prior to this conference President John. F. Kennedy while addressing United Nations General Assembly on Sept. 20, 1963, had said, "Never before has man had such capacity to control his own environment to end thirst and hunger to conquer poverty and diseases, to vanish illiteracy and massive human misery." With this backdrop there was a general realisation that we hold the earth and all its resources in trust for future generations and we are only entitled to use and benefit from these to the extent which is absolutely necessary. Mrs. Indira Gandhi the then Indian Prime Minister had attended the conference and concluded thus: "Environmental problems of developing countries are not the side effects of excessive industrialisation but reflect the inadequacy of development—are not poverty and need the greatest polluters?" The Stockholm Conference stressed upon the use of science and technology for solving environmental problems. It also emphasised the need for education in environmental matters, research and development in the field of conservation and also international co-operation to achieve the goals set by the conference. A National Committee of Environmental Planning and Co-ordination (NCEPC) was set up in 1972. In the aftermath of the 1972 declaration we brought about 46th amendments to the Constitution which inserted the new Article 48-A which says, "The States shall endeavour to protect and improve the environment and to safeguard the forests and wild life of the country." Article 51-A creates a duty for every citizen and says, "It shall be the duty of every citizen of India to protect and improve the natural environment including forests, lakes, rivers and wild life and to have compassion for living creatures."

Legislative Response after Stockholm Conference

Immediately after Stockholm Conference, Central Pollution Control Board (CPCB) was set up and the Water (Prevention and Control of Pollution) Act, 1974 was enacted. The Act provides for the prevention and control of water pollution and maintaining and restoring of wholesomeness of water.

The Act also provides for establishment of Central and States Boards to achieve the goals set by the Act. This Act was amended in 1978. The Act now requires that no person shall throw or discharge any poisonous, noxious or polluting matter in any stream or well. It also prohibited to discharge sewage or effluents into a stream without the consent of the Board. The Act also has penal provision for imprisonment of term of 3 months or a fine of Rs. 5000 or both for contravention of the regulatory provisions. In case of continuing failure, provision for additional fine upto Rs. 1000 per day has also been provided.

The Air (Prevention and Control of Pollution) Act, 1981 came into force from May 16, 1981. This Act also provides for establishment of Central and States Board vested with powers to devise ways and means to improve the quality of air and control pollution. The Boards are also authorised to lay down standard for industrial units. This Act also provides for Penal Provision for contravention of the Act.

As has been discussed earlier the pressure on forest land has become almost unbearable since independence, specially in the wake of green revolution in India. The first Forest Act was enacted in 1865. Later on it was thoroughly revised in 1927. With the change of environmental awareness and international pressure it was considered incumbent to revise that therefore the Forest (Conservation) Act, 1980 has come into being, with utmost emphasis on conservative aspect. It is a very comprehensive Act which provides that no State Government or other authority shall make rules without the prior approval of the Central Government or permit with respect to any reserved forest or any portion thereof to seize to be reserved or any forest or any portion thereof to be used for non-forest purposes. This enactment was brought into force to provide for the conservation of forest by completely banning indiscriminate diversion of forest lands for non-forest purposes. The Act was further amended to define 'Non-Forest Purposes' and it was specifically mentioned that plantation of tea, coffee, spices, rubber, palm oil bearing plants, medicinal plants and horticulture plants shall be treated non-forest activity. The penal provisions were also introduced into the Act to provide for contravention of this Act.

As a sequel to the recommendations made by Tiwari Committee constituted in 1980 wide-ranging changes were brought about in the legislation concerning environmental protection. The study made by Tiwari Committee pointed out lack of comprehensive approach to the problem and also that administrative set up is not properly tuned to tackle such problems.

The Government took immediate decision and the Environment (Protection) Act of 1986 came into being. This Act was enacted with a view to protecting and improving environment in integrated manner thereby reducing hazards to human life that also provided list of subjects with respect to which Central Government will exercise power. The Act also empowered the Central Government to issue directions to close or order, prohibition or regulation of any industry, stoppage or regulation of supply of electricity, water or any other services. The Act defines environment which includes water, air and land, the inter-relationship which exists between human beings and other living creatures, micro organism and property.

EPA also provided for stringent punishment including fine upto Rs. 1 lakh and imprisonment upto 5 years. In case of company, firm or government departments the officer incharge was made responsible for the lapses and contraventions hence made liable for the punishment.

The Earth Summit of 1992 at Rio-de-Janeiro stressed the need for fixing liability of owners and also the compensation of the victims. Government of India enacted National Environmental Tribunal Act, 1995 for fixing liability and expeditious disposal of claims for damages. In this connection Government of India have also issued an ordinance for the establishment of National Environmental Appellate Authority in 1997. The authority shall have a former Judge of Supreme Court and a Judge of High Court as its chairperson, a vice-chairperson and 3 expert members. This authority will hear appeals made by the persons aggrieved by the orders of appropriate authority in connection with grant of environmental clearance.

After independence Democratic Socialistic Governments both at the Centre and the states remained very sensitive to issues of environment protection and all efforts have been made to provide necessary legislative support to the international declarations and the constitutional provisions but law has not been very effective and in this connection one tends to agree with Shri T.N. Dhar when he says, "It is now widely realised that if a constructive complementarity between development and conservation is to be evolved in terms of sustainability, in addition to policies and resources, legal strategies and procedure as well as the mechanisms for compliance and enforcement are essential to combat environmental degradation, hazards to life forms, and neglect of air, earth or water resources."[8] The implementation of the agenda items could not keep pace with the legislative action, partly because of lack of awareness and commitment of the masses and partly because of paucity of funds.

Law dealing with Environmental Crime

The offences created to deal with violations of standards prescribed for protection of environment and conservations of resources are very recent in origin. The 'first generation legislations' were satisfied with setting up regulatory procedure with respect to disposal of effluents from factories causing harm to public at large. These legislations were enacted in a hurry. Later on some of the discoveries made in the field of medical science brought to light relationship between certain chemicals and cancer and certain deformities in human beings. Such discoveries coupled with accidents in some of the factories producing dangerous substances necessitated 'second generation' legislations to impose control on the production of such chemicals and also introduced strict standards for safety of the workers and public at large.

After 1972 conference, the emphasis has been on "both aspects of man's environment, the natural and the man-made, are essential to his well being and to the enjoyment of basic human rights, even the right to life itself." The conference observed with grave concern", the dangerous level of pollution of water and air and living beings, major and undesirable disturbances to ecological balance of the bio-sphere, destruction and gross deficiencies harmful to the physical, mental and social health of man, in the man-made environment, particularly in living and working environment". The African Community of Nations in view of above observation decided that, "all people shall have the right to a general satisfactory environment favourable to their development."[9]

The deliberations of these conferences enjoined upon the national governments to take more serious measures in the interest of mankind. The third generation legislations are the direct result of these conferences and the concern shown by community of nations towards tragedies like Bhopal gas leak in India and Flixborough and Seveso in Europe. In India we came out with very comprehensive law in 1986 (E.P. Act, 1986) while in US, France and Canada also new legislations were enacted with a view to giving effect to the declarations made from international fora and also to meet the challenge of the disasters of the Bhopal magnitude.

Sanction Behind Environmental Crime

The 'State of Environment' reports produced by the UN Environment Programme indicate that regulations have failed to improve the general environmental conditions. The UN programmes has given a direction which to a large extent arrested rapid deterioration and has motivated national governments to embark upon programmes of mass awareness to successfully launch project of preventive measures but they have failed to improve the environment or to compensate the victims.

With a view to ameliorating the situation some countries have introduced fines or imprisonment to penalize environmental offences. In some countries the maximum limits of fine have been enhanced besides increasing term of imprisonment. In some countries minimum fines as well as minimum term of imprisonment has been prescribed for continuing offences, special care has been taken to prescribe daily fines. For repeat offenders, enhanced punishment has been prescribed in most of the countries but in Nigeria it is even life imprisonment.

Environmentally dangerous conduct has been declared crime very recently therefore there is no unanimity on definition of environmental crime. In most cases the environmental crime remains tagged up with specific violation of regulatory provisions which means that it is subordinate to administrative sanction and continuous monitoring thereafter. The Jurists while studying environmental law have found out three theories of criminal sanctions[10] :

(a) Anthropocentric view which defines environmental crime as crime against life health, property etc. through deterioration of environment. To be a crime it requires harm or at least abstract danger to some fundamental human interest to justify the use of criminal sanction.

(b) Quasi-anthropocentric view defines environmental crimes as crimes against life, health, property etc. and against environment. It requires some relationship with some human interest to justify criminal sanction.

(c) Eccentric view may also be termed as post-modern view which defines them as crime against ecosystem itself and no relationship is required for criminal sanction to be applied.

In the context of environmental crime a new jurisprudence has to be evolved otherwise the principles of law applied to criminal cases will not be useful and effective in dispensing justice.

The problems in fixing criminal liability is also of utmost importance in dispensation of justice in environmental crime. In absence of any administrative law or rules with punitive provisions tagged, the very existence of offence can be knocked off further. The responsibility of administering regulations rests with monitoring or inspecting agencies therefore more often than not joint responsibility can be argued in court of law further diluting the punitive responsibility of the offender. Unless we make environmental offences free from accessorial bondage with administrative and regulative sanctions, it will be difficult to successfully combat environmental offences.

The problems of jurisdiction will cause another difficulty specially in trans-border offences. In cases of offences against humanity such as damaging ozone layer or disposing nuclear waste on high seas the problem is almost insurmountable even now when the declarations of the Hague Conference and the Earth Summit are still fresh in the minds of national leaders who attended and felt very strongly about the same. In this connection the recommendations of the "Preparatory Colloquium to the 15th International Congress on Penal Law" (Ottawa- Canada 2-6 Nov. 1992) are noteworthy:

(a) When the harm or threat of harm which underlies environmental offences that are recognized by the State, it should be possible to prosecute the offender either in the state when the offence was committed wholly or partly or in the state when the effects or harm from the offences are suffered or in both States.

(b) In cases when the offence has been committed on high seas or places where no one state has jurisdiction then the states should agree to a convention which would enable them to prosecute the offender in any one of the states where the offender is found.

(c) If an International Criminal Court is created in pursuance of some international convention then such court may be authorised to have jurisdiction of international recognised environmental offences.

Corporate Offenders

In case of juridical persons or corporations the problems of identifying the human being behind the dangerous conduct becomes difficult. A corporation or a firm can be held guilty and monetary penalty can be imposed but sentencing for imprisonment causes problems. Vicarious liability has been fixed in cases of torts and in civil law but to apply this principle in criminal cases may not be found very sound. Such interpretations tend to remain uncertain depending largely upon the legal philosophy of the presiding officer of the court.

Non-Criminal Sanction

Besides declaring non-conformity with the standards an offence to be visited by as stringent a punishment as prescribed for culpable homicide (life imprisonment in Nigeria) some countries have introduced provisions in their respective constitutions to give them respectability and direction to the interpreters of law. Some member State of United Nations have recognised the right to a Safe, clean and ecologically balanced environment as Fundamental Right (Brazil—Article 262, Cuba—Article 39, Portugal—Article 66, Spain—Article 45).

Some other states have incorporated provisions in their constitutions as guidelines to courts and also states under an obligation to provide general protection to the environment and this category includes countries like India, Sri Lanka, China, Greece, Malta, Bahamas and Seychelles.

The public at large can also approach courts of justice for compensation by way of civil suits in case they feel that environment has been damaged or polluted. In this connection Public Interest Litigations (PIL) have been quite effective at least in India. Besides awarding compensation to victims the courts have issued preventive and corrective orders in the interest of common man.

Other non-criminal sanctions include the empowerment of administrative machinery to arbitrate, order improvement or suspension or cessation of operation, cancellation of permit and stoppage of supplies like power and water and other such measures to force the polluters or potential polluters to conform to rules.

Public Co-operation

Nothing can be achieved and sustained without public

co-operation. In case of environment protection and preservation, general awareness and education is fundamental to any project launched by national or international agencies. Besides legislating on every probable violation, the monitoring and supervising agencies to be created, empowered and insulated against pressure of groups to make them really effective in protecting and preserving our environment for all living beings and also to future generations.

REFERENCES

1. 'The Earth Charter' prepared by non-Governmental organisations in Rio-de-Janeiro. (June, 3, 4 of 1992).
2. योनिबालवधं पुंस्त्वोपघातं च प्रतिषेधयेत्।
3. पांसुन्यासे रथ्यायामष्टभागो दण्डः। पङ्कोदकसन्निरोधेपादः राजमार्गे द्विगुणः

(55/36/3(5)

(कौटिल्य अर्थशास्त्र)

पुण्यस्थानोदकस्थादेवगृहराजपरिग्रहेषु पणोत्तरा विष्ठादण्डाः।
मूत्रेष्वर्धदण्डाः।
भैषाज्यब्याधिमयनिमित्तमदण्डयाः।
मार्जारश्वनकुलसर्पप्रेतानां नगरस्यान्तरूत्सर्गे त्रिपणो दण्डः।
खरोष्ट्राश्वतराश्वपशुप्रेतानां अट्पणः। मनुष्यप्रेतानां पञ्चाशत्पणः।
मार्गविपर्यासे शवद्वारादन्यतः शवनिर्णयेने पूर्वः साहसदण्डः।
द्वाः स्थानां द्विशतम्। श्मशानादन्यत्र न्यारो दहने च द्वादशपणो दण्डः।

(55/36/4 (1 से 4)

(कौटिल्य अर्थशास्त्र)

4. मूलतो ब्रह्मरूपाय मध्यतो विष्णु रूपिणे।
अग्रतः शिवरूपाय वृक्षराजाय ते नमः।
यं दृष्टवा मुच्यते रोगैः, स्पृष्टवा पापैः प्रमुच्यते।
यदाश्रितः चिरञ्जीवी तमश्वत्वं नमाम्यहम्।।
5. गा वै पश्चाम्यहं नित्यं
गावः पश्यन्तु मां सदा।
गावोऽस्मांक वयं तासां
यतो गावस्ततो वयम्।।

(महाभारत–अनु. 78/24)

6. Central Acts dealing with subjects of Environmental Protection in pre-independence India—
(1) The Shore Nuisance (Bombay and Colaba Act), 1853.
(2) Orient Gas Company Act, 1857.

(3) Indian Penal Code, 1860.
(4) Police Act, 1861.
(5) Indian Forest Act, 1865.
(6) The Serail Act, 1867.
(7) Cattle Trespass Act, 1871.
(8) North Canal and Drainage Act, 1873.
(9) Indian Forest Act, 1878.
(10) Obstruction in Airways Act, 1881.
(11) Indian Fisheries Act, 1897.
(12) The Code of Criminal Procedure 1898 (Repealed).
(13) Explosives Act, 1908.
(14) Indian Ports Act, 1908.
(15) Indian Steam Vessels Act, 1917.
(16) Poison Act, 1919.
(17) Indian Boilers Act, 1923.
(18) Indian Forest Act. 1927.
(19) Petroleum Act, 1934.
(20) Motor Vehicles Act, 1939 (Repealed).
(21) Inflammable Substances Act, 1942.

7. List of Acts after 1947.

(1) Factories Act, 1948.
(2) Damodar Valley Corporation (Prevention of Pollution of Water) Act, 1948.
(3) Constitution of India, 1950.
(4) The Industries (Development Regulation) Act, 1951.
(5) The Food Adulteration Act, 1954.
(6) River Boards Act, 1956.
(7) Merchant Shipping Act, 1958.
(8) Insecticides Act, 1968.
(9) Atomic Energy Act, 1969.
(10) Merchant Shipping (Amendment) Act, 1970.
(11) Rediation Protection Rules, 1971.
(12) Wild Life (Protection) Act, 1972 (Since amended).
(13) Code of Criminal Procedure, 1973.
(14) The Water (Prevention and Control of Pollution) Act, 1974.
(15) The Water (Prevention and Control of Pollution) Rules, 1975.
(16) The Territorial Waters and Maritime Zone Act, 1976.
(17) The Water (Prevention and Control of Pollution) Cess Act, 1977.
(18) The Water Prevention and Control Amendment Act,1978.
(19) The Water Supply and Sewerage Corporation Act 1979.
(20) Forest Conservation Act, 1980.
(21) The Air (Prevention and Control of Pollution) Act, 1981.
(22) The Water (Prevention and Control of Pollution) Amendment

Act, 1983.
(23) Environment Protection Act, 1986.
(24) Environment Protection Rules, 1986.
(25) The Air (Prevention and Control of Pollution Amendment) Act, 1987.
(26) The Motor Vehicles Act, 1988.
(27) Public Liability Insurance Act, 1991.
(28) The National Environmental Tribunal Act, 1995.

8. Document-1/97 I.I.P.A. (U.P. Regional Branch) Evolution of Environmental Legislation. (By T.N. Dhar).
9. African Charter on the Man and People's Rights, 1981.
10. UNAFEI- Dec. 1994 Resources Material Series 45 (p. 329) (Fuchu, Tokyo, Japan).

■■

Index